NOVELS

IN THE MAKING

Novels

IN THE MAKING

WILLIAM E. BUCKLER
NEW YORK UNIVERSITY

HOUGHTON MIFFLIN COMPANY · BOSTON

The Riverside Press
CAMBRIDGE • MASSACHUSETTS
PRINTED IN THE U.S.A.

CONTENTS

INTRODUCTION

When Daniel Defoe sat down, in 1722, to write the Preface to *Moll Flanders*, the modern novel had not been born. The novel was in the making, certainly. A rich collection of prose tales had been gradually accumulating for centuries — in Boccaccio's Italy, in Rabelais' France, in Cervantes' Spain. The travel literature, memoirs (sometimes called "scandal chronicles"), and character books of the seventeenth century also helped to engender the novel.

But these were not the thing itself — these were not novels. Before the novel as an individually distinctive literary form could come into being, certain conditions had to exist and — by one of those seemingly fortuitous concourses of significant pressures which tend to betray the purely analytical literary historian — they had to coalesce.

One of the conditions was a "popular" audience. The invention of printing by movable type had, of course, led inevitably toward a multiplied reading public. But an audience is not truly popular until it begins to press the hand of the printer, until its pleasure becomes an integral part of the writer's creative effort. The printing presses of the eighteenth century could have issued thousands of editions of Homer and Virgil, Petronius and Apuleius without ever creating a popular audience. The closed coterie had to be forfeited, and the pound of the patron had to give way to the pence of the people.

Another condition was the relaxation of rigid standards of literary respectability and an exaggerated reverence for traditional literary forms. The examples of Homer and Sophocles and the prescriptions of Aristotle had dominated the "grand style" in literature for more than two thousand years. Shakespeare's tragedies and Milton's *Paradise Lost* have, in this sense, the same high lineage. But the age of kings was past; the seat of authority — political, ethical, religious, even artistic — had shifted. Society was being leveled, and writers were coming more and more to feel that, to be useful to their own creative efforts, the rules formulated on classical examples must be radically modified. Thus the death of the serious epic as a practical literary form coincided with the birth of the novel.

The indispensable condition was the inventor himself — the gifted writer who had clearly perceived what it was that he was trying to do and who had sufficient faith in his adopted formulae to enable him to achieve his objective. In Henry Fielding, the man and the moment met, and the modern novel was born.

Fielding brought exceptional qualifications to the shaping of the novel. From his practical experience of stagecraft, he had learned the importance of such qualities as movement, relevance, length, and tone to the making of the well-tailored literary production. Further, he had an analytical understanding both of epic principles at work in ancient literature and of that transmuted quasi-epic tradition represented in the work of Cervantes and Le Sage. (Thus Fielding defined the novel as "a comic epic poem in prose" and asserted that *Joseph Andrews* was "*Written in the Manner of Cervantes.*") Fielding's respect for aesthetic and moral categories and distinctions enabled him not only to formulate important prefaces for *Joseph Andrews* and *Jonathan Wilde*, but also to press his doctrines into service in the making of *Tom Jones* — the first novel, at least in English, possessed of true organic unity. The fact that Fielding was a serious social critic made him a worthy predecessor of that long line of novel-writers who have taken as their major subject the anatomy of modern society. Finally, Fielding gave to the novel the dignity of a frank and unequivocal avowal that he was, indeed, writing novels. He did not apologize for the fact; rather, he saw the novel as the logical modern modification and continuation of an ancient epic tradition. (The suspicion that there is something not quite dignified about the novel still lingers on: as late as 1950, the dean of a large Midwestern arts college wondered aloud to a faculty committee "if a course in fiction can ever be quite respectable.")

It is often said that only lately — that is, since the prefaces of Henry James and studies in "the craft of fiction" largely built upon them — have we learned to talk about the novel, have we found an appropriate descriptive vocabulary. This is, in a special sense, true, and it was not to be expected that Henry Fielding would bring to his critical prefaces (including the introductory chapters to the various books of *Tom Jones*) a fully developed lexicon. On the other hand, it is curiously revealing to compare critical vocabularies of two English novelists more than two hundred years apart:

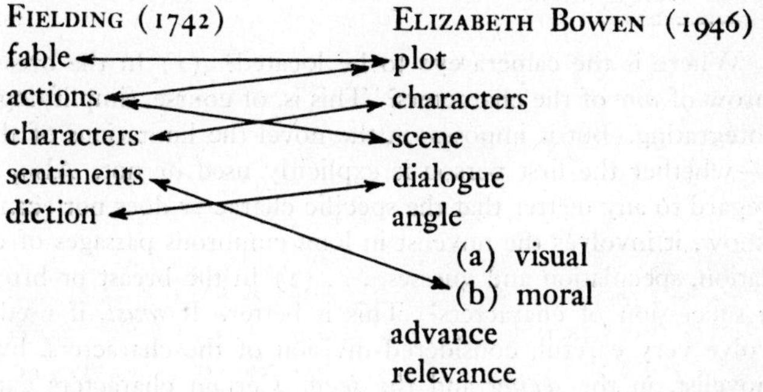

Setting aside "advance" and "relevance" — which are not really "parts" of the novel, but rather prescribe the manner in which those parts should be put together — one finds between Fielding and Miss Bowen striking agreement on what, in the broad, constitute the stock ingredients of the novel. There are basic differences in detail, emphasis, and elaboration — Fielding's "diction" is a broader term than Miss Bowen's "dialogue," though he relates diction specifically to dialogue; Fielding, though he had been a playwright and draws an analogy between the art of the novelist and the art of the painter, shows only a vaguely developed sense of "scene" as Miss Bowen uses the term; Fielding's "fable" is in several ways an apter term than "plot"; sentiment ("a mental attitude, thought, or judgment permeated or prompted by feeling"), in the sense in which Fielding understood it, is at least as satisfactory as "moral angle."

The one contemporary concept of which Fielding shows no awareness is "visual angle" — or angle of vision, or point of view. He adopted a visual angle, certainly: he saw his characters as an imaginative historian would have seen them — clearly, omnisciently, and in his own person. From the time of Richardson, on the other hand, novelists have experimented with other ways of telling their story, have attempted to achieve effects of subtlety, immediacy, and drama through narrative centers other than that of the omniscient author. Since Henry James, no single concept related to the craft of fiction has received as much serious consideration as the concept of point of view.

Point of view may be analyzed in various ways and into varying numbers of parts. Elizabeth Bowen (below, p. 260) puts the matter as well as most:

> Where is the camera-eye to be located? (1) In the breast or brow of *one* of the characters? This is, of course, simplifying and integrating. But it imposes on the novel the limitations of the 'I' — whether the first person is explicitly used or not. Also, with regard to any matter that the specific character does not (cannot) know, it involves the novelist in long cumbrous passages of cogitation, speculation and guesses. . . . (2) In the breast or brow of a succession of characters? This is better. It *must*, if used, involve very careful, considered division of the characters, by the novelist, in the *seeing* and the *seen*. Certain characters gain in importance and magnetism by being only *seen:* this makes them more romantic, fatal-seeming, sinister. In fact, no character in which these qualities are, for the plot, essential should be allowed to enter the *seeing* class. (3) In the breast or brow of omniscient story-teller (the novelist)? This, though appearing naïve, would appear best. The novelist should retain right of entry, at will, into any of the characters: their memories, sensations and thought-processes should remain his, to requisition for appropriate use.

Although Miss Bowen's statement seems to vindicate Fielding's earliest "point of view" as, after all, the best, it is clear that Fielding had no notion of the numerous ways of telling a story which have significantly controlled the shape of the novel.

The concern of novelists over point of view, although it has often been very technical, should not be looked upon as something arid and arbitrary: more than any other single element, it represents the novelist's attempt to accommodate the forms of modern fiction to the pressures of modern life. Between Fielding and Faulkner, man has witnessed the rapid dissolution of a robust, rational, external view of life and the growing awareness that life, if its true nature is to be probed at all, must be approached from the inside — from fancies rather than facts, from patterns of the private rather than the public mind and heart. If, as critics as disparate as Walter Pater and R. P. Blackmur have been inclined to say, "art is life at the remove of form," then it was inevitable that novelists should find new "forms" through which to control and interpret life. And ultimately it is to the form that we must look to discover a writer's values and intentions.

* * * * *

In *Novels in the Making* the editor's object has been to provide representative primary documents — distributed by time, type, and nationality — which suggest the problems and perceptions that have gone into the making of the modern novel. Within the limits of this broad aim the book can be used in a number of ways; for example, (*a*) as a resource, either in itself or in conjunction with one or more novels, for short critical papers dealing with the development of the genre or of particular novels; (*b*) as a springboard for full-length papers which involve use of the library and additional reading and draw on the ability to handle the techniques and problems of both research and criticism; (*c*) as a collection of source readings for advanced study of the history and theory of the novel. These selections make no pretense at a complete coverage of the novel, as a glance at some of the major omissions makes plain: Richardson and Sterne; Scott and Jane Austen; Balzac, Victor Hugo, Gautier, Proust; Hawthorne, Melville, Howells, Dreiser; Thackeray, Hardy, Joyce; Faulkner and Hemingway. The aim, rather, has been simply to give enough central source material to plot a curve, sketch the broad line of development. For those who wish to treat the materials in documentary fashion, the page numbers of original sources are given in heavy type immediately *after* the material from the page.

I wish to express my gratitude to various colleagues at New York University whose personal and intellectual sympathy has encouraged me in this work: Professor Nelson Adkins, Professor Joseph Bram, Professor Ilse Lind, Professor L. Ruth Middlebrook, Professor Aron Pressman, and Professor George Winchester Stone.

THREE BIBLIOGRAPHICAL NOTES

Note A
(refer to pages 27–48)

Dickens was essentially a "serial" novelist — that is, he willingly adopted and exploited the nineteenth-century convention of publishing novels in instalments of a prescribed length at regular monthly intervals. Most of Dickens' novels were published in twenty instalments of thirty-two pages, with two engraved illustrations, the last two instalments (numbers nineteen and twenty) being combined into a "double number" of sixty-four pages.

Publication regularly took place on the last day of the month, known as "magazine day." The price of a single monthly number was one shilling; of a double number, two shillings. Further, Dickens regularly allowed serial publication of a 640-page novel to begin with less than seventy-five pages of the novel actually written, and on several occasions the writing of two novels in this piecemeal fashion overlapped.

As Dickens began to develop his characteristic style of novel-making, he felt increasingly the need "to keep a steadier eye upon the general purpose and design" of his novels. Thus from the mid-'forties onwards Dickens regularly prepared "number plans" for those novels designed as monthly serials. (*Great Expectations* and *A Tale of Two Cities*, which were published as serials in a weekly magazine, are to be excepted.) Dickens took a sheet of paper and folded it in the middle to form two half-sheets. He headed the right half-sheet with the title of the novel and the number of the monthly part; then he sketched the chapters into which the number was to be subdivided. On the left half-sheet, he jotted down general memoranda — queries, cautions, relationships, and so forth.

The "number plans" for *David Copperfield* are now in the Forster collection in the Victoria and Albert Museum, London. Forster, the famous confidant and biographer of Dickens, removed from the manuscript the plan for Number I and did not replace it; it has disappeared. However, in his *Life of Dickens*, Forster used a facsimile of the first two-thirds of this number plan to illustrate "the lightness and confidence of handling" in *David Copperfield.* Thus the only parts of Dickens' plans for the novel which are lost to us are the general memoranda and outline of Chapter III.

John Butt and Kathleen Tillotson, the first scholars to publish *in extenso* the number plans of *David Copperfield,* describe their method of transcription as follows: "Though it is impossible to convey in print all that the number plans reveal, in their manuscript form, of hesitation and decision, of haste and excitement, and of afterthought squeezed into what might seem the least inconvenient space unfilled, our transcription is as exact as it is practicable to make it. A line in the manuscript is invariably represented by a line of type, and in position it matches as closely as possible an entry on the half-sheet of paper facing it. Capitalization and underlining have been preserved. Erasures, where legible, are printed within angle-brackets." The Butt-Tillotson transcription has been followed in the present text.

Note B
(refer to pages 97–118)

Anna T. Kitchel, first editor of George Eliot's "Quarry for Middlemarch," has described it as "a small, black leather notebook, 4⅛ by 6½ in. On the cover an undecipherable title in gilt script is concealed by a paper label inscribed in George Eliot's hand, 'Quarry for Middlemarch.' About half the book is devoted principally to notes on scientific, and especially medical, matters, with three pages, 23, 24, and 26, listing mottoes for chapters, and one, 25, presenting political dates drawn from the *Annual Register.* This first half of the notebook we shall speak of as *Quarry I.* The notebook was then turned over and again almost exactly half of it was used, chiefly for the working out of the structure of the novel, though a few pages are devoted to political dates concerned with the passage of the First Reform Bill. This part of the notebook we shall call *Quarry II.*" The *Quarry* was bought by Miss Amy Lowell on June 27, 1923, and, at her death in 1925, was left to Harvard University.

The student is advised to use this notebook in conjunction with three other works: John W. Cross (ed.), *George Eliot's Life as*

Related in Her Letters and Journals, 3 vols. (London and Edinburgh, 1885); Gordon S. Haight (ed.), *The George Eliot Letters*, 7 vols. (New Haven, 1954–1955); and Jerome Beaty, "*Middlemarch*" *from Notebook to Novel: A Study of George Eliot's Creative Method*, Illinois Studies in Language and Literature, Vol. 47 (Urbana, 1960).

Note C

(*refer to pages 215–251*)

The special daybook in which André Gide kept a record of the genesis and growth of *The Counterfeiters* was originally published in 1926 as *Journal des Faux-Monnayeurs.* First published in English in 1951, the *Journal of "The Counterfeiters"* — according to Justin O'Brien, the translator — "has always been considered as a unit distinct from Gide's monumental *Journals* of the years 1889–1949." Gide gave the *Journal of "The Counterfeiters"* to his friend Jacques De Lacretelle — "and to those who are interested in questions of technique."

DANIEL DEFOE

Moll Flanders (1722)

Author's Preface

The world is so taken up of late with novels and romances, that it will be hard for a private history to be taken for genuine, where the names and other circumstances of the person are concealed; and on this account we must be content to leave the reader to pass his own opinion upon the ensuing sheets, and take it just as he pleases.

The author is here supposed to be writing her own history, and in the very beginning of her account she gives the reasons why she thinks fit to conceal her true name, after which there is no occasion to say any more about that.

It is true that the original of this story is put into new words, and the style of the famous lady we here speak of is a little altered; particularly she is made to tell her own tale in modester words than she told it at first, the copy which came first to hand having been written in language more like one still in Newgate than one grown penitent and humble, as she afterwards pretends to be.

The pen employed in finishing her story, and making it what you now see it to be, has had no little difficulty to put it into a dress fit to be seen, and to make it speak language fit to be read. When page xvii / a woman debauched from her youth, nay, even being the offspring of debauchery and vice, comes to give an account of all her vicious practices, and even to descend to the particular occasions and circumstances by which she first became wicked, and of all the progressions of crime which she ran through in three-score years, an author must be hard put to it to

---

The Fortunes and Misfortunes of the Famous Moll Flanders. Reprinted from *The Works of Daniel Defoe* (New York: The Jenson Society, 1905), Volume VII.

wrap it up so clean as not to give room, especially for vicious readers, to turn it to his disadvantage.

All possible care, however, has been taken to give no lewd ideas, no immodest turns in the new dressing up this story; no, not the worst part of her expressions. To this purpose some of the vicious part of her life, which could not be modestly told, is quite left out, and several other parts are very much shortened. What is left 'tis hoped will not offend the chastest reader or the modestest hearer; and as the best use is to be made even of the worst story, the moral, 'tis hoped, will keep the reader serious, even where the story might incline him to be otherwise. To give the history of a wicked life repented of, necessarily requires that the wicked part should be made as wicked as the real history of it will bear, to illustrate and give a beauty to the penitent part, which is certainly the best and brightest, if related with equal spirit and life.

It is suggested there cannot be the same life, the same brightness and beauty, in relating the penitent part as is in the criminal part. If there is any truth in that suggestion, I must be allowed to say, 'tis because there is not the same taste and relish in the reading; and indeed it is too true that the differ- page xviii / ence lies not in the real worth of the subject so much as in the gust and palate of the reader.

But as this work is chiefly recommended to those who know how to read it, and how to make the good uses of it which the story all along recommends to them, so it is to be hoped that such readers will be much more pleased with the moral than the fable, with the application than with the relation, and with the end of the writer than with the life of the person written of.

There is in this story abundance of delightful incidents, and all of them usefully applied. There is an agreeable turn artfully given them in the relating, that naturally instructs the reader, either one way or another. The first part of her lewd life with the young gentleman at Colchester has so many happy turns given it to expose the crime, and warn all whose circumstances are adapted to it, of the ruinous end of such things, and the foolish, thoughtless, and abhorred conduct of both the parties, that it abundantly atones for all the lively description she gives of her folly and wickedness.

The repentance of her lover at Bath, and how brought by the

just alarm of his fit of sickness to abandon her; the just caution given there against even the lawful intimacies of the dearest friends, and how unable they are to preserve the most solemn resolutions of virtue without divine assistance; these are parts which, to a just discernment, will appear to have more real beauty in them than all the amorous chain of story which introduces it.

In a word, as the whole relation is carefully garbled page xix / of all the levity and looseness that was in it, so it is applied, and with the utmost care, to virtuous and religious uses. None can, without being guilty of manifest injustice, cast any reproach upon it, or upon our design in publishing it.

The advocates for the stage have, in all ages, made this the great argument to persuade people that their plays are useful, and that they ought to be allowed in the most civilised and in the most religious government; namely, that they are applied to virtuous purposes, and that, by the most lively representations, they fail not to recommend virtue and generous principles, and expose all sorts of vice and corruption of manners; and were it true that they did so, and that they constantly adhered to that rule, as the test of their acting on the theatre, much might be said in their favour.

Throughout the infinite variety of this book, this fundamental is most strictly adhered to; there is not a wicked action in any part of it, but is first or last rendered unhappy and unfortunate; there is not a superlative villain brought upon the stage, but either he is brought to an unhappy end, or brought to be a penitent; there is not an ill thing mentioned but it is condemned, even in the relation, nor a virtuous, just thing but it carries its praise along with it. What can more exactly answer the rule laid down, to recommend even those representations of things which have so many other just objections lying against them? namely, of example of bad company, obscene language, and the like.

Upon this foundation this book is recommended to page xx / the reader, as a work from every part of which something may be learned, and some just and religious inference is drawn, by which the reader will have something of instruction if he pleases to make use of it.

All the exploits of this lady of fame, in her depredations upon mankind, stand as so many warnings to honest people to beware of them, intimating to them by what methods innocent people are drawn in, plundered, and robbed, and by consequence how to avoid them. Her robbing a little child, dressed fine by the vanity of the mother, to go to the dancing-school, is a good memento to such people hereafter, as is likewise her picking the gold watch from the young lady's side in the park.

Her getting a parcel from a hare-brained wench at the coaches in St. John's Street; her booty at the fire, and also at Harwich, all give us excellent warning in such cases to be more present to ourselves in sudden surprises of every sort.

Her application to a sober life and industrious management at last, in Virginia, with her transported spouse, is a story fruitful of instruction to all the unfortunate creatures who are obliged to seek their re-establishment abroad, whether by the misery of transportation or other disaster; letting them know that diligence and application have their due encouragement, even in the remotest part of the world, and that no case can be so low, so despicable, or so empty of prospect, but that an unwearied industry will go a great way to deliver us from it, will in time raise the meanest creature to appear page xxi / again in the world, and give him a new cast for his life.

These are a few of the serious inferences which we are led by the hand to in this book, and these are fully sufficient to justify any man in recommending it to the world, and much more to justify the publication of it.

There are two of the most beautiful parts still behind, which this story gives some idea of, and lets us into the parts of them, but they are either of them too long to be brought into the same volume, and indeed are, as I may call them, whole volumes of themselves, viz.: 1. The life of her governess, as she calls her, who had run through, it seems, in a few years, all the eminent degrees of a gentlewoman, a whore, and a bawd; a midwife and a midwife-keeper, as they are called; a pawnbroker, a child-taker, a receiver of thieves, and of stolen goods; and, in a word, herself a thief, a breeder up of thieves, and the like, and yet at last a penitent.

The second is the life of her transported husband, a highwayman, who, it seems, lived a twelve years' life of successful villainy upon the road, and even at last came off so well as to be a volunteer transport, not a convict; and in whose life there is an incredible variety.

But, as I said, these are things too long to bring in here, so neither can I make a promise of their coming out by themselves.

We cannot say, indeed, that this history is carried on quite to the end of the life of this famous Moll Flanders, for nobody can write their own life to the **page xxii /** full end of it, unless they can write it after they are dead. But her husband's life, being written by a third hand, gives a full account of them both, how long they lived together in that country, and how they came both to England again, after about eight years, in which time they were grown very rich, and where she lived, it seems, to be very old, but was not so extraordinary a penitent as she was at first; it seems only that indeed she always spoke with abhorrence of her former life, and every part of it.

In her last scene, at Maryland and Virginia, many pleasant things happened, which makes that part of her life very agreeable, but they are not told with the same elegancy as those accounted for by herself; so it is still to the more advantage that we break off here. **page xxiii /**

HENRY FIELDING

Joseph Andrews (*1742*)

Author's Preface

As it is possible the mere English reader may have a different idea of romance from the author of these little volumes, and may consequently expect a kind of entertainment not to be found, nor which was even intended, in the following pages, it may not be improper to premise a few words concerning this kind of writing, which I do not remember to have seen hitherto attempted in our language.

The Epic, as well as the Drama, is divided into tragedy and comedy. Homer, who was the father of this species of poetry, gave us a pattern of both these, though that of the latter kind is entirely lost; which Aristotle tells us, bore the same relation to comedy which his Iliad bears to tragedy. And perhaps, that we have no more instances of it among the writers of antiquity, is owing to the loss of this great pattern, which, had it survived, would have found its imitators equally with the other poems of this great original.

And farther, as this poetry may be tragic or comic, I **page 17 /** will not scruple to say it may be likewise either in verse or prose: for though it wants one particular, which the critic enumerates in the constituent parts of an epic poem, namely metre; yet, when any kind of writing contains all its other parts, such as fable, action, characters, sentiments, and diction, and is deficient in metre only, it seems, I think, reasonable to refer it to the epic;

The History of the Adventures of Joseph Andrews and of his Friend Mr. Abraham Adams. Reprinted from *The Complete Works of Henry Fielding,* Drury Lane Edition (New York: Croscup & Sterling Company, 1902), Volume I.

at least, as no critic hath thought proper to range it under any other head, or to assign it a particular name to itself.

Thus the Telemachus of the archbishop of Cambray appears to me of the epic kind, as well as the Odyssey of Homer; indeed, it is much fairer and more reasonable to give it a name common with that species from which it differs only in a single instance, than to confound it with those which it resembles in no other. Such are those voluminous works, commonly called Romances, namely, Clelia, Cleopatra, Astræa, Cassandra, the Grand Cyrus, and innumerable others, which contain, as I apprehend, very little instruction or entertainment.

Now, a comic romance is a comic epic poem in prose; differing from comedy, as the serious epic from tragedy: its action being more extended and comprehensive; containing a much larger circle of incidents, and introducing a greater variety of characters. It differs from the serious romance in its fable and action, in this; that as in the one these are grave and solemn, so in the other they are light and ridiculous: it differs in its characters by introducing persons of inferior rank, and consequently, of inferior manners, whereas the grave romance sets the highest before us: lastly, in its sentiments and diction; by preserving the ludicrous instead of the sublime. In the diction, I think, burlesque itself may be sometimes admitted; of which many instances will occur in this work, as in the description of the battles, and some other places, not necessary to be pointed out to the classical reader, for whose entertain- **page 18 /** ment those parodies or burlesque imitations are chiefly calculated.

But though we have sometimes admitted this in our diction, we have carefully excluded it from our sentiments and characters; for there it is never properly introduced, unless in writings of the burlesque kind, which this is not intended to be. Indeed, no two species of writing can differ more widely than the comic and the burlesque; for as the latter is ever the exhibition of what is monstrous and unnatural, and where our delight, if we examine it, arises from the surprising absurdity, as in appropriating the manners of the highest to the lowest, or *è converso;* so in the former we should ever confine ourselves strictly to nature, from the just imitation of which will flow all the pleasure we can this way convey to a sensible reader. And perhaps there is one reason why a comic writer should of all others be the least excused for deviating from nature, since it may not be always so easy for a serious poet to meet with the great and the admirable; but life everywhere furnishes an accurate observer with the ridiculous.

I have hinted this little concerning burlesque, because I have often heard that name given to performances which have been truly of the comic kind, from the author's having sometimes admitted it in his diction only; which, as it is the dress of poetry, doth, like the dress of men, establish characters (the one of the whole poem, and the other of the whole man), in vulgar opinion, beyond any of their greater excellences: but surely, a certain drollery in stile, where characters and sentiments are perfectly natural, no more constitutes the burlesque, than an empty pomp and dignity of words, where everything else is mean and low, can entitle any performance to the appellation of the true sublime.

And I apprehend my Lord Shaftesbury's opinion of mere burlesque agrees with mine, when he asserts, There is no **page 19 /** such thing to be found in the writings of the ancients. But perhaps I have less abhorrence than he professes for it; and that, not because I have had some little success on the stage this way, but rather as it contributes more to exquisite mirth and laughter than any other; and these are probably more wholesome physic for the mind, and conduce better to purge away spleen, melancholy, and ill affections, than is generally imagined. Nay, I will appeal to common observation, whether the same companies are not found more full of good-humour and benevolence, after they have been sweetened for two or three hours with entertainments of this kind, than when soured by a tragedy or a grave lecture.

But to illustrate all this by another science, in which, perhaps, we shall see the distinction more clearly and plainly, let us examine the works of a comic history painter, with those performances which the Italians call Caricatura, where we shall find the true excellence of the former to consist in the exactest copying of nature; insomuch that a judicious eye instantly rejects anything *outré*, any liberty which the painter hath taken with the features of that *alma mater;* whereas in the Caricatura we allow all licence — its aim is to exhibit monsters, not men; and all distortions and exaggerations whatever are within its proper province.

Now, what Caricatura is in painting, Burlesque is in writing;

and in the same manner the comic writer and painter correlate to each other. And here I shall observe, that, as in the former the painter seems to have the advantage; so it is in the latter infinitely on the side of the writer; for the Monstrous is much easier to paint than describe, and the Ridiculous to describe than paint.

And though perhaps this latter species doth not in either science so strongly affect and agitate the muscles as the other; yet it will be owned, I believe, that a more rational and useful pleasure arises to us from it. He who should page 20 / call the ingenious Hogarth a burlesque painter, would, in my opinion, do him very little honour; for sure it is much easier, much less the subject of admiration, to paint a man with a nose, or any other feature of a preposterous size, or to expose him in some absurd or monstrous attitude, than to express the affections of men on canvas. It hath been thought a vast commendation of a painter to say his figures seem to breathe; but surely it is a much greater and nobler applause, that they appear to think.

But to return. The Ridiculous only, as I have before said, falls within my province in the present work. Nor will some explanation of this word be thought impertinent by the reader, if he considers how wonderfully it hath been mistaken, even by writers who have professed it: for to what but such a mistake can we attribute the many attempts to ridicule the blackest villainies, and, what is yet worse, the most dreadful calamities? What could exceed the absurdity of an author, who should write the comedy of Nero, with the merry incident of ripping up his mother's belly? or what would give a greater shock to humanity than an attempt to expose the miseries of poverty and distress to ridicule? And yet the reader will not want much learning to suggest such instances to himself.

Besides, it may seem remarkable, that Aristotle, who is so fond and free of definitions, hath not thought proper to define the Ridiculous. Indeed, where he tells us it is proper to comedy, he hath remarked that villainy is not its object: but he hath not, as I remember, positively asserted what is. Nor doth the Abbé Bellegarde, who hath written a treatise on this subject, though he shows us many species of it, once trace it to its fountain.

The only source of the true Ridiculous (as it appears to me) is affectation. But though it arises from one spring only, when we consider the infinite streams into which this one branches, we shall presently cease to admire at the **page 21 /** copious field it affords to an observer. Now, affectation proceeds from one of these two causes, vanity or hypocrisy: for as vanity puts us on affecting false characters, in order to purchase applause; so hypocrisy sets us on an endeavour to avoid censure, by concealing our vices under an appearance of their opposite virtues. And though these two causes are often confounded (for there is some difficulty in distinguishing them), yet as they proceed from very different motives, so they are clearly distinct in their operations: for indeed, the affectation which arises from vanity is nearer to truth than the other, as it hath not that violent repugnancy of nature to struggle with, which that of the hypocrite hath. It may be likewise noted, that affectation doth not imply an absolute negation of those qualities which are affected; and, therefore, though, when it proceeds from hypocrisy, it be nearly allied to deceit; yet when it comes from vanity only, it partakes of the nature of ostentation: for instance, the affectation of liberality in a vain man differs visibly from the same affectation in the avaricious; for though the vain man is not what he would appear, or hath not the virtue he affects, to the degree he would be thought to have it; yet it sits less awkwardly on him than on the avaricious man, who is the very reverse of what he would seem to be.

From the discovery of this affectation arises the Ridiculous, which always strikes the reader with surprise and pleasure; and that in a higher and stronger degree when the affectation arises from hypocrisy, than when from vanity; for to discover any one to be the exact reverse of what he affects, is more surprising, and consequently more ridiculous, than to find him a little deficient in the quality he desires the reputation of. I might observe that our Ben Jonson, who of all men understood the Ridiculous the best, hath chiefly used the hypocritical affectation.

Now, from affectation only, the misfortunes and calami- **page 22 /** ties of life, or the imperfections of nature, may become the objects of ridicule. Surely he hath a very ill-framed mind who can look on ugliness, infirmity, or poverty, as ridiculous in themselves: nor do I believe any man living, who meets a dirty fellow riding through the streets in a cart, is struck with an idea of the Ridiculous from it; but if he should see the same figure descend from his coach and six, or bolt from his chair with his hat under his arm, he would then begin to laugh, and with justice. In the same manner, were we to enter a poor house and behold a wretched family shivering with cold and languishing with hunger, it would not incline us to laughter (at least we must have very diabolical natures if it would); but should we discover there a grate, instead of coals, adorned with flowers, empty plate or china dishes on the sideboard, or any other affectation of riches and finery, either on their persons or in their furniture, we might then indeed be excused for ridiculing so fantastical an appearance. Much less are natural imperfections the object of derision; but when ugliness aims at the applause of beauty, or lameness endeavours to display agility, it is then that these unfortunate circumstances, which at first moved our compassion, tend only to raise our mirth.

The poet carries this very far:

> None are for being what they are in fault,
> But for not being what they would be thought.

Where if the metre would suffer the word Ridiculous to close the first line, the thought would be rather more proper. Great vices are the proper objects of our detestation, smaller faults, of our pity; but affectation appears to me the only true source of the Ridiculous.

But perhaps it may be objected to me, that I have against my own rules introduced vices, and of a very black kind, into this work. To which I shall answer: first, that it is very difficult to pursue a series of human actions, and keep clear from them. Secondly, that the vices to be found here are rather the accidental consequences of some **page 23 /** human frailty or foible, than causes habitually existing in the mind. Thirdly, that they are never set forth as the objects of ridicule, but detestation. Fourthly, that they are never the principal figure at that time on the scene: and, lastly, they never produce the intended evil.

Having thus distinguished *Joseph Andrews* from the productions of romance writers on the one hand and burlesque writers on the other, and given some few very short hints (for I intended no more) of this species of writing, which I have affirmed to be hitherto unattempted in our language; I shall leave to my good-natured reader to apply my piece to my observations, and will detain him no longer with a word concerning the characters in this work.

And here I solemnly protest I have no intention to vilify or asperse any one; for though everything is copied from the book of nature, and scarce a character or action produced which I have not taken from my own observations and experience; yet I have used the utmost care to obscure the persons by such different circumstances, degrees, and colours, that it will be impossible to guess at them with any degree of certainty; and if it ever happens otherwise, it is only where the failure characterised is so minute, that it is a foible only which the party himself may laugh at as well as any other.

As to the character of Adams, as it is the most glaring in the whole, so I conceive it is not to be found in any book now extant. It is designed a character of perfect simplicity; and as the goodness of his heart will recommend him to the good-natured, so I hope it will excuse me to the gentlemen of his cloth; for whom, while they are worthy of their sacred order, no man can possibly have a greater respect. They will therefore excuse me, notwithstanding the low adventures in which he is engaged, that I have made him a clergyman; since no other office could have given him so many opportunities of displaying his worthy inclinations.

page 24 /

TOBIAS SMOLLETT

Roderick Random (1748)

Author's Preface

Of all kinds of satire, there is none so entertaining, and universally improving, as that which is introduced, as it were, occasionally, in the course of an interesting story, which brings every incident home to life; and, by representing familiar scenes in an uncommon and amusing point of view, invests them with all the graces of novelty, while nature is appealed to in every particular.

The reader gratifies his curiosity in pursuing the adventures of a person in whose favour he is prepossessed; he espouses his cause, he sympathises with him in distress; his indignation is heated against the authors of his calamity; the humane passions are inflamed; the contrast between dejected virtue and insulting vice appears with greater aggravation; and every impression having a double force on the imagination, the memory retains the circumstance, and the heart improves by the example. The attention is not tired with a bare catalogue of characters, but agreeably diverted with all the variety of invention; and the vicissitudes of life appear in their peculiar circumstances, opening an ample field for wit and humour.

Romance, no doubt, owes its origin to ignorance, vanity, and superstition. In the dark ages of the page xxxix / world, when a man had rendered himself famous for wisdom or valour, his family and adherents availed themselves of his superior qualities, magnified his virtues, and represented his character and person as sacred and supernatural. The vulgar easily swallowed the bait,

---

The Adventures of Roderick Random. Reprinted from *The Works of Tobias Smollett*, edited by George Saintsbury (London: The Navarre Society, Ltd., n.d.), Volume I.

implored his protection, and yielded the tribute of homage and praise even to adoration; his exploits were handed down to posterity with a thousand exaggerations; they were repeated as incitements to virtue; divine honours were paid, and altars erected to his memory, for the encouragement of those who attempted to imitate his example; and hence arose the heathen mythology, which is no other than a collection of extravagant romances. As learning advanced, and genius received cultivation, these stories were embellished with the graces of poetry; that they might the better recommend themselves to the attention, they were sung in public, at festivals, for the instruction and delight of the audience; and rehearsed before battle, as incentives to deeds of glory. Thus tragedy and the epic muse were born, and in the progress of taste, arrived at perfection. It is no wonder that the ancients could not relish a fable in prose, after they had seen so many remarkable events celebrated in verse, by their best poets; we, therefore, find no romance among them, during the era of their excellence, unless the *Cyropædia* of Xenophon may be so called; and it was not till arts and sciences began to revive, after the irruption of the Barbarians into Europe, that anything of this kind appeared. But when the minds of men were debauched, by the imposition of priestcraft, to the most absurd pitch of credulity, the authors of romance arose, and, losing sight of probability, filled their performances with the most monstrous hyperboles. If they could not equal the ancient poets in point of genius, they were resolved to excel page xl / them in fiction, and apply to the wonder rather than the judgment of their readers. Accordingly they brought necromancy to their aid, and instead of supporting the character of their heroes by dignity of sentiment and practice, distinguished them by their bodily strength, activity, and extravagance of behaviour. Although nothing could be more ludicrous and unnatural than the figures they drew, they did not want patrons and admirers, and the world actually began to be infected with the spirit of knight-errantry, when Cervantes, by an inimitable piece of ridicule, reformed the taste of mankind, representing chivalry in the right point of view, and converting romance to purposes far more useful and entertaining, by making it assume the sock, and point out the follies of ordinary life.

The same method has been practised by other Spanish and French authors, and by none more successfully than by Monsieur

Le Sage, who, in his *Adventures of Gil Blas*, has described the knavery and foibles of life, with infinite humour and sagacity. The following sheets I have modelled on his plan, taking the liberty, however, to differ from him in the execution, where I thought his particular situations were uncommon, extravagant, or peculiar to the country in which the scene is laid. The disgraces of Gil Blas are, for the most part, such as rather excite mirth than compassion: he himself laughs at them; and his transitions from distress to happiness, or at least ease, are so sudden, that neither the reader has time to pity him, nor himself to be acquainted with affliction. This conduct, in my opinion, not only deviates from probability, but prevents that generous indignation which ought to animate the reader against the sordid and vicious disposition of the world.

I have attempted to represent modest merit struggling page xli / with every difficulty to which a friendless orphan is exposed, from his own want of experience, as well as from the selfishness, envy, malice, and base indifference of mankind. To secure a favourable prepossession, I have allowed him the advantages of birth and education, which, in the series of misfortunes, will, I hope, engage the ingenuous more warmly in his behalf; and though I foresee that some people will be offended at the mean scenes in which he is involved, I persuade myself the judicious will not only perceive the necessity of describing those situations to which he must of course be confined, in his low state, but also find entertainment in viewing those parts of life, where the humours and passions are undisguised by affectation, ceremony, or education; and the whimsical peculiarities of disposition appear as nature has implanted them. But I believe I need not trouble myself in vindicating a practice authorised by the best writers in this way, some of whom I have already named.

Every intelligent reader will, at first sight, perceive I have not deviated from nature in the facts, which are all true in the main, although the circumstances are altered and disguised, to avoid personal satire.

It now remains to give my reasons for making the chief personage of this work a North Briton; which are chiefly these: I could at a small expense bestow on him such education as I thought the dignity of his birth and character required, which could not possibly be obtained in England, by such slender means as the nature of my plan would afford. In the next place, I could represent simplicity of manners in a remote part of the kingdom, with more propriety than in any other place near the capital; and, lastly, the disposition of the Scots, addicted to traveling, justifies my conduct in deriving an adventurer from that country. page xlii /

That the delicate reader may not be offended at the unmeaning oaths which proceed from the mouths of some persons in these memoirs, I beg leave to premise, that I imagined nothing could more effectually expose the absurdity of such miserable expletives, than a natural and verbal representation of the discourse in which they occur. page xliii /

Ferdinand Count Fathom (1753)

Author's Prefatory Address

To Doctor . . . . . .

You and I, my good friend, have often deliberated on the difficulty of writing such a dedication as might gratify the self-complacency of a patron, without exposing the author to the ridicule or censure of the public; and I think we generally agreed that the task was altogether impracticable.—Indeed, this was one of the few subjects on which we have always thought in the same manner. For, notwithstanding that deference and regard which we mutually pay to each other, certain it is, we have often differed, according to the predominancy of those different passions, which frequently warp the opinion, and perplex the understanding of the most judicious.

The Adventures of Ferdinand Count Fathom. Reprinted from *The Works of Tobias Smollett,* edited by George Saintsbury (London: The Navarre Society, Ltd., n.d.), Volume VIII.

In dedication, as in poetry, there is no medium; for, if any one of the human virtues be omitted in the enumeration of the patron's good qualities, the whole address is construed into an affront, and the writer has the mortification to find his praise prostituted to very little purpose.

On the other hand, should he yield to the transports of gratitude or affection, which is always apt to exaggerate, and produce no more than the genuine effusions of his heart, the world will make no allowance for the warmth of his passion, but ascribe the praise he bestows to interested views and sordid adulation.

Sometimes too, dazzled by the tinsel of a character which page 1 / he has no opportunity to investigate, he pours forth the homage of his admiration upon some false Mæcenas, whose future conduct gives the lie to his eulogium, and involves him in shame and confusion of face. Such was the fate of a late ingenious author,[1] who was so often put to the blush for the undeserved incense he had offered in the heat of an enthsiastic disposition, misled by popular applause, that he had resolved to retract, in his last will, all the encomiums which he had thus prematurely bestowed, and stigmatise the unworthy by name — a laudable scheme of poetical justice, the execution of which was fatally prevented by untimely death.

Whatever may have been the fate of other dedicators, I, for my own part, sit down to write this address, without any apprehension of disgrace or disappointment; because I know you are too well convinced of my affection and sincerity to repine at what I shall say touching your character and conduct. And you will do me the justice to believe, that this public distinction is a testimony of my particular friendship and esteem.

Not that I am either insensible of your infirmities, or disposed to conceal them from the notice of mankind. There are certain foibles which can only be cured by shame and mortification; and whether or not yours be of that species, I shall have the comfort to think my best endeavours were used for your reformation.

Know then, I can despise your pride, while I honour your integrity, and applaud your taste, while I am shocked at your ostentation. — I have known you trifling, superficial, and obstinate in dispute; meanly jealous and awkwardly reserved; rash

[1] The Author of the "Seasons."

and haughty in your resentments; and coarse and lowly in your connexions. I have blushed at the weakness of your conversation, and trembled at the errors of your conduct — yet, as I own you possess certain good qualities, which overbalance these defects, and distinguish you on this occasion as a person for whom I have the most perfect attachment and esteem, you have no cause to complain of the indelicacy with which your faults are reprehended. And as they are chiefly the excesses of a sanguine disposition and looseness of thought, impatient of caution or control, you may, thus stimulated, watch over your own intemperance and infirmity with redoubled vigilance and consideration, and for the future profit by the severity of my reproof.

page 2 /

These, however, are not the only motives that induce me to trouble you with this public application. I must not only perform my duty to my friends, but also discharge the debt I owe to my own interest. We live in a censorious age; and an author cannot take too much precaution to anticipate the prejudice, misapprehension, and temerity of malice, ignorance, and presumption.

I therefore think it incumbent upon me to give some previous intimation of the plan which I have executed in the subsequent performance, that I may not be condemned upon partial evidence; and to whom can I with more propriety appeal in my explanation than to you, who are so well acquainted with all the sentiments and emotions of my breast?

A novel is a large diffused picture, comprehending the characters of life, disposed in different groups, and exhibited in various attitudes, for the purposes of an uniform plan, and general occurrence, to which every individual figure is subservient. But this plan cannot be executed with propriety, probability, or success, without a principal personage to attract the attention, unite the incidents, unwind the clue of the labyrinth, and at last close the scene, by virtue of his own importance.

Almost all the heroes of this kind, who have hitherto succeeded on the English stage, are characters of transcendent worth, conducted through the vicissitudes of fortune, to that goal of happiness, which ever ought to be the repose of extraordinary desert. — Yet the same principle by which we rejoice at the remuneration of merit, will teach us to relish the disgrace and discomfiture of vice, which is always an example of extensive use and influence, because it leaves a deep impression of terror upon the minds of those who were not confirmed in the pursuit of morality and virtue, and, while the balance waivers, enables the right scale to preponderate.

In the drama, which is a more limited field of invention, the chief personage is often the object of our detestation and abhorrence; and we are as well pleased to see the wicked schemes of a *Richard* blasted, and the perfidy of a *Maskwell* exposed, as to behold a *Bevil* happy, and an *Edward* victorious.

The impulses of fear, which is the most violent and interesting of all the passions, remain longer than any other upon the memory; and for one that is allured to virtue, by the contemplation of that peace and happiness which it page 3 / bestows, a hundred are deterred from the practice of vice, by that infamy and punishment to which it is liable, from the laws and regulations of mankind.

Let me not, therefore, be condemned for having chosen my principal character from the purlieus of treachery and fraud, when I declare my purpose is to set him up as a beacon for the benefit of the unexperienced and unwary, who, from the perusal of these memoirs, may learn to avoid the manifold snares with which they are continually surrounded in the paths of life; while those who hesitate on the brink of iniquity may be terrified from plunging into that irremediable gulf, by surveying the deplorable fate of *Ferdinand Count Fathom.*

That the mind might not be fatigued, nor the imagination disgusted, by a succession of vicious objects, I have endeavoured to refresh the attention with occasional incidents of a different nature; and raised up a virtuous character, in opposition to the adventurer, with a view to amuse the fancy, engage the affection, and form a striking contrast which might heighten the expression, and give a *relief* to the moral of the whole.

If I have not succeeded in my endeavours to unfold the mysteries of fraud, to instruct the ignorant, and entertain the vacant; if I have failed in my attempts to subject folly to ridicule, and vice to indignation; to rouse the spirit of mirth, wake the soul of compassion, and touch the secret springs that move the heart; I have, at least, adorned virtue with honour and applause, branded iniquity with reproach and shame, and carefully avoided every hint or expression which could give umbrage to the most delicate reader — circumstances which (whatever may be my fate with the public) will with you always operate in favour of,

Dear sir, your very affectionate friend and servant,

THE AUTHOR. page 4 /

JAMES FENIMORE COOPER

The Leather-Stocking Tales (1823–1841)

Author's Preface

This series of Stories, which has obtained the name of *The Leather-Stocking Tales*, has been written in a very desultory and inartificial manner. The order in which the several books appeared was essentially different from that in which they would have been presented to the world had the regular course of their incidents been consulted. In *The Pioneers*, the first of the series written, the Leather-Stocking is represented as already old, and driven from his early haunts in the forest by the sound of the axe and the smoke of the settler. *The Last of the Mohicans*, the next book in the order of publication, carried the readers back to a much earlier period in the history of our hero, representing him as middle-aged, and in the fullest vigor of manhood. In *The Prairie*, his career terminates, and he is laid in his grave. There, it was originally the intention to leave him, in the expectation that, as in the case of the human mass, he would soon be forgotten. But a latent regard for this character induced the author to resuscitate him in *The Pathfinder*, a book that was not long after succeeded by *The Deerslayer*, thus completing the series as it now exists.

While the five books that have been written were originally published in the order just mentioned, that of the incidents, insomuch as they are connected with the career of page iii / their principal character, is, as has been stated, very different. Taking the life of the Leather-Stocking as a guide, *The Deerslayer* should have been the opening book, for in that work he is seen just

---

"Preface to the Leather-Stocking Tales." Reprinted from *The Works of James Fenimore Cooper*, Mohawk Edition (New York: G. P. Putnam's Sons, [1895–1900]), [Volume I], *The Deerslayer*.

emerging into manhood; to be succeeded by *The Last of the Mohicans*, *The Pathfinder*, *The Pioneers*, and *The Prairie*. This arrangement embraces the order of events, though far from being that in which the books at first appeared. *The Pioneers* was published in 1822; *The Deerslayer* in 1841; making the interval between them nineteen years. Whether these progressive years have had a tendency to lessen the value of the last-named book, by lessening the native fire of its author, or of adding somewhat in the way of improved taste and a more matured judgment, is for others to decide.

If anything from the pen of the writer of these romances is at all to outlive himself, it is, unquestionably, the series of *The Leather-Stocking Tales*. To say this, is not to predict a very lasting reputation for the series itself, but simply to express the belief it will outlast any, or all, of the works from the same hand.

It is undeniable that the desultory manner in which *The Leather-Stocking Tales* were written, has, in a measure, impaired their harmony, and otherwise lessened their interest. This is proved by the fate of the two books last published, though probably the two most worthy an enlightened and cultivated reader's notice. If the facts could be ascertained, it is probable the result would show that of all those (in America, in particular) who have read the three first books of the series, not one in ten has a knowledge of the existence even of the two last. Several causes have tended to produce this result. The long interval of time between the appearance of *The Prairie* and that of *The Pathfinder*, was itself a reason why the later books of the series should be overlooked. There was no longer novelty to attract attention, and the interest was materially impaired by the manner in which events were necessarily anticipated, in laying the last of the series first before the world. With the generation that is now coming on the stage this fault will be partially removed by the edition contained in the page iv / present work, in which the several tales will be arranged solely in reference to their connection with each other.

The author has often been asked if he had any original in his mind for the character of Leather-Stocking. In a physical sense, different individuals known to the writer in early life certainly presented themselves as models, through his recollections; but in a moral sense this man of the forest is purely a creation. The idea of delineating a character that possessed little of civilization but its highest principles as they are exhibited in the uneducated, and all of savage life that is not incompatible with these great rules of conduct, is perhaps natural to the situation in which Natty was placed. He is too proud of his origin to sink into the condition of the wild Indian, and too much a man of the woods not to imbibe as much as was at all desirable, from his friends and companions. In a moral point of view it was the intention to illustrate the effect of seed scattered by the wayside. To use his own language, his "gifts" were "white gifts," and he was not disposed to bring on them discredit. On the other hand, removed from nearly all the temptations of civilized life, placed in the best associations of that which is deemed savage, and favorably disposed by nature to improve such advantages, it appeared to the writer that his hero was a fit subject to represent the better qualities of both conditions, without pushing either to extremes.

There was no violent stretch of the imagination, perhaps, in supposing one of civilized associations in childhood, retaining many of his earliest lessons amid the scenes of the forest. Had these early impressions, however, not been sustained by continued, though casual connection with men of his own color, if not of his own caste, all our information goes to show he would soon have lost every trace of his origin. It is believed that sufficient attention was paid to the particular circumstances in which this individual was placed, to justify the picture of his qualities that has been drawn. The Delawares only attracted the attention of the missionaries, and were a tribe unusually influenced by their precepts and example. In many instances they became Christians, and cases occurred in which their subsequent page v / lives gave proof of the efficacy of the great moral changes that had taken place within them.

A leading character in a work of fiction has a fair right to the aid which can be obtained from a poetical view of the subject. It is in this view, rather than in one more strictly circumstantial, that Leather-Stocking has been drawn. The imagination has no great task in portraying to itself a being removed from the everyday inducements to err, which abound in civilized life, while he retains the best and simplest of his early impressions; who sees God in the forest; hears Him in the winds; bows to Him in the firmament that o'ercanopies all; submits to his sway in a humble belief of his justice and mercy; in a word, a being who finds the impress of the Deity in all the works of nature, without any of the blots produced by the expedients, and passion, and mistakes of man. This is the most that has been attempted in the character of Leather-Stocking. Had this been done without any of the drawbacks of humanity, the picture would have been, in all probability, more pleasing than just. In order to preserve the *vraisemblable,* therefore, traits derived from the prejudices, tastes, and even the weaknesses of his youth, have been mixed up with these higher qualities and longings, in a way, it is hoped, to represent a reasonable picture of human nature, without offering to the spectator a "monster of goodness."

It has been objected to these books that they give a more favorable picture of the redman than he deserves. The writer apprehends that much of this objection arises from the habits of those who have made it. One of his critics, on the appearance of the first work in which Indian character was portrayed, objected that its "characters were Indians of the school of Heckewelder, rather than of the school of nature." These words quite probably contain the substance of the true answer to the objection. Heckewelder was an ardent, benevolent missionary, bent on the good of the redman, and seeing in him one who had the soul, reason, and characteristics of a fellow-being. The critic is understood to have been a very distinguished agent of the government, one very familiar with Indians, as they are **page vi /** seen at the councils to treat for the sale of their lands, where little or none of their domestic qualities come in play, and where indeed, their evil passions are known to have the fullest scope. As just would it be to draw conclusions of the general state of American society from the scenes of the capital, as to suppose that the negotiating of one of these treaties is a fair picture of Indian life.

It is the privilege of all writers of fiction, more particularly when their works aspire to the elevation of romances, to present the *beau idéal* of their characters to the reader. This it is which constitutes poetry, and to suppose that the redman is to be represented only in the squalid misery or in the degraded moral state that certainly more or less belongs to his condition, is, we apprehend, taking a very narrow view of an author's privileges. Such criticism would have deprived the world of even Homer. **page vii /**

The Deerslayer (1841)

Author's Preface

As has been stated in the preface to the series of *The Leather-Stocking Tales, The Deerslayer* is properly the first in the order of reading, though the last in that of publication. In this book the hero is represented as just arriving at manhood, with the freshness of feeling that belongs to that interesting period of life, and with the power to please that properly characterizes youth. As a consequence, he is loved; and, what denotes the real waywardness of humanity, more than it corresponds with theories and moral propositions, perhaps, he is loved by one full of art, vanity, and weakness, and loved principally for his sincerity, his modesty, and his unerring truth and probity. The preference he gives to the high qualities named, over beauty, delirious passion, and sin, it is hoped, will offer a lesson that can injure none. This portion of the book is intentionally kept down, though it is thought to be sufficiently distinct to convey its moral.

The intention has been to put the sisters in strong contrast; one, admirable in person, clever, filled with the pride of beauty, erring, and fallen; the other, barely provided with sufficient capacity to know good from evil, instinct, notwithstanding, with the virtues of woman, reverencing and loving God, and yielding only to the weakness of her sex, in admiring personal attractions in one too coarse and unobservant to distinguish or to understand her quiet, gentle feeling in his favor.

As for the scene of this tale, it is intended for, and believed to be a close description of the Otsego, prior to the **page ix /** year 1760, when the first rude settlement was commenced on its banks, at that time only an insignificant clearing near the outlet,

---

Reprinted from *The Works of James Fenimore Cooper*, Mohawk Edition (New York: G. P. Putnam's Sons, [1895–1900]), [Volume I].

with a small hut of squared logs, for the temporary dwelling of the Deputy Superintendent of Indian affairs. The recollections of the writer carry him back distinctly to a time when nine tenths of the shores of this lake were in the virgin forest, a peculiarity that was owing to the circumstance of the roads running through the first range of valleys removed from the water side. The woods and the mountains have ever formed a principal source of beauty with this charming sheet of water, enough of the former remaining to this day to relieve the open grounds from monotony and tameness.

In most respects the descriptions of scenery in the tale are reasonably accurate. The rock appointed for the rendezvous between the Deerslayer and his friend the Delaware still remains, bearing the name of the Otsego Rock. The shoal on which Hutter is represented as having built his "castle" is a little misplaced, lying, in fact, nearer to the northern end of the lake, as well as to the eastern shore, than is stated in this book. Such a shoal, however, exists, surrounded on all sides by deep water. In the dryest seasons a few rocks are seen above the surface of the lake, and rushes, at most periods of the year, mark its locality. In a word, in all but precise position, even this feature of the book is accurate. The same is true of the several points introduced, of the bay, of the river, of the mountains, and of all the other accessories of the place.

The legend is purely fiction, no authority existing for any of its facts, characters, or other peculiarities, beyond that which was thought necessary to secure the semblance of reality. page x /

CHARLES DICKENS

David Copperfield (*1850*)

AUTHOR'S "NUMBER PLANS"

The Personal History, Adventures, Experience, and Observation of David Copperfield the Younger of Blunderstone Rookery (Which He never meant to be Published on any Account.) Author's "Number Plans" reprinted by permission from *Dickens at Work*, by John Butt and Kathleen Tillotson (Fairlawn, New Jersey: Essential Books, Inc., 1958). These notes are printed on a double page. See Bibliographical Note A, page xiii.

page 116 /

Lobsters & Crawfish

The people living on the Barge.

Mr Hasden
Murdle Murdstone
Murden

The progress of his mother's second courtship

Brooks of Sheffield
Goes to Peggotty's

(Personal History and Adventures of
David Copperfield — No I)

chapter I.

I am born

Father dead — Gravestone outside the house
Young mother — Tendency to weakness and vanity
Miss Betsey — Her old wrongs — Peggotty
Why rookery? — Ham Peggotty

Morgan the Dr

chapter II.

I observe

The things that come out of the blank of his infancy on looking back. — child at church —
— The future father in law "at this minute I see him turn round in the garden with his damned black eyes" — &c

page 120 /

Miss Murdstone
Their religion
Picture of all that, and its effect on Davy's life.
Cast off and getting sullen.
qy His books and reading?
His offence, and confinement upstairs. Child's remembrance of the latter.
Sent away

⟨I attend church⟩

⟨hospitably received⟩
⟨I am received ∧ by Mr Peggotty⟩

page 121 /

experience
(Personal History and ⟨adventures⟩ of
David Copperfield — N° II.)

chapter IV.

I fall into disgrace

Progress of his mother's weakness under the Murdstones.
Miss Murdstone
Beat's him
Bites
Shut up and dismissed

chapter V.

— And am sent away from home.

The carrier & Peggotty.
Waiter — Glass of ale — chops — pudding — himself
journey
to be left till called for
School with the boys all at home
"Take care of him. He bites"

chapter VI.

I enlarge my circle of acquaintance.

Mr Creakle.
return of the boys
spending his money
Steerford
Steerforth.

page 122 /

School. Master

Steerforth

The Afternoon

Peggotty's enquiries about school
Tells her of Barkis

Goes home — Mother says she is not to leave her.
It may not be for long.

Mother with a baby.
comes back, & receives news of her death.
Goes home ∧ again, to the funeral.

⟨I enjoy one afternoon's holiday⟩

⟨The holidays are concentrated into one afternoon.⟩

⟨My holidays.⟩

page 123 /

(Personal History and Experience of
David Copperfield — Nº III.)

chapter VII.

My First half at Salem House.

School — His progress
Steerforth's character.
Traddles. Dº
Mr Mell's poverty and mother, and dismissal.

Visit from ⟨Peggotty⟩ Mr Peggotty? Yes. And Steerforth
Summing up, & going home.

chapter VIII.

My holidays. Especially one happy Afternoon

The Afternoon. The baby
Peggotty & his mother.
The Murdstones — progress of their influence &c
Holding up the baby

chapter IX.

I have a memorable Birthday.

Mrs Creakle breaks it to him
His state of mind — childish incidental whimsicalities
The undertaker's, Mr Omer's
State of home, and recollection of funeral
Peggotty's narrative
close with the idea of his mother as she was, with him as he was, in her arms.

page 126 /

what I know so well

I become neglected and am provided for

I begin life on my ⟨account⟩ own account.

I go on with life, rather uncomfortably
on my own account and don't like it

I make a resolution

page 127 /

(Personal History and Experience of
David Copperfield — N° IV.)

chapter X.

I become neglected, and am provided for.

Go away with Peggotty — Barkis
Mr Peggotty's
Her marriage ride with the two children
neglect
Quinion. — arrangement
"Behold me" &c

chapter XI.

I begin life on my own account, and don't like it.

all the ⟨Murdstone and⟩ life at the warehouse
Murdstone and Grinby
Mr and Mrs Micawber — Prison — Insolvent Court

chapter XII.

Liking life on my own account no better,
I form a great resolution.

The young man with the donkey cart

run away to Aunt Betsey

page 128 /

Chatham — Canterbury sunshine
Tramps — pint of beer?

Your sister, Betsey Trotwood

Mr Dick's history? qy Yes, very briefly. by Miss Betsey

Donkies
Miss Murdstone comes on a donkey

Mr Dick and his memorial

His delusion

Introduction of the real heroine

page 129 /

(Personal History and Experience of
David Copperfield — No V.)

chapter XIII.

The sequel of my resolution.

His journey
Goes to his aunts
Miss Betsey — "Janet! Donkies!"
Mr Dick

chapter XIV.

My Aunt makes up her mind about me.

Mr Dick again
Mr and Miss Murdstone come
conversation — ends with his Aunt adopting him.
Trotwood Copperfield

chapter XV.

I make another beginning

old House at Canterbury
Mr Wickfield
His one motive. Agnes Wickfield
Uriah Heep.

page 132 / Dictionary

The good old Doctor & the young wife
Uriah Heep? qy Yes.
Mr Micawber? qy Yes. and Mrs
"Turn his attention to coals." The Medway Coal Trade

Mr Micawber's letter

The Progress from childhood to youth.

My aunt? qy No. only generally

Mr Dick? qy Yes. With the Dr.

Peggotty's half guinea to be repaid.

Mems for the Progress.

The cathedral

Miss Wilkins — No. Shepherd

Head boy.
Tail-coat
Loving a grown woman, much too old.

page 133 / (Personal History and Experience of David Copperfield — No VI.)

chapter XVI.

I am a new boy, in more senses than one.

Doctor Strong's
The Doctor and his young wife
Mr Jack Maldon   Wife's mother. The old soldier
Mr Wickfield & Agnes.
Uriah Heep.
Mr Jack Maldon's going away. The cherry colored ribbon.
Close with her face.

chapter XVII.

Somebody turns up.

Mr Dick — The man who frightens my aunt.
Mr Dick & the Doctor walking up & down
Uriah Heep and his mother
Their lemon-squeezing process
Mr & Mrs Micawber.

Mr Micawber makes Uriah's acquaintance.

chapter XVIII.

A Retrospect.

Two loves.
Miss Shepherd. In the responses — put her in among the Royal family.
Fight with a butcher
Growing up — Agnes grows up.
In love with the eldest Miss Larkins
ring — Bear's grease — &c &c

page 136 /

Janet? qy?

Steerforth's mother? ⟨Yes⟩

Steerforth?	Yes.
Little Em'ly?	Yes.
The two partners?	No
Mr Mell?	No.

Lirrimer?
Littimer.

page 137 /

(Personal History and Experience of
David Copperfield — No VII.)

chapter XIX.

I look about me, and make a discovery.

Pave the way with Mr Wickfield
Do Agnes
Do Mrs Strong
Goes away to see Peggotty
First Fall in life Play.
Waiter Golden Cross Charing Cross
meets Steerforth

chapter XX.

Steerforth's Home.

Mrs Steerforth
Miss Dartle. "Threw a hammer at her?"
"Eh? But is it really though? I want to know

chapter XXI.

Little Em'ly.

The servant. Littimer.
Little Em'ly at Mr Omer's — Mr Omer "Two parties."
Peggotty
Mr Barkis a little nearer
Mr Peggotty's account of her being engaged to Ham.

page 140 /

Aiguille and Tanguille
Tranguille and Jorker] For the Proctors
No. Spenlow & Jorkins

Miss Croodledey
Miss Croodledy
Miss Croodlejeux | No. Miss Mowcher.

His first time of getting tipsy.
Description of it exactly.

page 141 /

(Personal History and Experience of
David Copperfield — N° VIII.)

chapter XXII.

Some old scenes and some new faces.

Steerforth's misgivings
Em'ly's misgivings] still tending onwards, Miss Mowcher

Ham — Martha. The girl already lost.
Omer. haberdasher &c

chapter XXIII.

I corroborate Mr Dick and choose a profession

Aunt Betsey — Afraid of fire
Proctor's — Doctors Commons
Chambers in Buckingham Street
Mrs Crupp

Chapter XXIV.

My First Dissipation

Dinner Party
Guests
"A man" &c
Agnes at the Theatre
Amigoarawayso?

page 142 /

No Steerforth this time. Keep him out.

Doctors Commons? Yes

Traddles? Yes

Dora Spenlow? Yes

Uriah Heep? Yes

The Micawbers? Yes

page 143 /

(Personal History and Experience of
David Copperfield — N° IX.)

chapter XXV.

Good and bad Angels.

Start from last point, with Agnes — His good angel. Steerforth, she tells him, his bad

at Papa's agent's — Mr Waterbrook.
Dinner — Aristocracy — Blood
Tommy Traddles.
Uriah Heep and Agnes — told to David at his chambers
sleeps there.

chapter XXVI.

I fall into captivity.

In love with Dora Spenlow
Miss Murdstone, her duenna
all his love
close with Mrs Crupp

chapter XXVII.

Tommy Traddles.

Traddles engaged
His furnishing
His story
M^r^ and Mrs Micawber.
all engaged to dine with David

page 144 /

qy Em'ly to go? No. — Yes.

qy Aunt ruined? — Next time

qy Miss Mowcher? Impossible. Try next time

Littimer? Yes
Steerforth? Yes

First chapter funny

Then on to Em'ly.

Gauntlet to society
"Going out with the tide"

Divide last chapter in two

Mrs Gummidge

page 145 /

(Personal History and Experience of
David Copperfield — No X.)

chapter XXVIII.

Mr Micawber's Gauntlet

Mr & Mrs Micawber
& Traddles

Glimpse of Littimer
Mr Micawbers relieving himself
by legal phraseology

Mrs Micawber's projects
Mr Micawber's letter.

Steerforth

chapter XXIX.

I visit Steerforth at his home, again.

Rosa Dartle.
"Never more to touch that passive hand"

chapter XXX.

A loss. Omer and Joram — lead up.
Barkis is willin

chapter XXXI.

A greater loss. The candle in the window
Ham comes alone & takes
Davy outside
Her letter.

Close with Mrs Gummidge

page 146 /

Mr Peggotty to begin his search. ✓
Mrs Steerforth. qy Yes. And Rosa Dartle

Miss Mowcher. ✓ Yes
The Doctor and his wife. qy. No
Agnes? qy. Only an allusion
Aunt & Mr Dick Yes
Is engaged to Dora. Yes (Miss Mills)

Tommy Traddles qy

What an idle time! What an insubstantial, happy, foolish, time! of all the times of mine, that ⟨he⟩ Time has in his grip, there is none that in retrospection I can smile at half so much, and think of half so tenderly!

page 147 /

(Personal History and Experience of
David Copperfield — No XI.)

chapter XXXII.

The beginning of a ⟨pilgrimage⟩ long journey.

chapter XXXIII.

Blissful.

The used-up young friend. Miss Mills — blighted affection.
Sings about the echoes in the Caverns of Memory.

chapter XXXIV.

My Aunt astonishes me.

page 150 /

Agnes. ⟨Her ⟩ Yes
Dr & Mrs Strong? Yes
Jack Maldon? Yes.
Mr Micawber engaged by Uriah.

Progress of David to a working state, still tinged, romantically, by his youth and character, and overdone. No similar progress on the part of Dora. Poor little Dora, not bred for ⟨the world⟩ a working life
My aunt
⟨Miss Betsey⟩ "And not silly?"

Express that, very delicately

Carry the thread of Agnes through it all

page 151 / (Personal History and Experience of
David Copperfield — No XII.)

chapter XXXV.

Depression.

My Aunt.
"and not silly?
"Blind, Blind, Trot!"
Agnes
My Aunt's Property
Mr Wickfield and Uriah. Agnes — Blind, blind, blind

chapter XXXVI.

Enthusiasm.

David's New State. Forest of Difficulty
Glimpse of Rosa Dartle
Bring up Dr Strong and Annie, & Mr Jack Maldon. Mr Dick useful
Mr Micawber "a member of one of the learned professions
I.O.U. Foot on his native heath — Judge or Chancellor.
Kettle Drums.

"Walks erect before his fellow men"

chapter XXXVII

A little cold water.

⟨ ⟩ Poor little Dora
"Oh Take me to Julia Mills and go away, please!"
Taking a Guitar case through the Forest of difficulty.
"I used to sit thinking of it of a night, sometimes, until I felt quite grey

page 154 /

The Doctor, Annie, and Mr Jack Maldon? No.

Agnes and her father? Yes

Mrs Heep? Yes. Touched

To carry on the thread of Uriah, carefully, and not obtrusively, also of David and Agnes

Mr Spenlow. Dead
Mr Peggotty's story of his search.
Miss Murdstone / Mr Murdstone } qy Not yet

Traddles Next No

page 155 /

(Personal History and Experience of
David Copperfield — No XIII.)

chapter XXXVIII.

A Dissolution of Partnership.

David found out
Mr Spenlow & Miss Murdstone
Will-making Two Maiden Aunts
Putney
Miss Mills's Journal. "Self and Young Gazelle. J.M."

chapter XXXIX.

Wickfield and Heep.

Touting in Doctors Commons.
Canterbury. Agnes.
Uriah and his mother. Why "Umble"
Mr Wickfield. Agnes.

chapter XL.

The Wanderer

Snowy night.
Martha. — a shadow of it.

Mr Peggotty.
His travels.
Letter from Little Em'ly. Close with him going away again — through the snow — hushed.

page 156 /

David's Marriage to Dora

Back to the Strong incidents, and clear the way

Mr Dick

Clear Julia Mills off

Bring Agnes and Dora together.

page 157 /

(Personal History and Experience of
David Copperfield — No XIV.)

chapter XLI.

Dora's Aunts.

Traddles & David go to them
Their house at Putney
The old ladies like birds
arranged — Little Dora behind the door
"If I should like a nice Irish Stew for instance.

chapter XLII.

Mischief.

Uriah Heep, jealous of interlopers, works it out, about the Strongs
Old Doctor, generous & good. Agnes & Dora
Dora — suppose — to David
Slap Uriah's face
Close chapter with Mrs Micawber's letter describing change in Micawber

chapter XLIII.

Another Retrospect.

Let me stand aside, and see the phantoms of those
days go by me.
Licence — dressmaker — Agnes, Sophy, church

Peggotty in the gallery Dora Jip
House. Aunt don't live with them
"Are you happy now, you foolish boy?"

page 160 /

M^r^ and Mrs Strong. To be adjusted — Mrs Markleham — Mr Jack Maldon

David's Married Life.

qy. M^r^ and Miss Murdstone? No. consider for next N^o^

qy Little Em'ly? And through Martha? ?

qy My Aunt's persecutor? And any indication of Mr Micawber in communication with her? — No consider for next N^o^

Mrs Steerforth and Miss Dartle. Carry Steerforth through by means of them.

page 161 / (Personal History and Experience of David Copperfield. N° XV.)

chapter XLIV.

Our Housekeeping

⟨ ⟩ Mary Anne — Paragon
Ordeal of Servants
First quarrel Carry through incapacity of Dora — but affectionate
Salmon. One pound six.

chapter XLV.

Mr Dick fulfils my aunt's prediction.

The Explanation brought round by Mr Dick
Shew the faults of mothers, and their consequences
"No disparity in marriage like unsuitability of mind and purpose" — "Saved from the first mistaken impulse of an undisciplined heart" — My love was founded on a rock."
all brought to bear on David, and applied by him to himself
old unhappy feeling going by, upon the wind

chapter XLVI.

Intelligence.

Miss Dartle — ⟨ ⟩ Garden seat — Prospect
respectable Mr Littimer, and his account of
Em'ly's having left Steerforth, and why
"Don't address yourself to me" — "Nor to me" —
"You have no mother? It is a pity she would have been proud of you
closing prospect, and mist like a rising sea. Next
time seen, sea risen. — Then with Mr Peggotty following Martha

page 162 /

Carry through, the unravelling of Uriah Heep. always by

Mr Micawber.

Carry through, also, the married life √

Dora in declining health. First intimation? Yes.

Little Em'ly and Mr Pegotty. qy. To close the No with

her discovery? Yes

qy Omer and Joram? No

qy. Mr and Miss Murdstone? From last Number

No.

qy. My Aunt's Persecutor? From last Number

Yes.

page 163 / (Personal History and Experience of

David Copperfield. No XVI.)

chapter XLVII.

Martha

Vauxhall Bridge
Oh the river oh the river!
Emily will be the means of her redemption.

My Aunt's husband
"This is my grumpy
frumpy, story Trot."

chapter XLVIII

Domestic.

Dora & David again — Page — transported page
Progress of his mind about his marriage — Tries to "form Dora's mind."
David's mind — old feeling — suppose not married —
Dora's illness begun — Jip growing old Carrying her upstairs

Little Blossom. O what a fatal name it was, and how the blossom withered in its bloom!

chapter XLIX

Mysterious.

Mr Micawber's letter to David — fallen tower
Mrs Micawber's letter to Traddles. Oyster knife at the twins
Mr Micawber contemplating King's Bench
rascal-Heep — Gray's Elegy. Pastoral note.

page 163 / chapter L.

Mr Peggotty's dream comes true.

Martha takes them to her
old street — about Golden Square
Scene between Emily and Rosa Dartle
"Uncle!"
covers her face with a handkerchief.

page 166 /

Dora to die in this No? Yes. at the end. "I

want to speak to Agnes." alone with her, before dying.

Smash Uriah Heep, by means of Mr Micawber.

Mr Micawber triumphant. restored to Mrs Micawber's arms.

page 167 / (Personal History and Experience of David Copperfield — No XVII.)

chapter LI.

The beginning of a longer journey.

Mr Peggotty's narrative
Fever — forgot recently acquired language — "Fisherman's daughter
"here's a shell!" / saved by Martha
David & Peggotty go down to Yarmouth
Clear the way for Emigration   Farewell of old boat
Mrs Gummidge

Chapter LII.

I assist at an Explosion.

Uriah Heep's office
Mr Micawber's letter — revelation — Traddles. my Aunt's property.
Mrs Heep "Be umble Ury, and tell all!
Emigration proposed by my Aunt
restoration of mutual confidence
between Mr & Mrs Micawber.
Australia.

page 166 /

Brought from last No. Omer & Joram? Yes.

Mr and Miss Murdstone? Not yet.

page 167 /

Chapter LIII.

Another Retrospect.

Three times — White line before each [?]
Speaks of herself as past.

Jip grown old. The chinese House before the fire. David looking at him
Present little Dora's death, through Jip's Death. David sees him lie down on the rug, and die — Agnes comes down — all over —

page 168 /

To finish from last No — Uriah

To bring up — Mr and Miss Murdstone? No. last No.

The Emigration No = Mr Peggotty, Mrs Gummidge, Em'ly, Martha }

Mr Micawber, Mrs Micawber, The children }

page 169 /

(Personal History and Experience of
David Copperfield — No XVIII.)

chapter LIV.

Mr Micawber's Transactions

Mr & Mrs Micawber
Her family.
Uriah Heep's business finished
Mr Micawber arrested — over and over again

My Aunt's money recovered. She composed.

Her husband. "He is gone, Trot. God forgive us all!

page 168 /

Agnes. Carry through.
Ham and Steerforth. Steerforth in a sinking ship in a great storm in Yarmouth Roads. Ham goes off in a life boat, — or with a rope round his waist? — through the surf. Both bodies washed ashore together?
No.

a mighty wind.

To remember — the last parting — "he was lying easily with his head upon his arm".

Mrs Micawber — Her "family" and "never will desert Mr Micawber".

Close with David going on a tour abroad.

(Lapse between this N^o and the next)

page 169 /

chapter LV.

Tempest.

David goes down to Yarmouth with letter from Emily to Ham
The storm
The wind — The spray — the coming to the sea
The town — Flying sand, seaweed — and flakes of foam seen in blotches.

Wreck. Bell at Broadstairs here, last night. Flying Boat, blown down
I saw him lying with his head upon his arm, as I had often seen him lie at school.

chapter LVI.

Two chapters here. The New wound and the old

Home to Mrs Steerforth & Rosa Dartle.
"I loved him better than you ever did! I loved him better than you ever did!" Mother, a mere statue

chapter LVII.

The Emigrants.

The Micawbers. Preparation and Nauticality
arrested again — Hungerford
her family — Sunset
Tween Decks
close with Emily & her uncle

page 172 /

after Lapse — dreamily described — in Italy &c
David to come back from abroad
All his love for Agness and all her love for him to be worked out

Traddles married, & living in chambers. Himself and his wife putting themselves to all kinds of inconvenience for her sisters

Uriah Heep "a Pet Prisoner" — continually singing hymns and exhorting everybody who visits him — regarded as a model Penitent — but quite true to himself & exactly the same infernal scoundrel as ever.
His Mother, ditto. Never were people so "umble".
No. Change that. Let him profess to be converting her.

Peggotty. Little Em'ly. The Micawbers

Order
Absence
Return
Agnes
Interesting Penitents
Agnes
Visitor
Retrospect

David and Agnes married.
Close with ⟨ ⟩ a Retrospect
What Dora said to Agnes, to come out at last.

page 173 / (Personal History and Experience of David Copperfield — Nos XIX and XX.)

chapter LVIII.

Absence

His state of mind
Despondency changed by Agnes — Switzerland
Loves her and finds dreamily that he has long loved her.
Too late. For he made her his sister! Her, & her own noble heart

chapter LIX.

Return.

Gray's Inn Coffee House
unpromising appearance of England
Happiness of Traddles married. Hope for him, after all.
Mr Chillip

chapter LX.

Agnes.

Tells of the Murdstones.
Finishes them

My Aunt (1st time)
The old house
Looking out of a window how he had looked out as a boy
Brother and sister   Agnes mother

chapter LXI.

I am shewn two interesting Penitents

Middlesex Magistrates Separate System
Uriah Heep & Mr Littimer

page 172 /

To bring up.

Creakle, as ^a Middlesex Magistrate. remember his son
Mr Mell?
Mr and Miss Murdstone
Janet — Donkeys — Dr and Mrs Strong — Julia Mills
⟨order⟩

Transition state return home? Murdstones? Agnes? Agnes 1 Traddles and his wife Interesting Penitents & Miss Mowcher? Agnes 2. and marriage	Visitor? Mrs Steerforth and Rosa? Last Retrospect

page 173 /

The Beef & the Cocoa. "Hoping you and your families will amend & see your wickedness"! Everybody ought to come here"
Mowcher

chapter LXII.

A light shines on my way   Agnes —

My Aunt (2nd time) David declares "I have loved you all my life"
"That only I should occupy this vacant place"

chapter LXIII.

A Visit

Mr Peggotty. Tells of them all. "That's Em'ly"
— Mrs Gummidge

Port Middlebay newspaper. Micawber.   Dr Mell of Colonial Salem House

chapter LXIV.

A last Retrospect.

Wind up. Julia Mills &c.
Traddles a Judge
Close with Agnes.

GUSTAVE FLAUBERT

Madame Bovary (1856)

Author's Letters

23 [305]

To Ernest Chevalier

Croisset, *January 17th* [1852]

No, my dear Ernest, I have not forgotten you. You are as important to me as I am to you, which accounts for the fact that I had been thinking most seriously of you for five or six days when your letter arrived. I had fully meant to write; in fact, our intentions coincided. . . .

Here I am back at Croisset, beside my own fire, and heavy as a log myself. I have turned back to my implacable task, and given up all idea of making any sort of splash. What I am doing is for myself and for myself alone, done in the same spirit as one plays dominoes in, to prevent life from being too much of a burden. If I publish (which I doubt) it will be solely to oblige the people who are always advising me to, and so as not to appear proud or pigheaded. Nothing could be more monotonous than my life; as it passes by, it presents no more features to the eye than the river that flows beneath my windows. Our little girl brings a bit of gaiety into the house, but my mother is growing old, both physically and mentally. A sad listlessness is creeping over her, and she is exhausted by insomnia. So here I am with the two of them. Only on Sundays Bouilhet comes; we chat a little, and that is all for a week. **page 65 /**

. . . .

Reprinted, by permission, from *Letters of Gustave Flaubert*, translated by J. M. Cohen (London: George Weidenfeld & Nicholson Limited, 1950). Based on *Correspondence, G. Flaubert, Nouvelle Edition Augmentée* (Paris: Louis Conard, 1926–1933), to which the numbers in brackets at the head of each letter refer.

. . . I am the only one to remain for ever unplaced, the same wayward scholar I was at eighteen. I see all my comrades either married, or established in life, or on the point of being. By the way, a certain friend of mine wants me to enter into marriage, to the tune of two hundred thousand pounds invested, with a mulatto lady who speaks six languages. She was born in Havana and has a most charming nature. Can you see me engendering a bunch of blackamoors? *Oi me!* I have not the least desire for wife or children. With age I have grown out of a number of little lusts, which it once seemed to me needful to satisfy. If one goes on long enough saying the grapes are sour, does not one end by believing it? So I go on from day to day, working for working's sake, without a plan in life, or schemes (I have made too many schemes), and without any desire, except to write better. page 66 /

24 [327]

To Maxime du Camp

Croisset, 1852 [*June 26th*]

My dear friend,

You seem to have some sort of interfering mania about me. Not that it worries me, never fear. My mind has been made up on these matters for a long time.

I shall only say that all these expressions: *make haste*, *now is the time*, *the moment has come*, *filling a place*, *taking up a position*, *ultra vires*, etc., are to me a meaningless language. You might just as well be speaking to a Red Indian. Don't you understand?

To *get there*, but where? To the position of Messrs. Murger, Feuillet, Monselet, etc., Arsène Houssaye, Taxile Delord, Hippolyte Lucas and seventy two more of them. Thank you very much.

To be well known is not my main business; it can only be entirely satisfying to those with a poor conceit of themselves. Besides, even then does one ever know when to rest content? The utmost renown never slakes a man's appetite and, unless he is a fool, he almost always dies uncertain of his own fame. For prominence is no more help towards a true self-estimate than obscurity.

I am aiming at something better, at pleasing myself. To me success appears to be a by-product, not a goal. Now I have been marching on this goal for what seems to me a long time, without the slightest deflection; nor have I ever stopped to pay court to ladies by the wayside, or to sleep on the greensward. If it is an illusion I am pursuing, at least I prefer the highest illusions. page 67 /

I had rather see the whole United States perish than sacrifice a single principle. I would sooner die like a dog than hurry my sentence by so much as a second before it is ripe.

I have in my head the method of writing and the choice of language that I wish to attain. When I think I have plucked the fruit, I shall not refuse to sell it, nor reject the world's applause if it is good. But, in the meantime, I do not want to diddle the public. There it is.

And if when that time comes it is too late and people have lost their appetite, that will be too bad. Believe me, I wish I were much more facile, and could draw larger profits for much less work. But I can see no remedy.

There may well be favourable moments in business, a lucky run on such and such an article, a passing craze which sends up the price of rubber or printed cottons. Let would-be manufacturers of such goods hurry to put their factories up, of course. But if your work of art is good, if it is *right*, it will evoke its response, it will find its place, in six months time, in six years or when you are dead. What does it matter?

You talk of finding the *breath of life* in Paris. To my mind your breath of life very often stinks of decayed teeth. You invite me to breathe the air of that Parnassus, but I find it rather noxious than heady. The laurels plucked there are, you must agree, a little dung-spattered. page 68 /

. . . .

There is certainly one thing you gain in Paris, and that is cheek. But it costs you a few grey hairs.

Anyone who has turned out to be a man of real strength, despite a Paris upbringing, must have been born a demi-god. He will have grown up with his ribs compressed and a weight on his head; whereas a man has to be absolutely devoid of native originality, if solitude, concentration, and years of work do not finally make something of him.

As for your bitter outcry at the stultifying nature of my life, you might as well blame a cobbler for making shoes, or a blacksmith for hammering his iron, as reproach an artist for living in his workshop. As I work every day from one in the afternoon till one in the morning, except for an interval between six and eight, I can hardly see anything to spend the remainder of my time on. If I really lived in the provinces or in the country, and spent my days playing dominoes or growing melons, I should understand your criticism. But if I am becoming stupid, it is Lucian, Shakespeare and the writing of a novel that are the cause.

I told you that I should come and live in Paris when my book was finished, and that I should publish it if I were satisfied with it. I have not altered my decision. That is all I can say, nothing more.

Really, old chap, one must take things as they come. I don't care about any fresh literary disputes that may arise. I care even less for Augier's success, and I don't give a damn if Vacquerie and Ponsard spread themselves till they have crowded me right out. I shall not come and push them from my place.

And here I send you my love. page 69 /

25 [332]

To Louise Colet

[Croisset] Tuesday [*July 6th*, 1852]

. . . If all you needed to be a poet were to have sensitive nerves, I should be greater than Shakespeare — or Homer either, for I imagine he was without nerves. But this is blasphemy. . . .

You often find children who are upset by music. They show great talent and remember tunes at a single hearing. When they play the piano they grow excited and their hearts beat faster. They get thin and pale, and fall ill; and like dogs they feel their nerves shrivel with pain at the very sound of music. It is not they that are the future Mozarts. Their *vocation* has been displaced; the spirit has passed into the flesh where it remains sterile, and the flesh decays; the result is neither genius nor good health.

It is the same with art. Feeling does not make poetry; and the more personal you are, the poorer you will be. That has always been my sin; I have always put myself into everything I have done. There I am, for instance, in Saint Anthony's place; the *Temptation* was mine and not the reader's. *The less one feels a thing, the more fit one is to express it in its true nature* (as it always is, in itself, in its generic being and divorced from all ephemeral conditions). But one must have the faculty for *making oneself feel.* This faculty is neither more nor less than genius; *which is,* to have the object posed in front of one. . . .

It is such lovely weather, Louise, and there is such sunshine! All my shutters are closed, and I am writing page 70 / in the shade! We have had two or three really lovely nights, with such moonlight! I feel in a good state physically and mentally, and I am hoping that *Bovary* will pick up a bit. Heat acts on me like spirits, it hardens my sensibility and excites me.

I am expecting Bouilhet. . .

26 [341]

TO THE SAME

[Croisset] Saturday, 5 o'clock [*September*, 1852]

. . . Another saddening letter from you this morning. My poor dear creature, I *do* love you. Why did you let yourself be hurt by a sentence which I had intended to convey the most unequivocal love that one human being can feel for another? Oh, woman, woman, be less feminine! Keep your femininity for bed. Does not your body kindle me when I am with you there? Have not you seen me gaze at you open-mouthed, and slide my hands with delight over your skin. Even in memory you excite me; and if I do not dream of you more often, it is because one does not dream of what one desires. Breathe in the woodland air this week, and look at the leaves for their own sakes; if you would understand nature you must be as calm as she is.

Let us regret nothing; to bewail our pains and irritations is to bewail the very nature of existence. People page 71 / like us were created to describe it, and for no other purpose. Let us have faith. Everything tiresome that befalls me, great or small, drives me further back on my eternal preoccupation. I hang on to it with both hands and close both my eyes. If I call on Grace it comes. God has mercy on the simple, and the sun always shines on stalwart hearts that climb to the mountain summits.

I am turning to a kind of aesthetic mysticism (if the two words can be used together), and I wish my faith were stronger.

When no encouragement comes from others, when the external world disgusts, weakens and corrupts, *honest* and *sensitive* people are forced to look within themselves for a fitter dwelling place. If society continues on its present course, we shall see mystics again, I think, as we have done in every dark age. Denied an outlet, the soul will retire into itself. Very soon we shall see the reappearance of universal apathy, of beliefs in the end of the world, of Messianic claims. But lacking a theological foundation, where can this unconscious fervour find a basis? Some will seek it in the flesh, others in the old religions, and yet others in Art; and like the Children of Israel in the desert, humanity will adore all sorts of idols. Our kind have come a little too early; in twenty-five years time the nodal point will respond magnificently to an artist's touch. Then prose (prose especially, the younger medium) will be capable of a grand humanitarian symphony. There may be a return to books like the *Satyricon* and the *Golden Ass*, but in place of their abounding sensuality, their successors will have an equally abounding psychological wealth.

This is what the world socialists, with their eternal materialistic prophecies, have refused to see. They have denied *pain;* they have blasphemed against three-quarters page 72 / of modern poetry, the blood of Christ which runs in our veins. Nothing will exhaust it or dry it up. The problem is not to drain it away, but to make it flow in a stream. If the consciousness of human insufficiency, of the vanity of life, were to perish (which would result from their hypothesis) we should be sillier than the birds, who at least perch on the trees. At present man's soul is asleep, drugged by the words she has heard; but she will have a frenzied awakening, and give herself over to the joys of liberty; for she will have no restraints left to hold her back, no government, no religion, no principles of any sort. Republicans of all complexions are to me the cruellest pedagogues in the world, with their dreams of organisation, legislation, and a monastically rigid society. I believe, on the other hand, that rules of all kinds are breaking down, that barriers are tumbling, and the earth falling to a dead level. This vast disorder may perhaps bring liberty. At least Art, which is always in the vanguard, has followed this road. What is the prevalent poetic form nowadays? Broad construction itself is becoming more and more impossible, with our limited and precise vocabulary and our vague, confused and fugitive ideas. All that we can do then is, out of sheer virtuosity, to tighten the strings of the overstrummed guitar and become primarily virtuosi, seeing that simplicity in our age is an illusion. At this point the picturesque has almost completely died out. Poetry, however, will not die, but where poetry will come into things in future I can hardly see. Who knows? Perhaps beauty will become a useless quality to humanity, and Art will be something halfway between algebra and music.

Since I cannot see yesterday I should like to see page 73 / tomorrow. Why did I not live at least under Louis XIV, with a great wig and stockings without a crease, in the company of M. Descartes? Or in Ronsard's time. Or in Nero's. How I should have argued with the Greek orators, and travelled in their great chariots along Roman roads, and slept at night in wayside inns with the wandering priests of Cybele. But best of all, why could not I have lived in the time of Pericles, to sup with the violet-crowned Aspasia, singing her verses in a white marble-walled room? Well, all that is over; that dream will not return. No doubt I have lived in all those places in some previous existence. I was the manager of a troupe of strolling players under the Roman Empire, I'm certain, one of those queer creatures who went to Sicily to bring women to train as actresses, and were a combination of schoolmaster, pimp and artist. They make an attractive bunch of scoundrels in Plautus's comedies; and when I read them, I seem to have memories. Have you ever felt it, the thrill of antiquity?

Good-bye, all my love, everywhere.

27 [355]

TO THE SAME

Saturday, *Dec. 11th*, 1852. 1 o'clock

First I will cover you with kisses, out of sheer joy. This morning's letter took a heavy weight from my page 74 / mind. It was time. Yesterday I could not work all day. At every movement I made, my brain — quite literally — gave a start inside my skull, and I had to go to bed at 11. I had a temperature and general prostration. For three weeks I have been suffering under dreadful apprehensions; I thought of you every single minute, but not in at all an agreeable way. Yes, the idea did torture me. It knocked me right out two or three times; Thursday was one of them. I should need a whole book to explain my thoughts on the subject comprehensively. The idea of bringing anyone into the world *horrifies me*. I could never forgive myself if I were a father. A son of mine! Oh, no, no, no! Let my seed die out. I will not hand on to anyone the stupidities and ignominies of existence. . . .

28 [360]

TO THE SAME

[Croisset] Monday, 5 o'clock [*December 27th* 1852]

At the moment I seem absolutely terror stricken, and I am writing to you perhaps only in order not to be alone with myself, as one lights a lamp at night when one is afraid. It is very strange, and I do not know if you will understand me. Have you ever read a book of Balzac's called *Louis Lambert?* I finished it five minutes ago, and it has stunned me. It is the story of a man who goes mad through dwelling on intangible ideas. It has fastened on to, and hooked itself into my flesh. Lambert is, with page 75 / trifling differences, my poor Alfred. I found some of *our* old sayings in it almost word for word; the conversations of the two student friends are ours, or just like them. One incident, concerning a manuscript stolen from these two and some observations by the master in charge, actually happened to me. Do you remember my telling you about a tale of the supernatural in which a man thinks himself into such a state of hallucination that the ghost of his friend finally appears to him, to draw the (ideal, absolute) conclusion from his (mundane, tangible) premises? Well, that idea is sketched out there, and the whole of *Louis Lambert* is a preface to it. In the end the hero tries to castrate himself, in a kind of mystical mania. In the midst of my Paris troubles, when I was nineteen, I had the same thought (I will show you a shop in the Rue Vivienne, where I stopped one evening, seized by this idea with overwhelming intensity); I spent two whole years at that time without so much as looking at a woman. (Last year when I talked to you of the idea of entering a monastery, it was my old leaven rising). There comes a time when *one has to torture oneself*, to loathe one's flesh, and throw mud in its face, it seems so hideous. If it were not for my love for beauty I might perhaps have been a great mystic. There are my nervous attacks, too, which are nothing but an involuntary weakening of thoughts and images. The psychic element then gets control of me, and consciousness, together with sense of being, departs. I am certain that I know what dying is. I have often clearly felt my spirit flowing out of me, as one feels blood pouring out of an open wound.

That wretched book made me dream of Alfred all night. At nine I woke up and went to sleep again. Then page 76 / I dreamt of the Château de la Roche-Guyon; it lay behind Croisset, and I was amazed to see it for the first time. I was woken up when they brought me a letter. Could it have been that letter, jolting along the road in the postman's box, that conveyed to me from afar off the idea of la Roche-Guyon? You used to come to me by that way. Was it *Louis Lambert* that made me dream of Alfred that night? (Eight months ago I dreamt of lions, and at the time I was dreaming a boat with a menagerie on board was passing under my windows). Oh, how very close one feels to madness sometimes! I certainly do. You know what an influence I have on madmen, how much they like me. I am in a state of fear at present, let me tell you, though as I sat down to write to you, the sight of white paper made me feel calmer. But for the last month, since the day of my departure, I have been in a strangely exalted, or rather vibrant, state. If the slightest idea comes into my head, I have the kind of strange sensation you feel in your nails when you go near a harp.

Confound the book! It has disturbed me; it is so real to me.

Another coincidence: my mother showed me a passage in Balzac's *Country Doctor* (she discovered it yesterday) a scene *straight out of my Bovary*, a visit to an old nurse. (I had never read the book, any more than I had read *Louis Lambert*). The *details are identical*, the scene is the same, and it serves the same purpose. You might suppose I had copied it, if (I am not boasting) my pages were not infinitely the better written. If Du Camp knew all this he would say I was comparing myself with Balzac as I did with Goethe. Once I used to get annoyed with page 77 / people who found me so like so-and-so — or so-and-so. Now things are worse; it is my thoughts. I find them everywhere, everything recalls them. Now why?

Louis Lambert begins, just like *Bovary*, with a first day at school, and there is one identical sentence; it is where he is describing details of school life even more tiresome than those in the *Livre posthume.*

Bouilhet did not come yesterday. He stayed in bed with a boil, and sent me a charming piece of Latin verse on the subject. I replied with a letter in sixteenth century language, which I feel rather pleased with.

By all means let Hugo send me your letters, if they come from London; but from Jersey it might be too obvious. Let me advise you once more to send nothing in writing. I will keep your letter to show it to Bouilhet on Sunday, if you do not mind. Are you reading the *Golden Ass* at last? I will write you at the end of this week, and send you my opinion about the alternative reading you suggest for the *Peasant Girl.* Be brave, my poor dear Muse. I think that my Bovary will go ahead; but I am bothered by my sense of metaphor, which has too much control over me. Comparisons consume me like flies, and I spend my whole time squashing them; my sentences are swarming with them. Good-bye....

29 [362]

TO THE SAME

[Croisset] 3 o'clock, Saturday afternoon
[*January 15th,* 1853]

The beginning of the week was dreadful, but since page 78 / Thursday I have been getting along better. I have still six to eight pages to do before I get to a point when I can go and see you. I think it will be in a fortnight. Bouilhet will probably come with me. If he does not write to you more often, it is either that he has nothing to say, or that he has not the time. Do you know that the poor devil works eight hours a day at his teaching? ...

I spent *five days on one page* last week, and I gave up everything for it, my Greek and my English; I did nothing else. One thing worries me about my book, and that is its *entertainment* value, which is poor. It is deficient in events. I maintain that *ideas* are events. It is more difficult to make them interesting, I know, but if you fail the style is at fault. At present, for instance, I have fifty pages on end without a single thing happening. It is one uninterrupted description of a middle-class existence and a passion which remains unexpressed, and is all the more difficult to describe because it is both timid and deep. Alas, though, there are no internal fireworks, for my man is of a temperate nature. I have had something of the kind already in my first part: my husband loves his wife in rather the same way as my lover. [They] are a couple of mediocrities with the same background, but they must be differentiated all the same. If I am successful it will be really good, I think, for to paint one colour on another, without sharp differences of tone, is no light task. But I am afraid that all these subtleties may be tedious, and that the reader would just as soon see a bit more movement. But one must follow out one's own conception. If I decided to introduce action, I should be working according to a theory and I should spoil everything. One must sing with one's own voice; and mine will never be **page 79 /** dramatic or attractive. Besides I am convinced that it is all a matter of style, or rather of shape and angle.

. . . .

30 [314]

TO THE SAME

[Trouville] Sunday [*August*] 14*th*, 4 o'clock **page 80 /**

. . . .

The day before yesterday, at a charming spot in the Forêt de Touques, just near a spring, I found cigar ends put out with scraps of meat pie. They had been there *on a trip*. I wrote about it in November, eleven years ago. It was pure imagination then, and the other day it proved true. All one's inventions are true, you can be sure of that. Poetry is as exact a science as geometry. Induction is as good as deduction, and when one reaches a certain point, one makes no more mistakes with regard to the things of the mind. No doubt my poor *Bovary* is suffer- **page 81 /** ing and weeping in twenty different French villages, at this very moment. **page 82 /**

. . . .

Nature cares precious little for us — the trees, the grass and the waves present us with a cruelly impassive front. The Havre steamship's bell is ringing so furiously that I must stop. What a din industry does make in the world! The machine is a rowdy object. Talking of industry, have you ever thought of the number of stupid professions it gives rise to, and of the mass of inanity it will eventually produce? That would be an alarming piece of research. What can you expect from a population which, like Manchester's, spends its life making pins? And the making of a single pin requires five or six different processes. As the work is split up, you get, beside the machines proper, a quantity of human machines. Think of the job of a railway car attendant or a feeder in a printing works, etc. Man is indeed becoming an animal. Leconte is right; the way he set that theory out I shall never forget. The *contemplatives* of the Middle Ages were very different men from our modern *men of action*. page 83 /

Humanity hates us; we do not minister to it and we hate it because it wounds us. Therefore, we must love one another in *Art*, as the mystics love one another *in God*, and everything must grow pale before that love. Let all life's other lamps (which stink, one and all) vanish before this great sun. In an age when all common bonds are snapped, and when Society is just one huge brigandage (to use official parlance) more or less well organised, when the interests of flesh and spirit draw apart like wolves and howl in solitude, one must act like everyone else, cultivate an ego (a more beautiful one naturally) and live in one's den. The distance between myself and my fellow men widens every day. I feel this process working in my heart and I am glad, for my sensitivity towards all that I find sympathetic continually increases, as a result of this very withdrawal. . . .

31 [418]

TO THE SAME

[Trouville] Sunday, 11 o'clock
[and Monday, *August 21st and 22nd*, 1853]

. . . *Remarks on morals and æsthetics:* a local man, who has been mayor for *forty years*, told me that all that time he had only known *two* convictions for theft, out of a population of more than three thousand. That strikes me as illuminating. If sailors and workmen are of a different **page 84 /** kidney, what is the reason? I believe that it arises from *contact with greatness*. A man who has always before his eyes as wide a stretch as human sight can cover must derive from that very familiarity a scornful habit of equanimity (think of the wastefulness of sailors of all sorts, of how little they care for their lives or their money). I believe that is the direction in which to look for the *moral effect of Art*. Its intrinsic sublimity, like nature's, will lead to a higher morality; by virtue of its very superiority it will serve a useful purpose. The sight of a cornfield brings more joy to a philanthropist's heart than a view of the Ocean, for everyone agrees that Agriculture encourages good habits. But what a poor creature a carter is beside a sailor! The ideal is like the sun; it sucks up all the filth in the world....

32 [444]

TO THE SAME

[Croisset] 1 o'clock, Wednesday night
[*December* 14*th*, 1853] **page 85 /**

. . . .

You are in love with life; you are a pagan and a southerner; you believe in the passions and hope for happiness. Oh, that was all right when we went about in purple, and lived under a blue sky; when ideas, freshly hatched, sang in fresh shapes in the mild air, like so many cheerful sparrows among the April leaves. But I loathe life. I am a Catholic with something of the green effluence of Norman Cathedrals in my heart. My intellectual weakness is for the passive, the ascetic, the dreamer. Dressing and undressing and eating, etc., exasperate me. If I were not afraid of hashish I would gorge myself on it instead of bread and, if I have still thirty years to live, I would spend them like that, on my back, log-like and inert. I had thought that you would keep me spiritual company, and that we would draw a great circle around to cut ourselves off from the rest. But I was wrong. You need the ordinary conventional things. I am not 'what a lover ought to be!' In fact, almost nobody finds me 'what a young man ought to be.' What you need are proofs and deeds. You love me tremendously, much more than I have ever been loved or ever shall be. But you love me as anyone else might, with the same pre- page 86 / occupation with secondary concerns and the same incessant worries. . . .

How can you expect a man as besotted with Art as I am, perpetually hungry for an ideal he never attains, a man with a sensibility sharper than a razor blade, a man who spends his life striking on it to raise a spark, etc., etc. (a practice which makes notches in the said blade) — how can you expect such a man to love with the heart of a twenty year old, and with the *ingenuous* passions proper to that age? You speak of your last great days. Mine were over long ago, and I do not regret them. That was all done with at eighteen. But people like us should use a different language in speaking of themselves. We should not have great or poor days. Heraclitus put out his eyes the better to see that sun I am speaking of. . . .

Good-bye. . . . yours

33 [446]

TO THE SAME

[Croisset] Friday night, 2 o'clock
[*December* 23*rd*, 1853]

I must love you, to be writing to you this evening, for I am *whacked*. I have an iron weight on my head. I have been writing *Bovary* since two o'clock in the afternoon (except for about twenty-five minutes for dinner). I am deep in it, well in the middle; it makes me sweat and page 87 / catches my throat. This has been one of the rare days of my life that I have spent in a complete dream, from beginning to end. Just now, at six o'clock, just as I was writing the words 'nervous attack', I was so carried away that I groaned aloud, feeling in the depths of my being all that my little woman was then going through. I was afraid I should have a nervous crisis myself. To calm myself, I got up from the table and opened the window. My head was spinning. At present I have frightful pains in my knees, my back and my head. I am like a man who has over-copulated (pardon the expression) that is to say, in a kind of intoxicated swoon. And being on the subject of love, it would not be right for me to go to sleep without sending you a caress, a kiss and my remaining thoughts. Will it all be good? I really do not know. (I am hurrying a bit so as to show Bouilhet a whole piece when he comes). What is certain is that it has been going vigorously forward for the last week. I only hope it continues to, for I am sick of my sluggish pace. But I am afraid of a rude awakening, of disillusionment when I copy out all the pages. Never mind whether they are good or bad, it is grand to write, to cease to be *oneself*, and to move among the creatures one is describing. Today, for instance, I have been man and woman at the same time, lover and mistress together, riding in the forest on an autumn afternoon under the yellowing leaves; and I have been the horses, too, and the leaves, and the wind, and the words they spoke and the red sun that made them blink their eyes that swam with love. It may be out of pride or out of reverence, from a foolish gush of excessive self-conceit or a vague but lofty religious sense, but when I reflect, after experiencing these joys, I feel tempted to offer up a prayer of thanksgiving to God, page 88 / if only I knew he could hear me. But praised be His Name that I was not born a cotton merchant, a music hall artist or a wit, etc.

34 [480]

To Louis Bouilhet

Croisset, *September 17th*, 1855

Try and get me, my dear fellow, the following medical details for Sunday next, or earlier, if possible. They are going up the hill, Homais examines the blind man with red rims to his eyes (you know the condition I mean) and makes him a speech, using medical terminology. He believes he can cure him, and gives him his address. Of course, Homais is wrong, for the poor devil is incurable.

If you have not enough in your little black bag for five or six telling lines, draw on Follin and send me the results. I could go to Rouen, but that would cost me a day and I should have to do too much explaining.

I have been thick in the head for the last three days with a most deadly catarrh, but I have worked fairly well today. I hope that *Madame Bovary* will have the arsenic in her stomach in a month. Shall I bring her to you when she is buried? I wonder. . . . page 89 /

35 [511]

To Madame Maurice Schlésinger

Paris, *January 14th*, 1857

I was most touched, my dear Madame, by your kind letter. Rest assured that your questions concerning both author and book have come to the right address. Here is the whole story. The *Revue de Paris* in which my novel was serialised (from October 1st to December 15th) had already had two *cautions*, for its hostility to the government. Now, somebody decided that it would be a clever stroke to suppress it once and for all, on a charge of immorality and blasphemy. So they picked a few risky and irreverent passages out of my book at random, I was summoned before the prosecuting magistrate, and the case began. But I set my friends vigorously to work, and they stirred up some mud in high quarters in the capital. I am told in fact that proceedings have been suspended, though I have no official statement yet. I have no doubt of the result, the whole thing was too silly. So I shall be able to publish my novel in book form. You will receive it in about six weeks, I think, and for your amusement I will mark the offending passages. One of them, a description of the Extreme Unction, is simply a page of page 90 / the *Paris Liturgy* put into French, but the good folk who watch over the preservation of the faith are rather weak in their catechism.

All the same, I should have been found guilty and sentenced to a year's imprisonment, not to mention a fine of a thousand francs. What is more, every new book of mine would have been remorselessly examined and picked over by their excellencies the police, and a fresh offence would have brought me straight 'to the dread dungeon's reeking straw' for five years: in fact, I could not have printed a line. So I have learnt (1) that it is extremely unpleasant to be mixed up in a political affair, and (2) that popular hypocrisy must be taken seriously. But it was so stupid this time that it grew abashed, let go and returned to its burrow.

As for the book itself, it is moral, supermoral, and would receive the Montyon prize (an honour I hardly covet) if its manners were a little less free. It has been as successful as any novel can be in a revue.

I have received some very pretty compliments from my fellow authors, but whether they are genuine or not I do not know. I am even told that M. de Lamartine is loud in my praise — which I find very surprising, for everything about my book should annoy him! *La Presse* and *Le Moniteur* have made me very generous proposals. I have been asked for a comic opera (comic, mark you) and my *Bovary* has been noticed by several papers, large and small. There, my dear Madame, without false modesty, is my balance sheet of fame. Do not worry about the critics. They will treat me gently, for they know that I shall never creep into their shadows to steal their jobs. They will be charming, in fact, for it is so pleasant to break old pots with new crocks. page 91 /

I shall return to my poor, dull, quiet life, in which a phrase is an adventure and metaphors are the only flowers I pick. I shall write, as I have always done, for the mere pleasure of writing, for my self alone, without a thought of money or of making a splash. Apollo will remember me, no doubt, and one day, perhaps, I shall manage to produce something fine, for nothing can stand up against a strong and persistent passion, can it? Every dream finds a shape in the end; there is a draught to quench every thirst, and a love for every heart. And then there is no better way of passing the time than in ceaseless preoccupation with an idea — an ideal, as the tarts say. If it must be a folly, let us pursue the noblest. Since we cannot unhook the sun, we must shutter our windows and light the lamps in our rooms. . . .

36 [512]

To His Brother, Achille

Friday, half-past eight in the evening
[probably *January 16th*, 1857]

I did not write to you again, my dear Achille, because I believed the affair was completely over. Prince Napoleon had made three separate statements to that effect to three different people. M. Rouland himself went to speak to the Minister of the Interior, etc., etc. Edouard Delessert was instructed by the Empress (with whom he dined on page 92 / Tuesday) to tell his mother that the whole business was over.

It was not till yesterday morning that I learnt from old Sénard that I had been summoned before the magistrates. He had heard it from Treilhard the evening before, at the Courts.

I immediately sent a message to the Prince, and he replied that it was untrue; but it was he that was wrong. That is all I know. It is a whirlpool of slander and lies, and I am drowning in it. There is *something* behind it, some assiduous, invisible agent. At first I was nothing but a pretext, but now I believe the *Revue de Paris* is nothing but a pretext either. Has someone possibly a grudge against one of my patrons? They have been important rather for their *quality* than their numbers.

Everybody is very quick with his rejoinder: 'It is not me, not me.' What is certain is that proceedings were stopped and then resumed. How did this reversal arise? Everything originated with the Ministry of the Interior, the judiciary obeyed instructions; they were free, perfectly free, but . . . I do not expect justice, I shall serve my term. Naturally, I shall not ask for clemency; for that really would be disgraceful.

If you can get to *know* anything, or a clear sight of things, let me know.

I am not at all worried, I promise you. It is far too silly.

They will not shut my mouth, not a bit of it. I shall work as I always have done — that is to say conscientiously and independently. I will write novels — to spite them — and they will be *lifelike*. I have studied my subject and have taken my notes; only I shall wait for brighter skies to shine over Parnassus before I publish. page 93 /

The success of *Bovary* still continues; it is gathering weight and everybody has read it, is reading it, or intends to read it.

My persecution has brought me widespread sympathy. If my book is bad, that will serve to make it seem better. If, on the other hand, it has lasting qualities, that will build a foundation for it. There you are!

I am hourly awaiting the official document which will name the day when I am to take my seat (for the crime of having written in French) in the dock in the company of thieves and homosexuals.

Good-bye, dear brother. All my love.

Yours

37 [516]

To Theophile Gautier

Paris, 6 p.m. [*January*, 1857]

M. Abbatucci junior, who is much attached to you, is very well disposed towards me. A word from you this evening will carry very great weight. This I have been instructed to tell you. You will find a great number of *Bovary* lovers there. Join with them to save me, most powerful of men.

The case is going ahead.

Yours. page 94 /

38 [519]

To Eugène Crépet

Paris [*January*, 1857, between *26th* and *30th*]

My dear friend,

You know Abbé Constant. He should be able to furnish you with the following material, which I need this evening:

The greatest possible number of smutty passages drawn from ecclesiastical writers, particularly from contemporaries.

They have just ruled my written statement out of court, and on Sunday they stopped the *Independance Belge*, for an article in praise of your humble servant.

39 [520]

To His Brother, Achille

January 31st, 1857

This morning you will have received a telegram, sent to you at my request by a friend of mine. My case comes up for judgment a week today; the verdict is still in the balance. I have had an offer from the *Moniteur* to write for them at ten sous a line, which would add up to 8 to 10 thousand francs for a novel like *Bovary*. page 95 /

Maître Sénard's pleading has been splendid. He *crushed* the Public Prosecutor, who writhed in his seat and declined to answer. We overwhelmed him with quotations from Bossuet and Massillon, and scabrous passages from Montaigne, etc. The court was packed. It was splendid, and I had one grand opening. I was so bold as to contradict the Public Prosecutor flatly on one occasion, and convict him of dishonesty in open court. He withdrew his statement. You will see a verbatim account of the proceedings, for I had my own shorthand writer (at 60 francs an hour) to take it all down. Old Sénard spoke for four hours on end. It was a triumph for him, and for me.

He began by speaking of our father, then went on to you, and finally to me. After that he proceeded to a complete analysis of the book, refuting the indictment and defending the passages complained of. This is where he came in *strong*. The prosecutor must have got a flea in his ear later that evening. But the best thing of all was the passage on the Extreme Unction. The prosecutor was covered with confusion when Maître Sénard produced a Liturgy from under his seat and read from it. The passage in my book is only a *toned down* transcription of the words of the Liturgy. We gave it them there, hot and strong!

All through his pleading old Sénard presented me as a great man and my book as a masterpiece. Almost a third of it was read aloud. He made great play with Lamartine's commendation. Here is one thing he said: 'You owe him more than an acquittal. You owe him an apology'.

And another: 'Oh, you are making an attack on the younger son of M. Flaubert. Nobody, my honourable page 96 / friend, not even you, can give *him* lessons in morality!' And when he had twisted a passage, 'It is not your intelligence that I am attacking. It is your prejudice.'

It was a field day, in fact, and you would have enjoyed it if you had been there.

Say nothing, keep quiet; but if I lose, I shall go to the Court of Appeal; and if I lose there, to the Supreme Court.

Good-bye, my dear brother. All my love.

40 [523]

To Mademoiselle Leroyer de Chantepie

Paris, *February 19th* [1857]

I am very behind hand with you, Madame, not because I do not appreciate your charming letter nor out of forgetfulness, but I have been overwhelmed by the most unpleasant business. I have appeared (on account of the very book you paid me such compliments on) before the magistrate's courts on a charge of outraging public morals and the Catholic faith.

The *Bovary* whom you love has been dragged into the criminal's dock like any fallen woman. She was acquitted it is true—I had a perfectly clear defence—but I remain a writer *under suspicion* all the same, which is a poor sort of glory. I shall not be able to publish my novel in book form before the beginning of April. Will you accept a copy?

Needless to say, I am impatiently awaiting the arrival of some of your writings. I shall be most honoured, Madame, to receive them. page 97 /

41 [524]

To the Same

Paris, *February 19th* [1857]

. . . .

With a sympathetic reader like you, Madame, I am bound to be frank. I shall, therefore, reply to your questions. *Madame Bovary* has no foundation in fact. It is an entirely fictitious tale. I have put nothing into it of my own feelings or my own life. The illusion (if there is one) arises, on the contrary, from the impersonality of the work. It is one of my principles that one must not *write oneself in.* The artist must stand to his work as God to his creation, invisible and all powerful; he must be everywhere felt but nowhere seen. page 98 /

Then, Art must rise above private predilections and nervous idiosyncracies. The time has come to give it, by a pitiless method, the precision of the physical sciences. But the principal difficulty for me is still the style, the shape, the indefinable Beauty *resulting from the actual conception;* and that, as Plato said, is the resplendent quality of Truth.

For a long time I have lived a life like yours, Madame. I, too, spent several years completely alone in the country, with no other sound in the winter than the murmur of the wind in the trees and the cracking of the ice when the Seine brought it down under my window. If I have gained some understanding of life, it is by dint of having lived little, in the ordinary sense of the word. I have eaten sparely, but ruminated deeply. I have mixed with various sorts of people and visited different countries. I have travelled on foot and by dromedary. I know Paris stockbrokers and Damascus Jews, Italian pimps and negro jugglers. I have been on a pilgrimage to the Holy Land, and have lost my way on the snows of Parnassus — which facts can be taken symbolically.

Do not complain; I have mixed in the world a little, and I know the Paris of your dreams through and through; there is nothing so good as a book by the fireside . . . as reading *Hamlet* or *Faust* . . . on a *good* day. My own dream is to buy a small palace on the Grand Canal at Venice.

Well, Madame, there is some of your curiosity assuaged. To complete my biographical portrait, let me add that I am thirty-five, and five-foot-eight in height. I have the shoulders of a porter and the nervous irritability of a woman of fashion. I am a bachelor and a recluse. **page 99 /**

. . . .

42 [526]

TO THE SAME

[Paris] Monday [*March 30th*, 1857]

My dear fellow writer,

Your letter is so candid, so truthful, so *deeply* felt, and moves me so profoundly, that I cannot refrain from an immediate reply. First let me thank you for telling me your age. That puts me at greater ease. We will talk together like two men. I am flattered by your confidence, and feel not unworthy of it — but do not chaff me, do not call me a *scholar* again, for I am appalled by my own ignorance.

And do not compare yourself with Madame Bovary. You have hardly a thing in common with her. She was not your mental or emotional equal; for she was a slightly perverse character, given to false poetry and false emotion. My first idea was to make her a virgin, living in the depths of the country, growing bitter with age, and so ultimately reaching the depths of religiosity and page 100 / *imaginary* passion. Of this original plan I have kept the setting (dullish country and people), the atmosphere in fact. Only to make the story more comprehensible and more interesting, in the good sense of the word, I invented a more human heroine, a very ordinary sort of woman. Besides, I found my original plan so difficult to carry out, that I had not the courage to attempt it.

Write to me on any subject you like, at length and frequently, though I may take some time to reply; for since yesterday we have been old friends. I know you now, and like you. I have known, myself, all that you have undergone. I, too, have deliberately refused love and happiness. . . . Why, I do not know. Perhaps out of pride — or from fear? I have loved, too, deeply and in silence — and at twenty-one I almost died of a nervous complaint, brought on by a series of troubles and disappointments, and intensified by irritation and insomnia. This illness lasted two years. (I have experienced — yes, and I have *seen* — *every*thing described by Santa Teresa, Hoffmann, and Edgar Allan Poe, I understand delusions only too well.) But I emerged toughened, and suddenly enlightened on a variety of subjects I had scarcely touched in actual life. Sometimes I have taken a part in affairs, all the same, but hysterically, neurotically — and I have always very quickly returned to my true nature, which is contemplative. It is not virtue that has preserved me from excesses, but a sense of *irony*. It is not that vice disgusts me; it seems to me so pitifully, so ludicrously stupid.

I was born in a hospital (at Rouen, where my father was head surgeon; he died with a considerable reputation in his profession). I grew up amidst every human misery — separated from it by a mere wall. That is perhaps why page 101 / my manner is at once gloomy and cynical. I have no love of life and no fear of death. Even the hypothesis of absolute annihilation has no terrors for me. I am prepared to descend into the great black pit with equanimity.

And yet what attracts me most of all is religion. I mean all religions, one no more than another. Each separate dogma repels me, but what went to their making seems to me the most natural and poetical spirit in man. I have no love for the philosophers who see nothing in it but stupidity and fraud. I find religion both necessary and instinctive; and therefore I respect the negro kissing his idol as much as the Catholic at the feet of the Sacred Heart.

Now for more confidences; I have no sympathy for any political party, or rather I loathe them all. They seem to me equally limited, false and puerile, preoccupied with the ephemeral, lacking all breadth of vision and never rising above the *utilitarian*. I detest all despotism. I am a fervent liberal. That is why socialism strikes me as a pedagogic horror, which will be the death of all art and all morality. As a spectator, I have taken part in almost all the insurrections of my time.

You will realise that I am older than you — in spirit — and that you are my junior, despite your extra twenty years.

But from all I have seen and felt and read, I have retained an unquenchable thirst for truth. Goethe died crying: 'Light! More light!' Yes, light, even if it scorches us to the heart. It is a supreme sensual pleasure to learn, to absorb Truth by way of Beauty. The ideal state arising from that pleasure seems to me one variety of blessedness, which is perhaps higher than the other, because it is less self-absorbed. page 102 /

44 [534]

To the Same

Croisset, *May 18th* [1857]

I am very behind hand with you, my dear fellow-writer and reader. Do not take the rarity of my letters as a criterion of my affection. Put it down merely to the trials of Paris life, to the publication of my book, and the archaeological reading in which

I am at present engaged. But now I am back in the country again with more time to myself, and now we are going to spend the evening together. Let us talk first of ourselves, then of your books, and finally of certain social and political ideas on which we differ. page 106 /

You ask me how I cured myself of the nervous delusions from which I once suffered. In two ways: (1) by examining them scientifically—that is to say by trying to understand them—and (2) *by force of will.* I often felt the onset of madness. There was a whirl of ideas and images in my poor mind, and my consciousness, my ego, seemed to be foundering like a ship in a storm. But I clung tight to my reason. Though battered and beaten, it kept the upper hand. At other times I tried to reconstruct my appalling sufferings in my imagination. I played with fantasy and madness, as Mithridates did with his poisons. I was sustained by an intense pride, and conquered the disease by grappling with it hand to hand. There is one quality, or rather a habit, which you seem to lack, I mean *the love of contemplation.* Take life, the passions and yourself as a subject for intellectual exercise. You are in revolt against the injustice of the world, against its baseness, its tyranny and all the vileness and corruption of life. But do you thoroughly understand them? Have you fully studied them? Are you God? Who informed you that your human judgment is infallible, that your feelings do not lead you astray? How can we, with our limited senses and our circumscribed intelligence, attain to absolute knowledge of truth and goodness? Shall we ever grasp the absolute? In order to survive, one must give up having clear-cut opinions about anything at all. *Humanity is like that*; it is not a question of changing it, but of knowing it. *Think less about yourself.* Give up all hope of a solution. The answer is in our Father's heart. He alone possesses it, and does not communicate it. But there are in the *ardours of learning* pleasures of the mind befitting noble souls. Make mental contact with your brothers of three thousand years ago; relive all their page 107 / sufferings, all their dreams, and you will feel your heart and your mind expanding together till every phantom and every being is enveloped in the cloak of a deep and boundless sympathy. *Do try to cease living subjectively.* Do some deep reading. Draw up a plan of study; make it strenuous and consistent. Read history, especially ancient history.

Compel yourself to regular, exhausting work. Life is such a hideous business that the only method of bearing it is to avoid it. And one does avoid it by living in Art, in the ceaseless quest for Truth presented by Beauty. When you read the great masters, try to grasp their method, to draw near to the heart of them, and you will rise from your studies dazzled with joy. You will be like Moses descending Sinai, with the light shining from his face because he had seen God.

What is all this about remorse and guilt, and vague apprehensions and confession? Forget it all, my poor soul, for your own good. Since you feel your conscience entirely clear, you can stand before the Eternal Being and say 'Here am I'. If one is guiltless what has one to fear? And what can we humans be guilty of, inadequate as we are for evil as for good! All your troubles arise from too much idle thinking. Lacking external food, your greedy mind has turned in on itself and gnawed itself to the bone. You must *build it up again*, fatten it and, what is more, keep it from straying. Here is an example; you are greatly preoccupied with the injustices of this world, with socialism and politics. All right. Then start by reading *everyone* who has had the same ideals. Dig into the Utopians and the dry-as-dust dreamers. And next, before allowing yourself a definite opinion, you will have to study a new science, more discussed than studied — Political Economy, I mean. You will be amazed to find page 108 / yourself changing your ideas like a shirt, every day. No matter. There will be nothing bitter about your scepticism. It will be like watching the human drama, with History seeming to pass across the stage for your eyes alone.

Superficial, limited creatures, rash, feather-brained souls, demand a conclusion from everything; they want to know the purpose of life and the dimensions of the infinite. Picking up a handful of sand in their poor, puny grasp, they say to the Ocean: 'I shall now count the grains on your shores.' But when the sand slips through their fingers and the sum proves long, they stamp and burst into tears. Do you know what we should do on that shore? Either kneel down or walk. You must walk.

No great genius has come to final conclusions; no great book ever does so, because humanity itself is forever on the march and can arrive at no goal. Homer comes to no conclusions, nor does Shakespeare, nor Goethe, nor even the Bible. That is why I am so deeply revolted by that fashionable term, the *Social Problem*. The day on which the answer is found will be this planet's last. Life is an eternal problem; so is history and everything else. Fresh figures are always being added to the sum. How can you count the spokes of a turning wheel? The nineteenth century is like a slave so proud of his newly-won freedom that he imagines it is he that has discovered the sun. It is said, for example, that the Reformation was the prelude to the French Revolution. That would be true enough if matters could rest there; but the Revolution itself was a prelude to a different state of things, and so on, and so on. Our most advanced ideas will look very silly and out of date when people come to look back on them. I will wager that in a bare fifty years, the terms, page 109 / *Social Problem, raising the morals of the masses, progress* and *democracy*, will have passed into the realm of dead catchwords, and will seem as grotesque as *Sensibility, nature, crotchets* and *sweet ties of affection*, that were so fashionable towards the end of the eighteenth century.

I believe in the perpetual evolution of humanity and in its ever-changing forms, and consequently I abominate all those frames which men try to cram it into by main force, all the formulas by which they define it, and all the plans they devise for it. Democracy is no more man's last word than was slavery, or feudalism, or monarchy. No horizon perceived by human eyes is ever the shore, because beyond that horizon lies another, and so on for ever. Therefore it seems idiotic to me to seek the best religion or the best government. For me, the one on its deathbed is the best, since it is then making way for another.

I am rather cross with you for saying, in one of your earlier letters, that you are in favor of *compulsory* education for all. I loathe everything compulsory, all laws, governments and regulations. What is society, that it should *force* me to do anything at all? What God made it my master? See how it falls back into the old injustices of the past. It will no longer be a despot that oppresses the individual, but the masses, the public safety, the state that is always right, the universal catchword, Robespierre's maxim. I prefer the desert, and I shall return to the Bedouin who are free. page 110 /

. . . .

45 [539]

To Monsieur Cailleteaux

[Croisset, near Rouen, *June 4th*, 1857]

Dear Sir,

Your flattering letter compels me to answer your question frankly.

No, sir, I had no model before me. Madame Bovary is a pure invention. All the characters in the book are completely fictitious, and the district of Yonville l'Abbaye *does not exist*, nor does la Rieulle, etc. Though that has not prevented people here in Normandy from discovering a host of allusions in my novel. If they were right, my portraits would be the less telling, for I should have had personalities in mind, whereas what I wanted to do was to present types.

One of the dearest joys of the writer, sir, is to excite the sympathy of strangers. Accept my own in return.

With kind regards page 112 /

IVAN TURGENEV

Fathers and Sons (1862)

AUTHOR'S COMMENTS:

APROPOS OF *Fathers and Sons*

I was sea-bathing at Ventnor, a small town on the Isle of Wight — it was in August, 1860 — when the first idea occurred to me of *Fathers and Sons*, the novel which deprived me, forever I believe, of the good opinion of the Russian younger generation. I have heard it said and read it in critical articles not once but many times that in my works I always "started with an idea" or "developed an idea." Some people praised me for it, others, on the contrary, censured me; for my part, I must confess that I never attempted to "create a character" unless I had for my departing point not an idea but a living person to whom the appropriate elements were later on gradually attached and added. Not possessing a great amount of free inventive powers, I always felt the need of some firm ground on which I could plant my feet. The same thing happened with *Fathers and Sons;* at the basis of its chief character, Bazarov, lay the personality of a young provincial doctor I had been greatly struck by. (He died shortly before 1860.) In that remarkable man I could watch the embodiment of that principle which had scarcely come to life but was just beginning to stir at the time, the principle which later received the name of nihilism. Though very powerful, the impression that man left on **page 193 /** me was still rather vague. At first I could not quite make him out myself, and I kept observing and listening intently to everything around me, as though wishing to

---

Reprinted, by permission, from *Turgenev's Literary Reminiscences*, translated by David Magarshack (New York: Farrar, Straus and Company, 1958).

check the truth of my own impressions. I was worried by the following fact: not in one work of our literature did I ever find as much as a hint at what I seemed to see everywhere; I could not help wondering whether I was not chasing after a phantom. On the Isle of Wight, I remember, there lived with me at the time a Russian who was endowed with excellent taste and a remarkable "nose" for everything which the late Apollon Grigoryev called "the ideas" of an epoch. I told him what I was thinking of and what interested me so much and was astonished to hear the following remark: "Haven't you created such a character already in — Rudin?" I said nothing. Rudin and Bazarov — one and the same character!

Those words produced such an effect on me that for several weeks I tried not to think of the work I had in mind. However, on my return to Paris I sat down to it again — the *plot* gradually matured in my head; in the course of the winter I wrote the first chapters, but I finished the novel in Russia, on my estate, in July [1861]. In the autumn I read it to a few friends, revised something, added something, and in March, 1862, *Fathers and Sons* was published in *The Russian Herald*.

I shall not enlarge on the impression this novel has created. I shall merely say that when I returned to Petersburg, on the very day of the notorious fires in the Apraksin Palace, the word "nihilist" had been caught up by thousands of people, and the first exclamation that escaped from the lips of the first acquaintance I met on Nevsky Avenue was: "Look what *your* nihilists are doing! They are setting Petersburg on fire!" My impressions at that time, though different in kind, were equally painful. I became conscious of a coldness bordering on indignation among many friends whose ideas I shared; I received congratulations, and al- page 194 / most kisses, from people belonging to a camp I loathed, from enemies. It embarrassed and — grieved me. But my conscience was clear; I knew very well that my attitude towards the character I had created was honest and that far from being prejudiced against him, I even sympathised with him.[1] I have too great a respect for the vocation of an artist, a writer, to act against

[1] I should like to quote the following extract from my diary: "30 July, Sunday. An hour and a half ago I finished my novel at last. . . . I don't know whether it will be successful. *The Contemporary* will probably treat me with contempt for my Bazarov and . . . will not believe that while writing my novel I felt an involuntary attachment to him."

my conscience in such a matter. The word "respect" is hardly the right one here; I simply could not, and knew not how to, work otherwise; and, after all, there was no reason why I should do that. My critics described my novel as a "lampoon" and spoke of my "exasperated" and "wounded" vanity; but why should I write a lampoon on Dobrolyubov, whom I had hardly met, but whom I thought highly of as a man and as a talented writer? However little I might think of my own talent as a writer, I always have been, and still am, of the opinion that the writing of a lampoon, a "squib," is unworthy of it. As for my wounded vanity, all I can say is that Dobrolyubov's article on my last work before *Fathers and Sons* — *On the Eve* (and he was quite rightly considered as the mouthpiece of public opinion) — that that article, published in 1861, is full of the warmest and — honestly speaking — the most undeserved eulogies. But the critics had to present me as an offended lampoonist: *leur siège était fait*, and even this year I could read in Supplement No. 1 to *Cosmos* (page 96) the following lines: "At last, *everyone knows* that the pedestal on which Turgenev stood has been destroyed chiefly by Dobrolyubov. . . ." and further on (page 98) they speak of my "feeling of bitterness," which the critic, however, "understands and — perhaps even forgives." **page 195 /**

The critics, generally speaking, have not got quite the right idea of what is taking place in the mind of an author or of what exactly his joys and sorrows, his aims, successes and failures are. They do not, for instance, even suspect the pleasure which Gogol mentions and which consists of castigating oneself and one's faults in the imaginary characters one depicts; they are quite sure that all an author does is to "develop his ideas"; they refuse to believe that to reproduce truth and the reality of life correctly and powerfully is the greatness happiness for an author, even if this truth does not coincide with his own sympathies. Let me illustrate my meaning by a small example. I am an inveterate and incorrigible Westerner. I have never concealed it and I am not concealing it now. And yet in spite of that it has given me great pleasure to show up in the person of Panshin (in *A House of Gentlefolk*) all the common and vulgar sides of the Westerners; I made the Slavophil Lavretsky "crush him utterly." Why did I do it, I who consider the Slavophil doctrine false and futile? Because *in the given case life, according to my ideas, happened to be like that*, and what I wanted above all was to be sincere

and truthful. In depicting Bazarov's personality, I excluded everything artistic from the range of his sympathies, I made him express himself in harsh and unceremonious tones, not out of an absurd desire to insult the younger generation (! ! !),[1] but simply as a result of my observations of my acquaintance, Dr. D., and people like him. "Life happened to be *like that*," my experience told me once more, perhaps mistakenly, but, I repeat, not dishonestly. There was no need for me to be too clever about it; I just had to depict his character *like that*. My personal predilec-
page 196 / tions had nothing to do with it. But I expect many of my readers will be surprised if I tell them that with the exception of Bazarov's views on art, I share almost all his convictions. And I am assured that I am on the side of the "Fathers" — I, who in the person of Pavel Kirsanov have even "sinned" against artistic truth and gone too far, to the point of caricaturing his faults and making him look ridiculous![1*]

1 Among the multitude of proofs of my "spite against our youth" one critic cited the fact that I made Bazarov lose his game of cards to Father Alexey. "He simply doesn't know," the critic observed, "how most to hurt and humiliate him! He can't even play cards!" There can be no doubt that if I had made Bazarov win his game, the same critic would have exclaimed, "Isn't it abundantly clear? The author wants to suggest that Bazarov is a cardsharper!"

1* Foreigners cannot understand the crude accusations made against me for my Bazarov. *Fathers and Sons* has been translated several times into German. This is what one critic writes in analysing the last translation published in Riga *(Vossische Zeitung, Donnerstag, d. 10 Juni, zweite Beilage, Seite 3)*: "*Es bleibt für den unbefangenen . . . Leser schlechthin unbegreiflich, wie sich gerade die radicale Jugend Russlands über diesen geistigen Vertreter ihrer Richtung (Bazaroff), ihrer Ueberzeugungen und Bestrebungen, wie ihn T. zeichnete, in eine Wuth hinein erhitzen konnte, die sie den Dichter gleichsam in die Acht erklären und mit jeder Schmähung überhaüfen liess. Man sollte denken, jeder moderne Radicale könne nur mit froher Genungthuung in einer so stolzen Gestalt, von solcher Wucht des Charakters, solcher gründlichen Freiheit von allem Kleinlichen, Trivialen, Faulen, Schlaffen und Lügenhaften, sein und seiner Parteigenossen typisches Portrait dargestellt sehn.*"

That is: "To an unprejudiced . . . reader it is utterly incomprehensible how radical Russian youth could work itself into such a fury over the spiritual representative of their movement (Bazarov), their convictions and their aspirations, as Turgenev depicted him, and at the same time send the author to Coventry and hold him up to execration. One might have supposed that every modern radical would be only too glad to recognise himself and his comrades in such a proud personality, endowed with such a strength of character, such utter freedom from everything that is trivial, vulgar and false."

The cause of all the misunderstandings, the whole, so to speak "trouble," arose from the fact that the Bazarov type created by me has not yet had time to go through the gradual phases through which literary types usually go. Unlike Onegin and Pechorin, he had not been through a period of idealisation and sympathetic, starry-eyed adoration. At the very moment the *new* man — Bazarov — appeared, the author took up a critical, objective attitude towards him. That confused many people and — who knows? — that was, if not a mistake, an injustice. The Bazarov type had at **page 197 /** least as much right to be idealized as the literary types that preceded it. I have just said that the author's attitude towards the character he had created confused the reader: the reader always feels ill at ease, he is easily bewildered and even aggrieved if an author treats his imaginary character like a living person, that is to say, if he sees and displays his good as well as his bad sides, and, above all, if he does not show unmistakable signs of sympathy or antipathy for his own child. The reader feels like getting angry: he is asked not to follow a well-beaten path, but to tread his own path. "Why should I take the trouble," he can't help thinking. "Books exist for entertainment and not for racking one's brains. And, besides, would it have been too much to ask the author to tell me what to think of such and such a character or what he thinks of him himself?" But it is even worse if the author's attitude towards that character is itself rather vague and undefined, if the author himself does not know whether or not he loves the character he has created (as it happened to me in my attitude towards Bazarov, for "the involuntary attraction" I mentioned in my diary is not love). The reader is ready to ascribe to the author all sorts of non-existent sympathies or antipathies, provided he can escape from the feeling of unpleasant "vagueness."

"Neither fathers nor sons," said a witty lady to me after reading my book, "that should be the real title of your novel and — you are yourself a nihilist." A similar view was expressed with even greater force on the publication of *Smoke*. I am afraid I do not feel like raising objections: perhaps, that lady was right. In the business of fiction writing everyone (I am judging by myself) does what he can and not what he wants, and — as much as he can. I suppose that a work of fiction has to be judged *en gros* and while insisting on conscientiousness on the part of the author, the other *sides* of his activity must be regarded, I would not say, with indifference, but with calm. And, much as I should like to page 198 / please my critics, I cannot plead guilty to any absence of conscientiousness on my part.

I have a very curious collection of letters and other documents in connection with *Fathers and Sons.* It is rather interesting to compare them. While some of my correspondents accuse me of insulting the younger generation, of being behind the times and a reactionary, and inform me that they "are burning my photographs with a contemptuous laugh," others, on the contrary, reproach me with pandering to the same younger generation. "You are crawling at the feet of Bazarov!" one correspondent exclaims. "You are just pretending to condemn him; in effect, you are fawning upon him and waiting as a favour for one casual smile from him!" One critic, I remember, addressing me directly in strong and eloquent words, depicted Mr. Katkov and me as two conspirators who in the peaceful atmosphere of my secluded study, are hatching our despicable plot, our libellous attack, against the young Russian forces. . . . It made an effective picture! Actually, that is how this *plot* came about. When Mr. Katkov received my manuscript of *Fathers and Sons,* of whose contents he had not even a rough idea, he was utterly bewildered.[1] The Bazarov type seemed to him "almost an apotheosis of *The Contemporary Review,*" and I should not have been surprised if he had refused to publish my novel in his journal. "*Et voilà comme on écrit l'histoire!*" one could have exclaimed, but

page 199 /

[1] I hope Mr. Katkov will not be angry with me for quoting a few passages from a letter he wrote to me at the time. "If," he wrote, "you have not actually apotheosized Bazarov, I can't help feeling that he has found himself by some sort of accident on a very high pedestal. He really does tower above all those who surround him. Compared to him, everything is either rubbish, or weak and immature. Was that the impression one ought to have got? One can feel that in his novel the author wanted to characterize a principle for which he has little sympathy, but that he seems to hesitate in the choice of his tone and has unconsciously fallen under its spell. One cannot help feeling that there is something forced in the author's attitude towards the hero of his novel, a sort of awkwardness and stiffness. The author seems to be abashed in his presence, he seems not so much to dislike him as to be afraid of him!" Mr. Katkov goes on to express his regrets that I did not let Mrs. Odintsov treat Bazarov ironically, and so on — all in the same vein! It is clear, therefore, that one of the conspirators was not altogether satisfied with the other's work.

— is it permissible to give such a high-sounding name to such small matters?

On the other hand, I quite understand the reasons for the anger aroused by my book among the members of a certain party. They are not entirely groundless and I accept — without false humility — part of the reproaches levelled against me. The word "nihilist" I had used in my novel was taken advantage of by a great many people who were only waiting for an excuse, a pretext to put a stop to the movement which had taken possession of Russian society. But I never used that word as a pejorative term or with any offensive aim, but as an exact and appropriate expression of a fact, an historic fact, that had made its appearance among us; it was transformed into a means of denunciation, unhesitating condemnation and almost a brand of infamy. Certain unfortunate events that occurred at that time increased the suspicions that were just beginning to arise and seemed to confirm the widespread misgivings and justified the worries and efforts of the "saviours of our motherland," for in Russia such "saviours of the motherland" had made their appearance just then. The tide of public opinion, which is still so indeterminate in our country, turned back. . . . But a shadow fell over my name. I do not deceive myself; I know that that shadow will not disappear. But why did not others — people before whom I feel so deeply my own insignificance — utter the great words: *Périssent nos noms, pourvu que la chose publique soit sauvée* . . . i.e. may our names perish so long as the general cause is saved! Following them, I too can console my self with the thought that my book has been of some benefit. This thought compensates me for the unpleasantness of undeserved reproaches. And, indeed, what does page 200 / it matter? Who twenty or thirty years hence will remember all these storms in a teacup? Or my name — with or without a shadow over it.

But enough about myself, and besides it is time to finish these fragmentary reminiscences which, I am afraid, will hardly satisfy the reader. I just want to say a few parting words to my young contemporaries, my colleagues who enter upon the slippery career of literature. I have already said once and I am ready to repeat that I am not blinded about my position. My twenty-five-year-old "service to the Muses" has drawn to a close amid the growing coldness of the public, and I cannot think of any reason why it should grow warmer once more. New times have come and new men are needed; literary veterans, like the military ones, are almost always invalids, and blessed are those who know how to retire at the right time! I do not intend to pronounce my farewell words in preceptorial tones, to which, incidentally, I have no right whatever, but in the tone of an old friend who is listened to with half-condescending and half-impatient attention, provided he is not too longwinded. I shall do my best not to be that.

And so, my dear colleagues, it is to you that I am addressing myself.

Greif nur hinein ins volle Menschenleben!

I would like to say to you, quoting Goethe —

Ein jeder lebt's — nicht vielen ist's bekannt
Und wo ihr's packt — da ist's interessant!

[i.e. "put your hand right in (I am afraid I can't translate it any better), into the very depth of human life! Everyone lives by it, but few know it, and wherever you grasp it, there it is interesting!"] It is only talent that gives one the power for this "grasp-
page 201 / ing," this "catching hold" of life, and one cannot acquire talent; but talent alone is not enough. What one needs is the constant communion with the environment one undertakes to reproduce; what one needs is truthfulness, a truthfulness that is inexorable in relation to one's own feelings; what one needs is freedom, absolute freedom of opinions and ideas, and, finally, what one needs is education, what one needs is knowledge! "Oh, we understand! We can see what you are driving at!" many will perhaps exclaim at this point. "Potugin's ideas! Ci-vi-li-za-tion, *prenez mon ours!* [It's an old, old story!]" Such exclamations do not surprise me, but they will not make me take back anything I have said. Learning is not only light, according to the Russian proverb, it is also freedom. Nothing makes a man so free as knowledge and nowhere is freedom so needed as in art, in poetry; it is not for nothing that even in official language arts are called "free." Can a man "grasp," "catch hold of" what surrounds him if he is all tied up inside? Pushkin felt this deeply; it is not for

nothing that he said in his immortal sonnet, a sonnet every young writer ought to learn by heart and remember as a commandment —

. . . . by a free road
Go, where your free mind may draw you. . . .

The absence of such freedom, incidentally, explains why not a single one of the Slavophils, in spite of their undoubted gifts,[1] has ever created anything that is alive; not one of them knew how to remove — even for a moment — his rose-coloured spectacles. But the saddest example of the absence of true freedom, arising out of the absence of true knowledge, is provided by the last work of Count L. N. Tolstoy (*War and Peace*), which at the same time exceeds by its creative force and poetic gifts almost anything **page 202 /** that has appeared in our literature since 1840. No, without education and without freedom in the widest sense of the word — in relation to oneself and to one's preconceived ideas and systems, and, indeed, to one's people and one's history — a true artist is unthinkable; without that air, it is impossible to breathe.

As for the final result, the final appraisal of a so-called literary career — here, too, one has to remember the words of Goethe:

Sind's Rosen — nun sie werden blüh'n

— "if these are roses, they will bloom." There are no unacknowledged geniuses as there are no merits which survive their appointed time. "Sooner or later everyone finds his niche," the late Belinsky used to say. One has to be thankful if one has done one's bit at the right time and at the right hour. Only the few chosen ones are able to leave for posterity not only the content, but also the *form*, of their ideas and opinions, their personality, to which, generally speaking, the mob remains entirely indifferent. Ordinary individuals are condemned to total disappearance, to being swallowed up by the torrent; but they have increased its force, they have widened and deepened its bed — what more do they want?

[1] One cannot, of course, reproach Slavophils with ignorance or lack of education; but for the achievement of an artistic result one needs — to use a modern expression — the combined action of many *factors*. The factor the Slavophils lack is freedom; others lack education, still others talent, etc. etc.

I am laying down my pen. . . . One more last advice to young writers and one more last request. My friends, never try to justify yourselves (whatever libellous stories they may tell about you). Don't try to explain a misunderstanding, don't be anxious, yourselves, either to say or to hear "the last word." Carry on with your work — and in time everything will come right. At any rate, let a considerable period of time elapse first — and then look on all the old squabbles from an historical point of view, as I have tried to do now. Let the following example serve as a lesson to you: in the course of my literary career I have only **page 203 /** once tried "to get the facts right." Namely, when *The Contemporary Review* began assuring its subscribers in its announcements that it had dispensed with my services because of the *unfitness* of my convictions (while, in fact, it was I who, in spite of their requests, would have nothing more to do with them — of which I have documentary proof), I could not resist announcing the real state of affairs in public and — of course, suffered a complete fiasco. The younger generation were more indignant with me than ever. "How did I dare to raise my hand against their idol! What does it matter if I was right? I should have kept silent!" I profited by this lesson; I wish you, too, should profit by it.

As for my request, it is as follows: guard our Russian tongue, our beautiful Russian tongue, that treasure, that trust handed down to you by your predecessors, headed again by Pushkin! Treat this powerful instrument with respect; it may work miracles in the hands of those who know how to use it! Even those who dislike "philosophic abstractions" and "poetic sentimentalities," even to practical people, for whom language is merely a means for expressing thoughts, a means to an end, just like an ordinary lever, even to them I will say: respect at least the laws of mechanics and extract every possible use from every thing! Or else, glancing over some dull, confused, feebly longwinded diatribe in a journal, the reader will perforce think that instead of a *lever* you are using some antediluvian props — that you are going back to the infancy of mechanics itself. . . .

But, enough, or I shall become longwinded myself.

1868–69
Baden-Baden. **page 204 /**

COUNT LEO TOLSTOY

War and Peace (1865–1872)

AUTHOR'S COMMENTS:

A FEW WORDS CONCERNING THE BOOK *War and Peace*

In printing the work on which I have spent five years of constant and exclusive labour, under the best conditions of life, I should like in the introduction to this work to expound my view upon it and thus to disperse the misunderstandings which may arise in the readers. I wish my readers would not see or seek in my book what I did not want or could not express, and would direct their attention to what I meant to convey, but (considering the conditions of the production) did not think it suitable to dwell on. Neither my time nor my skill permitted me to do in full what I had intended to do, and I will make use of the hospitality of this special periodical for the purpose of expounding, even though briefly and incompletely, the author's view of his production for those readers who may be interested in the matter.

1. What is *War and Peace?* It is not a novel, still less is it a poem, still less a historical chronicle. *War and Peace* is what the author wanted and could express in the form in which it is expressed. Such an announcement as to the author's neglect to attend to the conventional forms of an artistic prose production might appear page i / as a bit of self-confidence if it were intentional and if it had no precedent. The history of Russian literature since the time of Púshkin not only furnishes many examples of such a departure from the European form, but does not offer even a single contrary example. Beginning with Gógol's

---

Reprinted, by permission, from *War and Peace*, translated by Leo Wiener (New York and Boston: Colonial Press Co., 1904).

Dead Souls and ending with Dostoévski's *Dead House*, in the new period of Russian literature, there is not a single artistic prose production, which ever so little rises above mediocrity, that is completely arranged in the form of a novel, epic, or story.

2. The character of the time, as some readers said to me at the appearance of the first part in print, is not sufficiently defined in my work. To this rebuke I have the following answer to make: I know in what consists that character of the time which is not found in my novel, — the horrors of the serf right, the immuring of wives, the flogging of grown sons, Saltýchikha, and so forth; but this character of that time, as it lives in our imagination, I do not consider correct and did not wish to express. In studying letters, diaries, and traditions, I did not find all the horrors of this savagery to any greater extent than I find them at present or at any other time. In those days they also loved, envied, searched after the truth and virtue, were carried away by passion; there was also a complex, mental, and moral life, at times even more refined than at present in the upper class. If in our conception there has been formed an opinion of arbitrariness and brute force as regards that time, this is so only because in the traditions, memoirs, stories, and novels there have come down to us exaggerated cases of violence and brutality. To conclude that the prevailing character of that time was brutality is as incorrect as it would be for a man, who beyond a mountain sees nothing but the tops of trees, to conclude that in that locality there is nothing but trees. There is a character of that time (just as there is a character to every epoch), which page ii / results from a greater alienation of the upper circle from the other classes, from the ruling philosophy, from the peculiarities of education, from the habit of using the French language, and so forth. It is this character that I tried to express as well as I could.

3. The use of the French language in a Russian production. Why in my work do not only Russians but also Frenchmen speak partly Russian and partly French? The reproach that persons speak and write French in a Russian book is like the reproach a man would make, who, looking at a picture, sees black spots (shadows) on it, which do not exist in reality. The artist is not to blame because to some the shadow which is made by him on the face of the picture appears as a black spot, which does not exist in reality; the artist is to blame only if these shadows are

put on wrongly and coarsely. Busying myself with the epoch of the beginning of the present century, and representing Russian persons of a certain class of society and Napoleon and the French, who took such a direct part in the life of that time, I was involuntarily carried away more than was necessary by the form of expression of that French manner of thinking. And so, without denying that the shadows put on by me are in all likelihood incorrect and coarse, I wish only that those to whom it will appear funny that Napoleon speaks now Russian and now French should know that this only seems so to them, because, like a man who is looking at a portrait, they do not see the face with its lights and shadows, but see a black spot under its nose.

4. The names of the acting persons, Bolkónski, Drubetskóy, Bilíbin, Kurágin, and so forth, remind one of well-known Russian names. In confronting acting non-historical persons, with other historical persons, I felt the awkwardness for the ear of making Count Rostopchín speak with Prince Prónski, with Stryélski, or with some other princes and counts, of an invented double or single page iii / family name. Bolkónski or Drubetskóy, although they are neither Volkónski nor Trubetskóy, sound familiar and natural in the Russian aristocratic circle. I was unable to invent for all persons such names as would seem to me to be false to the ear, such as Bezúkhi and Rostóv, and I was not able to avoid this difficulty in any other way than by taking at random names which were most familiar to the Russian ear and changing a few letters in them. I should be very sorry if the similarity between the invented names and the real ones could give any one the idea that I wanted to describe this or that actual person; especially, since that literary activity which consists in the description of actually existing persons has nothing in common with the one I busied myself with.

M. D. Akhrosímov and Denísov are the only persons to whom I involuntarily and without thinking gave names that closely approach two extremely characteristic and charming actual persons of the society of that time. That was my mistake, which arose from the peculiar intrinsic character of these two persons, but my mistake in this respect is limited to the mere introduction of these two persons. All the other persons are purely invented, and have not even for me any definite prototypes in tradition or reality.

5. My divergence in the description of historical events from

the narrative of the historians. It is not accidental, but inevitable. The historian and the artist, in describing a historical epoch, have two entirely different subjects before them. Just as the historian will be wrong if he shall try to represent a historical person in all his entirety, in all the complication of his relations to all the sides of life, so also will the artist not fulfil his work, if he always represents a person in his historical significance. Kutúzov did not always ride a white horse, with a field-glass in his hand, pointing to the enemy. Rostopchín did not always, with a torch in hand, burn the Voronóvski page iv / House (he even never did that), and Empress Márya Fédorovna did not always stand, clad in an ermine mantle, leaning with one hand on the code of laws; but it is as such that the popular imagination represents them to itself.

For the historian there are heroes, in the sense of people who contribute to some one purpose; but for the artist there cannot and must not be a hero, but must be a man, in the sense of this person's correspondence with all the sides of life.

The historian is at times obliged, by bending the truth, to subordinate all the actions of the historical person to the one idea which he has put into this person. The artist, on the contrary, in the very singleness of this idea finds an incompatibility with his problem and only tries to comprehend and show, not a certain actor, but a man.

In the description of the events themselves the distinction is still more sharp and essential.

The historian has to deal with the results of the event, the artist with the fact of the event. The historian, in describing a battle, says: "The left flank of such and such an army was moved toward such and such a village, defeated the enemy, but was compelled to retreat; then the cavalry which was sent to the attack overthrew," and so forth. The historian cannot speak otherwise. And yet these words have no meaning for the artist and do not even touch upon the event itself. Either from his own experience, or from letters, memoirs, and stories, the artist deduces his own conception about the course of the event, and frequently (as in the example of the battle) the deduction about the activity of such and such armies, which the historian permits himself to make, turns out to be the very opposite to the artist's deduction. The difference of the results obtained is also to be explained from those sources from which the two draw their information. For the historian (we continue the example of the battle) page v / the chief source is found in the reports of the private commanders and of the commander-in-chief. The artist can draw nothing from such sources, — they tell him nothing, explain nothing to him. More than that: the artist turns away from them, as he finds in them a necessary lie, to say nothing of the fact that every battle is described by the two enemies in absolutely opposite ways. In every description of a battle there is a necessity of lying, which results from the demand for a description in a few words of the actions of thousands of men scattered over several versts and acting under the strongest moral incitement, under the influence of fear, shame, and death.

In the descriptions of battles they generally say that such and such armies directed their attack upon such and such a point, and then they were commanded to retreat, and so forth, as though assuming that that discipline which submits tens of thousands of men to the will of one man on the parade-grounds will have the same effect where life and death are in the scale. Everybody who has been in a war knows how untrue that is;[1] and yet, on this assumption are based the reports, and upon them the military descriptions. Make the round of the troops immediately after a battle, even on the next day, or the day after, before the reports are written out, and ask all the soldiers, the superior and inferior commanders, how the affair took place; you will be told what all these men experienced and saw, and you will form a majestic, complex, infinitely varied and heavy, indistinct impression, page vi / and from no one, least of all from the commander-in-chief, will you find out how the affair took place. But two, three days later they begin to bring in the reports, the talkers begin to tell how that happened which they did not see; finally a general report is made out, and from this report the general opinion of the army is formed. It is a relief for any one to exchange his own

[1] After my first part was printed with the description of the battle of Schöngraben, I was told of the words of Nikoláy Nikoláevich Muravév-Kárski concerning this description of the battle, — words which confirmed for me my conviction. Nikoláy Nikoláevich Muravév, the commander-in-chief, said that he had never read a more correct description of a battle, and that he had become convinced through his own experience that it is impossible during a battle to carry out the orders of the commander-in-chief. — *Author's Note.*

doubts and questions for this deceptive, but clear and always flattering representation. Question a man who has taken part in this battle a month or two later, and you will no longer feel in his story that raw vital material which there was before, for he is telling it now in acordance with the report. Thus I was told about the battle of Borodinó by many wide-awake, clever participants in the battle. They all told one and the same thing, in accordance with the incorrect description of Mikhaylóvski-Danilévski, Glínka, and others; even the details which they told, though the narrators were several versts distant from one another, were all the same.

After the loss of Sevastopol, the commander of artillery, Kryzhanóvski, sent me the reports of the officers of artillery from all the bastions, asking me to make up a report from these more than twenty separate reports. I am sorry I have not described these reports. This was the best example of that naïve, unavoidable, military lie from which descriptions are made up. I assume that many of my comrades who at that time made up these reports will, as they read these lines, laugh at the recollection of how they, by order of the authorities, wrote what they could not know. All those who have experienced a war know how capable Russians are of doing their work in a war and how little fit they are to describe it with the necessary boastful lie. Everybody knows that in our armies this duty of writing out the reports is for the most part attended to by men of foreign birth.

All this I say in order to show the inevitableness of page vii / the lying in military descriptions, which serve as material for the military historians, and, therefore, to show the inevitableness of frequent disagreements between the artist and the historian in the comprehension of historical events. But besides the inevitableness of the untruth in the exposition of historical events, in the historians of the epoch in which I was interested, I observed (no doubt in consequence of the habit of grouping events, of expressing them briefly, and of complying with the tragic tone of the events) a special form of soaring diction, in which the lie and the distortion frequently pass, not only to the events, but even to the comprehension of the meaning of the events. In studying the two chief historical productions of this epoch, Thiers and Mikhaylóvski-Danilévski, I frequently marvelled how such books could have been printed and read. To say nothing of the fact that they treated the same events in a most serious, significant tone, with references to materials, and yet were diametrically opposed to one another, I came across such descriptions in these historians that I did not know whether to laugh or weep, considering that these two books are the only monuments of this epoch and have millions of readers. I will adduce but one example from the book by the famous historian Thiers. After telling how Napoleon brought with him counterfeit assignats, he says, "*Relevant l'emploi de ces moyens par un acte de bienfaisance digne de lui et de l'armée française, il fut distribuer des secours aux incendiés. Mais les vivres étant trop précieux être donné longtemps à des étrangers, la plupart ennemis, Napoleon aima mieux leur fournir de l'argent, et il leur fit distribuer des roubles papier.*"

This passage is striking in itself by its stupendous, I shall not say immorality, but simply stupidity; but in the whole book this is not so startling, because it fully corresponds to the general, soaring, solemn tone of the discourse, which makes no direct sense.

Thus the problem of the artist and of the historian in **page viii /** the description of events and persons in my book must not startle the reader.

But the artist must not forget that the representation of historical events, as formed among the people, is not based on fancy, but on historical documents, to the extent to which the historians have been able to group them; therefore, though the artist understands and represents these persons and events differently, he must, like the historian, be guided by historical material. Wherever historical persons in my novel speak and act, I have not invented, but have made use of material of which during my work a whole library has been formed, the books of which I do not find it necessary to cite here, but to which I can always refer.

6. Finally, the sixth and most important consideration for me refers to the small significance which, according to my ideas, is to be ascribed to so-called great men in the historical events.

In studying that epoch, so tragical, so rich in the grandeur of its events, and so near to us, in regard to which there live so many varied traditions, I arrived at the evident fact that the causes of the historical events, as they take place, are not accessible to our reason. To say (what to everybody seems very simple) that the causes of the events of the year 1812 consist in Napoleon's spirit of conquest and in the patriotic firmness of Emperor Aleksándr Pávlovich is as senseless as to say that the causes of the fall of the Roman Empire are these, that a certain barbarian led his nations to the west, and a certain Roman Emperor mismanaged the state, or that an immense hill which is being torn down fell because the last labourer struck it with his spade.

Such an event, where millions of people killed one another and in all killed half a million, cannot have for its cause the will of one man: just as one man could not have torn down the hill, so one man cannot cause five page ix / hundred thousand men to die. But what are the causes? Some historians say that the cause was the French spirit of conquest, the patriotism of Russia. Others speak of the democratic element which Napoleon's hosts carried abroad and the necessity for Russia of entering into an alliance with Europe, and so forth. But how did millions of people begin to kill one another,— who told them to do so? It is possible to make an endless number of retrospective conclusions as regards the causes of this senseless event, and these conclusions are actually made; but the great majority of these explanations and their coincidence in one purpose only proves that there is an endless number of these causes and that not one of them may be called the cause.

Why have millions of people killed one another, when it has been known ever since the creation of the world that this is both physically and morally bad?

Because that has been inevitably necessary, because, doing so, men have performed an elementary, zoological law, the one performed by the bees, when they destroy one another in the autumn, and the one according to which the male animals destroy one another. It is impossible to give any other answer to this terrible question.

This truth is not only apparent, but is so inherent in every man that it would not be worth while to prove it, if there did not exist another sentiment in man, which convinces him that he is free at any moment, whenever he is acting.

In viewing history from a common point of view, we are unquestionably convinced of the Pre-eternal Law according to which events take place. Looking at it from the personal point of view, we are convinced of the opposite.

A man who kills another, Napoleon who gives the order to

cross the Nyeman, you and I, petitioning about page x / a governmental appointment, raising and dropping our arms, are unquestionably convinced that every act of ours has for its base rational causes and our free will, and that it depended on us whether we should act in this manner or in that, and this conviction is to such a degree inherent in us and dear to every one of us that, in spite of the proofs of history and of the statistics of crimes (which convince us of the absence of freedom of the will in the acts of other men), we extend the consciousness of our freedom to all our acts.

The contradiction seems insoluble. In committing an act I am convinced that I commit it according to my will; but viewing this act in the sense of its participation in the general life of humanity (in its historical significance), I am convinced that this act was predetermined and inevitable. Where is the error?

The psychological observations concerning man's ability on the spur of the moment retrospectively to find a whole series of imagined free ratiocinations for an accomplished fact (this I intend to expound at a greater length in another place) confirm the assumption that man's consciousness of freedom, in the commission of a certain kind of acts, is erroneous. But the same psychological observations prove that there is another series of acts in which the consciousness of freedom is not retrospective, but sudden and unquestionable. No matter what the materialists may say, I am always able to commit an act or to keep from it, so long as the act refers to me alone. I have unquestionably by nothing but my will just raised and dropped my arm. I can at once stop writing. You can at once stop reading. Unquestionably I have by nothing but my own will and regardless of all obstacles just transferred myself mentally to America or to any desired mathematical question. I can, testing my freedom, raise and forcibly drop my hand in the air. I did so. But near me stands a child, and I raise my hand over page xi / him, and I want to drop it upon him with the same force. I cannot do so. A dog makes for this child, and I cannot help raising my hand against the dog. I am standing in the battle-line and I cannot help following the motions of the regiment. I cannot avoid in a battle making an attack with my regiment and running, when all men about me are running. When in the court-room I stand as a defender of a defendant, I cannot stop talking or knowing what I am going to say. I cannot help winking when a blow is directed against my eye. Thus there are two kinds of acts: some that depend on my will, others that do not depend on it. And the mistake which produces the contradiction is due only to this, that the consciousness of freedom (which legitimately accompanies every act that refers to my ego, up to the highest abstractions of my existence) is involuntarily transferred by me to my acts which are committed in conjunction with other men and which depend on the coincidence of other free wills with my own. It is very hard to determine the border between freedom and dependence, and the determination of this border forms the essential and only problem of psychology; but, observing the conditions of the manifestation of our greatest freedom and greatest dependence, it is impossible to avoid seeing that the more our activity is abstract and therefore the less it is connected with the activities of other men, the more it is free; and, on the other hand, the more our activity is connected with the activities of other men, the less free it is.

The most potent, indissoluble, heavy, and constant bond with other men is the so-called power exerted by one set of men against another, which in its true meaning is but the greatest dependence upon others.

Whether this is faulty or not, having become fully convinced of it in the course of my work, in describing the historical events of the years 1805, 1807, and es- page xii / pecially 1812, in which this law of predetermination appears boldly in relief,[1] I was unable to ascribe any significance to the acts of those men to whom it seemed that they guided the events, but who less than all the other participants of the events introduced into it a free human activity. The activity of these men was interesting to me only as an illustration of that law of predetermination which in my opinion guides history, and of that psychological law which compels a man who commits a most un-free act to find in his imagination a whole series of retrospective ratiocinations, the purpose of which is to prove his freedom to himself. page xiii /

[1] It is worthy of note that nearly all those who have written about the year '12, have seen in this event something peculiar and fatal. — *Author's Note.*

GEORGE ELIOT

Middlemarch, a Study of Provincial Life (1871–1872)

Author's "Quarry for *Middlemarch*": Quarry Two

[Second flyleaf, recto]

Dissolution of Parlt. April 22, 1831
General rejoicing & illuminations. Elections, May.
Parlt. Reopened, June 21.[1]

[Second flyleaf, verso]

Dates

1830 opening of Liverpool & Manchr. Railway, April
" George IV died, June 26 — Whigs come in
" French Revolution,* July, 27, 28, 29,
" Parliament Dissolved,† July 24
" King & Queen decline to visit the city, Nov. 9. Funds fall.
" Mr. Brougham's motion for Reform Nov. 16.
" Tory amendment carried. Machine breaking
" x (Writs returnable for
1831 Parliament dissolved April 22 & gen. election. Reopened. June 21

[1] For numbered notes to *Quarry II* see pages 65–66 below. [Pages 117–118 in this book.]

* Charles X published the Ordinances July 26, withdrew them, 29. "Too late!" said Laffitte, "Since yesterday, a century has passed away.

† Deaths from Cholera in Paris, Feb. & Mar., 1832 — 18,402

Reprinted, by permission and with the editor's notes, from *Quarry for "Middlemarch,"* edited by Anna Theresa Kitchel, first published in *Nineteenth-Century Fiction*, Volume 4, Supplement 1 (Los Angeles, 1950), pp. 43–66. See Bibliographical Note B, page xiv.

" x First cases of Cholera
" (Paganini) Reform Bill thrown out by the Lords Oct. 7
" Bristol Riots Oct. 29
Reintrod. 3rd time Dec. 12
1832 Cholera appears at Rotherhithe & London Feb. & Sep.
R.B. read in the Lords, Mar. Motion against it carried May 7‡
" Reform Bill passed, June 7.
" Capl. Punishment for sheep & cattle stealing abolished.
" First Nos. of Chambers' Journal & Penny Mag.
1833 Reformed Parliament, election Jan.
" Thanksgiving for departure of Cholera, Ap. 14[2] page 43 /

(1)

Queries

Periods of university examinations

	Oxford	Cambridge
Lent term	Jan. 14–April 1	Jan 13–Mar. 31
Easter	Ap. 12–May 26	April 14–June 23
Trinity	May 27–July 8	
Mich.	Oct. 10–Dec. 18	Oct. 1–Dec. 16

Notes from a letter on Hospitals

Chaplain. Chaplain at C honorary. Came when sent for & occasionally otherwise. At S. salaried £40. & had regular services &nd visitations.
Matron. At C factotum. At S. Housekeeper, with only power to report Nurses to the House Surgeon, who engaged or dismissed them.
House Surgeon. Always considered to carry out the treatment of the Surgeons & Physns, to attend urgent cases etc on his own account, & to keep the medical part of the house in order. Not allowed to attend cases out of the Hospital.
Physns. & Surgns. Attendance usually in forenoon ("At no decent institution is the term medical officer used as in C. viz. to express

‡ King threatening to create new peers, May 18 Carried in the Lords June 4

a license to attend medical & surgical cases — in fact to attend the Hospl as general practitioners

(2)[3]

Dr B. in 1869 refused to give a testimonial for the C. Hospital on the ground that such a state of things ought not to exist."[4]

Middlemarch

Directors	Votes for Tyke
Mr. Plymdale, Dyer	Votes for Tyke
Mr. Powderell, Retired ironmonger	" "
Mr. Hawley, Lawyer & town clerk	" Farebrother

page 44 /

Mr. Hackbutt, Tanner	" Farebrother
Mr. Larcher, Carrier	Tyke
Rev. E. Thesiger, Rector of St. Peter's	Tyke
Arthur Brooke Esq. of Tipton Grange	Tyke
Nicholas Bulstrode, Esq. Banker	Tyke[5]

Lowick

o

2 miles

Middlemarch

o

3 miles

Tipton

o

o

Freshitt

[Pen-drawn lines connect the places indicated by small circles]

(3)

Relations to be developed

1 of Dorothea to Mr. Casaubon
2 " Lydgate to Rosamond
3 " Fred Vincy to Mary Garth

4 " The Vincys to Old Featherstone
5 " Dorothea to Will Ladislaw
6 " Lydgate to Bulstrode
7 " Bulstrode to John Raffles
8 " Celia to Sir James
9 " Ladislaw to Mr Brooke
10 " Caleb Garth to Mr Brooke etc.
11 " Mr Farebrother to all, except Sir J. & Mr Brooke

(4)

Private dates[6]

Dorothea married, 1827. Featherstone dies & Ladislaw comes to Tipton, Ap. 1830. Celia married May
Lydgate's marriage 1830 — July or August **page 45 /**
Mr Brooke tries for Parliament May 1831
Mr Casaubon's death, 1831. March
Celia's baby born, 1831 — April
Dorothea's second marriage, 1832 Jan. or Feb.
Child born, 1833
Rosamond's baby born, June 1, 1831
Bulstrode buys Stone Court, June or July 1831
Raffles comes back, July 1831
Raffles dies, Aug. 1832. Two years after Lydgate's marriage.
" " "

Mr Casaubon's Death, March 1831
Dorothea settled at Lowick again June 1831
Bulstrode & Raffles at Stone Court, end of June 1831
Fred Vincy's adventure & choice July 1831
Lydgate's disclosure of trouble to Rosd. Aug.

(5)[7]

Middlemarch. Part I. Miss Brooke. Decr.

Chapter 1 The two sisters pp 1–13
2 Mr Casaubon & Sir James come to dine. 13–23
3 The two suitors persevere 23–36
4 Dorothea's eyes opened. A letter arrives 36–45
5 Mr Casaubon accepted 45–57
6 Mrs Cadwallader informed, & Sir James 57–70
7. Dorothea reads with Mr Casaubon 70–75
8. Sir James appeals to the Rector 75–82

9. Dorothea sees Lowick, & Will Ladislaw 82–92
10. The marriage approaching, & a party 92–103
11 Lydgate talked of at Fred Vincy's breakfast
12 Rosamond & Fred ride to Stone Court & Mr Featherstone asks for something awkward.

Ms. 134 pp.

(6)

Middlemarch Part II. Old and young. Feb.

Ch XI Lydgate is a subject of conversation at [*written above:* in] the Vincys' dining room, as the new doctor, 103–112 page 46 /
XII Fred & Rosamond go to Stone Court. Old F. asks for something awkward. Rosd. sees Lydgate — 135[8]
XIII. Bulstrode with Lydgate & Vincy. 135–145
XIV Fred carries a note to his uncle. Tells Mary of his love. Gives £80 to his mother to keep 145–160
XV Lydgate's history and present ambition 160–173
XVI Lydgate dines at Mr Vincy's. 173–189
XVII. Mr Farebrother at home. XVIII Tyke elected 189–220
XIX Fred Vincy tries to meet his debt 220–237[9]
XX Fred has to confess to Mr & Mrs Garth 237–246
XXI Fred confesses to Mary, & her father comes 246–256
Ch. IXX Mrs Casaubon in the Vatican Museum
XX Dorothea in tears. Receives a visitor
XXI Mr & Mrs Casaubon go to see a studio

MS. 126 pp.

(7)[10]

Part III. April

Ch. 22 Fred Vincy tries to meet his debt
23 Has to confess to Mr & Mrs Garth
24 Fred confesses to Mary & her father comes
25 Fred taken ill, & Mr Wrench dismissed
26 Lydgate & Rosamond in flirtation
27 Mr & Mrs Casaubon return to Lowick
28 Mr Casaubon taken ill
29 Lydgate advises & Mr Brooke writes a letter
30 The flirtation of Lydgate ends in engagement

31 The blood-relations at Stone Court
32 Old Featherstone's death

(8)[11]

Part III. April

Waiting for Death

Ch 22 Scene in the Museum of the Vatican
Tr 23 Dorothea in tears. Is called on by a relative **page 47 /**
to 24 Mr & Mrs Casaubon go to see a studio
pII [25 *cancelled*]
27 They return to Lowick
[26 *cancelled*]
28 Mr. Casaubon taken ill
[27 *cancelled*]
29 Lydgate advises, & Mr Brooke writes a letter
[28 *cancelled*]
25 Fred is taken ill, & Mr Wrench dismissed
29 26 Lydgate & Rosamond in flirtation
30. The flirtation ends in engagement
31. The blood-relations at Stone Court
32 Old Featherstone unable to do as he likes at the last

ch22 Fred Vincy tries to meet his debt
23 Has to confess to Mr & Mrs Garth
24 Fred confesses to Mary; & her father comes.

MS. 150 pages

(9)

Motives[12]

Featherstone's burial. Arrival of Ladislaw
Will read, & Family consternation
Advent of the new stranger, Rigg
Lydgate & Rosamond married
Mr Brooke seen to be making political tentatives. Ladislaw's relation to Dorothea & Mr Casaubon shown, a propos of appointment to edit the Pioneer.
Dismay of Sir James & the Cadwalladers.
Attacks on Mr Brooke as a Landlord.
He is induced to give the management of his estate to Caleb Garth

What Fred Vincy does.
How Lydgate goes on medically, & in relation to Bulstrode & the Hospital vide P. V
Looming of Raffles **page 48 /**

(10)

Part IV. June. Three Love Problems.

Ch. 33 Featherstone buried & Ladislaw resuscitated
" 34. The Reading of the Will
" 35. Lydgate & Rosamond advance toward marriage
" 36 Ladislaw's settlement at Middlemarch, in relation
" " to Dorothea & Mr Casaubon.
" 37 Sir James & the Cadwalladers attack Mr Brooke about
" " the management of the farms 249a
" 38 Dorothea goes to the Grange, & Dagley has his say 266
" 39 Caleb Garth at breakfast etc. 287
" 40 Mr Raffles visits Mr Rigg 296
" 41 Mr Casaubon in prospect of death.

pp. 164[13]

(11)[14]

Motives (in general)

Mr Casaubon dies.
Mr Brooke stands & falls
Embarrassment of Lydgate
Raffles comes on the scene
Scandal in Middlemarch
Raffles' Death
Lydgate accepts money from Bulstrode
Further scandal
Blight on Bulstrode & Lydgate
Rosamond's flirtation with Ladislaw
? Dorothea after severe struggles goes to Rosamond
? Action of Caleb Garth & Mr Farebrother

Continuation of Part V

1. About Mr Farebrother's appointment to Lowick
2. Mr Brooke goes to the hustings
3. Fred Vincy's choice of a career
4. Raffles' return?
5. Drama of Will & Dorothea advanced **page 49 /**

(12)[15]

Part V August. The Dead Hand

Chap. 41 Lydgate consulted by Mr Casaubon. Scene between
" Dorothea & her husband.
43 42 Dorothea goes into Middlemarch: calls at Lydgate's
44 43 Dorothea & Lydgate talk of the Hospital
45 44 Lydgate's medical position: scene between him &
" Rosamond.
46 45 Mr Brooke & Ladislaw. Lydgate & Ladislaw.
47 " Will goes to Lowick Church
48 Mr Casaubon's last wishes
49 Mr Casaubon dies
49 49 50 Sir James & Mr Brooke confer about the Will
50 50 51 Celia "prepares" Dorothea, & Lydgate exerts his influence for Mr Farebrother.
51 52 " Mr Brooke addresses the electors.
52 53 Mr Farebrother performs a difficult duty.
53. Raffles reappears

MS. pages 151

(13)

Part VI October: The Widow & the Wife

Ch. 54. Interview & goodbye between Dorothea & Will.
55. Dorothea declares she shall not remarry.
56. Fred Vincy chooses his vocation.
57 Lydgate embarrassed. Scene with R.
58. Fred Vincy becomes jealous.
59. Rosamond tells Will about the codicil
60 60 The Sale. Raffles recognizes Will
61 61 Interview between Will & Bulstrode.
62 Interview between Will & Dorothea.

MS. pp. 156 **page 50 /**

(14)

Part VII. December

Two Temptations.

Chap. 63. New Year. Mr Farebrother & Lydgate 12
64. Lydgate & Rosamond: house-letting 37

65 Sir Godwin's letter comes. 45
66 Lydgate in the Billiard Room: Fred called by Mr Farebrother 60
67 Lydgate applies to Bulstrode 72
68 Bulstrode's late experience, & consequent plans. 85
69 Caleb Garth informs Bulstrode that Raffles is at Stone Court. Lydgate called in. Goes home & finds the execution in his house.
70 Bulstrode's state of mind about Raffles — & Lydgate. Gives Lydgate the cheque for 1000. Struggles. Gives the key to the housekeeper. *Death.*
71 Scandal in Middlemarch. Mr Hawley's outburst against Bulstrode. Dorothea enters.

MS. pp. 149

(15)

Part VIII. February

Sunset & Sunrise.

Ch.72 Dorothea wants to help Lydgate —.
73 Lydgate's first anguish
74 Mrs Bulstrode learns her sorrow
75 Rosamond & Lydgate
76 Lydgate & Dorothea.
77 Dorothea, Rosamond & Will Ladislaw
78 Will & Rosamond [*interlineated, underscored:* 79] afterwards Will & Lydgate
[79 *cancelled*]
80 Dorothea in her anguish. 90
81 Dorothea & Rosamond. 105
82 Will Ladislaw 112 **page 51 /**
83 Will & Dorothea 123
84 Mr Brooke carries news 138
85 Mr & Mrs Bulstrode 143
86

(16)

Garth Family

Mary 22; Christy, at Glasgow, 19, Alfred, 15
James 12; Ben, 10, Letty 8.

Bulstrode 58

Raffles 51
Joshua Rigg 32
His mother 56

(17)
Sketch I.

Bulstrode, when young, was a banker's clerk in London & member of a dissenting church to wh. a wealthy couple living at Highbury also belonged. The husband had a business in the city, & on Bulstrode becoming an intimate offered him a place as clerk & accountant; which would be more profitable than his actual situation. Bulstrode accepted & found that the business was a pawnbroker's connected with the receipt of stolen goods.

Preliminary conversations had warned him that the wife was unacquainted with the nature of the business, & the facts were gradually opened to him as necessities which had crept into the management & could not be done away with.

Bulstrode showed ability, & became a confidential associate, winning his way at the same time with the pious wife on the ground of his gifts & divine grace.

(18)
Sketch II.

The couple had had three children, but the two sons had died, & this bereavement made them relent towards the daughter who had run away from them to go on the stage, & had married.

But this daughter had disappeared, & they knew no means of recovering her except by advertisement, which had hitherto failed, but was persevered in. page 52 /

Meanwhile, the husband died, & after a short time Bulstrode won the favour of the widow, who, however, before she made the settlements preliminary to her second marriage, was increasingly anxious to find her daughter & her daughter's possible offspring. Bulstrode, on the other hand, thought this extremely undesirable, as a possible diversion of her property into a less useful channel.

If she married him, he intended

(19)
Sketch III.

as occasion served, to draw away the capital from the criminal business & use it more irreproachably. But the advertising could not be evaded, or an apparent sympathy with the widow's wish.

Still there was no result. But at this stage of affairs a man named Raffles who had early been in service at Highbury but was now a subordinate in the city business was sent on some occasion to Dieppe, & there saw a young couple with their child, the man apparently in a reduced state from sickness, the woman closely resembling the girl whom Raffles had known as the pawnbroker's daughter & whom he knew to have been advertised for. She was holding her baby in her arms & showed a wedding ring.

Raffles came forward & said, "I beg pardon, ma'am, but was your name

(20)

Sketch IV.

Sarah Yorke? & did your parents live at Highbury?" She coloured, was startled & said "Yes." But Raffles then drew back, saying, "I thought so," & left them. He knew that the marriage was pending between Bulstrode & the widow York, & hence debated with himself to which of the two he should carry his information. He determined for Bulstrode, conjecturing that he should get more money there for silence than in the other direction for speech, & in no case should he lose the claim for speech ultimately. **page 53 /**

Bulstrode told Raffles that he himself would mention the matter: it was necessary to inquire into things & be cautious, for the sake of the widow's feelings. On certain hints from Raffles, he observed that R. had done a good

(21)

Sketch V.

service which should be well rewarded if he remained silent. After this, the advertising ceased, & Bulstrode married the widow, but not before Raffles had so presented the question to Bulstrode that he had secured a large sum in acquittance & had gone off to America.

Not long after the marriage the widow died, Bulstrode wound up the business & sought a position in the provinces; having among other changes, left the dissenting body & found all the edification he needed in the evangelical party of the Establishment.

The child of that couple is Will Ladislaw whose father is the son of Mr Casaubon's aunt Julia & her Polish husband, & inherits from the latter artistic faculties. In his extremity of illness & poverty he makes himself known to Mr Casaubon, having family guarantees, & from that time

(22)

Sketch VI.

Mr Casaubon provides for the mother & Will, the father having shortly died. Will's mother, Sarah York, had run away from home to go on the stage under peculiar circumstances, not only following a bent in opposition to her mother's dissenting tastes, but proximately determined by learning from a spiteful rejected suitor that her father's trade was dishonorable. Hence the choice of her husband's friends as sources of help, rather than her own, was doubly determined.

[The idea which governs the plot about Bulstrode is, that there is nothing which the law can lay hold of to make him responsible for: the Nemesis is wrought out by the public opinion determined against him.] **page 54 /**

(23)

How Ladislaw goes on in Middlemarch
Initiates relation to Rosamond
Scene of Fred Vincy's choice, after Mar. 31
Ladislaw's birth known
Mr Farebrother's appointment to the living

(24)

Elements.

1. Mr Casaubon makes the arrangements about his will, having been stimulated by Lydgate's answers to his inquiries about his health.
2. Lydgate again in colloquy with Dorothea, whence an occasion for her to apply some money.
3. Collision between Lydgate & medical men connected with Bulstrode.
4. Leading up to Mr Brooke's nomination in *April or May*
β 1831; his failure & loss of appetite for a public career.

5. Mr Casaubon's death. Sir James & Celia
6. Fred Vincy's debate about his career
7 δ Arrival of Raffles
8 Embarrassments of Lydgate
9 Second marriage of Dorothea
10 ϵ Lydgate attends Raffles' deathbed
11 Accepts money from Bulstrode
12 Scandal blighting him & Bulstrode

(25)[16]

Political dates

After the accession of William IV. Parliament was dissolved on the 23d. July. The writs were made returnable on the 14th. of September. Parliament opened Nov. 2. Duke of Wellington's declaration against reform.
King & Queen refuse to dine in the city, Nov. 9. Government defeated on Sir H. Parnell's motion for inquiry into the Civil List, Nov. 14 page 55 /
Brougham, having pledged himself to his constituency to bring forward a bill for reform had on the opening of Parliament given notice of a motion to that effect. Hence, lest they should be defeated on this question also, the ministry resigned. Lord Grey as prime minister explained his policy, Nov. 22.
Parliament reassembled after Xmas, Feb. 3 1831
Lord John Russell brought forth his measure of Reform on the 1st. of March. On Ap. 21, Ministers defeated on Mr. Bankes's motion to adjourn, Ap. 22. Parliament dissolved.

(26)

Elements of B. VI.

First meeting between Will & Dorothea after her husband's death
Will's increasing intimacy with the Lydgates
Lydgate gets more embarrassed, & moody in consequence
Rosamond makes him angry by writing to his uncle.
Will & Dorothea meet again & part with a sense that they can't marry, Will knowing all.
Rosamond flirting with Will.
Fred Vincy choosing his career

(27)

Will Ladislaw & Dorothea

An offence springs up between Mr Brooke & Will

Will, going on as editor of the Pioneer, comes to Lowick to see the Farebrothers, & has an interview with Dorothea. They part with a sense of being divided by destiny.

Dorothea has projects about filling her life: tells Sir James & Celia that she will never be married again — Celia's boy will have everything. She will go on some heroic errand of carrying away emigrants etc. Meanwhile, the cholera. Will does not go away & gets more intimate with Mrs. Lydgate. Learns the nature of Mr Casaubon's codicil; also about his mother's family from Bulstrode. There is another meeting & parting between him & Dorothea. She finds him with Mrs Lydgate. Scene between her & Will — anger, jealousy, reproach, ending in Dorothea's passionate avowal, & declaration that she will never **page 56 /** marry him. Will reproaches Rosamond with having ruined his happiness. Rosamond alarmed lest Dorothea should tell Lydgate. Dorothea goes to R. having conquered her jealousy by pity, & hears that Will has been true to her.[17]

(28)

Bulstrode & Raffles

Bulstrode buys Featherstone's land; Rigg having an ideal elsewhere. Raffles, not knowing where to find Bulstrode, his letter being dated from "The Shrubs" & containing no clue, comes again after Rigg, & finds Bulstrode riding about Stone Court. Rigg's ideal is a money-changing business.

Raffles comes again, recognizes Will & tells Bulstrode, who gets Raffles away by payment, & then under conscientious relenting offers amends to Will.

Rafflles comes back the third time.

(29)[18]

Scenes

1. First interview between Will & Dorothea after her husband's death.
2. Dorothea tells Sir James & Celia that she will not marry again. Entertaining projects of usefulness.

3. Fred Vincy has an adventure.
4 In consequence seeks employment with Mr Garth.
5 Lydgate embarrassed more & more, is moody. Rosamond, discontented, writes to Sir Godwin. Sir Godwin replies to Lydgate. His anger with R.
6. Will, not going away, gets more intimate with Rosamond, & she more disposed to conquer him.
7. Will learns the nature of Mr Casaubon's Will
8 Raffles comes back & recognizes Will
9 Raffles tells Bulstrode who Will is.
10 Bulstrode paying Raffles to go away, makes offers to Will, constrained by fear & conscience.* **page 57 /**
11 Will's struggles. Gets an interview with Dorothea. They part.
12 Will vacillating goes to Rosamond
13 Dorothea discovers them in emotion — together

(30)

Scenes

14 Scene of anger & jealousy between Will & Dorothea, ending in her avowal of love & resolve not to marry him
15 Will goes to Rosamond & reproaches her with having ruined his happiness.
16 Dorothea, wrought on by compassion, goes to Rosamond, & so moves her that R. tells D. how Will has been true.
17 Meeting & final reconciliation of Will & Dorothea.
18 Dorothea declares to Sir James her intention to marry Will
19. Lydgate in difficulties has half made up his mind to ask Dorothea for aid, & learns that she is going to marry Will.
20 Raffles comes back. Terror of Bulstrode. Disclosures.
21 Raffles' death. Bulstrode gives Lydgate £1000.
22 Scandal in Middlemarch. Blight on Lydgate & Bulstrode. . . .

Epilogue

23 Dorothea in her second married life (in London ?)

(31)

How to End the Parts

Part VI ends with the Farebrothers telling Dorothea of Will's sudden departure —

* Bulstrode expected to be cramped for money induces Dorothea to do more for the Hospital

VII. Ends with Lydgate's bribe [*written in above:* outpouring] to Dorothea

VIII. Epilogue of reconciliation with Dorothea's family

" " "

Remaining Scenes of Part VI.

1. Fred goes to see the Garth Family, finds Mary still away at Lowick.
2. Fred walks to Lowick & sees Mary
3. After Will has learned the nature of Mr Casaubon's codicil.

page 58 /

4 Raffles returns & recognizes Will & tells Bulstrode.
5. Scene between Bulstrode & Will
6. Will's struggles
7 Interview between Will & Dorothea. Parting
8. Will gone away.

(32)

Sketch 2.

Will declares his indifference as to what becomes of him & what career he shall pursue since the only woman he loves is debarred from him by honour. Departs.

Mrs. Cadwallader lets drop some phrase indicating some flirtation between Mrs Lydgate & Will, (in Dorothea's hearing).

Scene between Lydgate & Dorothea in which he exposes his whole life. Estrangement between him & Rosamond — her indifference to everything but Ladislaw & his singing etc.

Dorothea writes to him lending the sum: takes it herself to his house that it may fall into no other hands: also wishing to speak to Rosamond in the way of counsel —

Meanwhile Will has returned impatient to hear something about Dorothea

Calls on Lydgate. Rosamond who has been pining for him, overjoyed at his presence — thinks it is for her & pours out her feeling

Means to go to Utopia.

(33)

Mr Farebrother comes to Lydgate to see if anything can be done for him. Finds him in high spirits, released from trouble. Hears him speak of Raffles' illness.

α Bambridge tells what he has heard
β Raffles identified as just buried
γ Diffusion of the scandal among the Middlemarchers in connexion with Lydgate's release from debt
δ Scandal spreads to Freshitt & Lowick
ε Mr Hawley explodes at Vestry meeting
ζ Lydgate's misery. Rosamond's repulsion
η Mrs Bulstrode **page 59 /**

(34)

Dorothea enters. Their confusion. Will hurriedly departs. Rosamond shivering. Dorothea repressing her anguish, carries out her intended admonition, & quits Rosamond.

Scene between Will & Dorothea[19]

Part VII.

1. Lydgate's affairs
2. Fred & Mary
3 Bulstrode's terrors & wish to get rid of the hospital.*
4 Lydgate sounds him. He is deaf. Raffles' illness & death. Loan to Lydgate.
5 Middlemarch suspicious &
6 Lydgate's misery.
7 [Outpouring to Dorothea.][20] **Part VIII**

* Action of Caleb Garth

(35)[21]

Lydgate goes to the Billiard room at G.D.
(letter comes from Sir Godwin)
Fred Vincy is in the Billiard room
Mr Farebrother sends up for him
Walks with Fred to St Botolph's Parsonage & admonishes him that if he is not to lose Mary he must be careful.
Raffles having again been to Middlemarch — (seen by Lydgate in the billiard room) Bulstrode is meditating removal from Middlemarch going somewhere where he will have a less marked position & suffer less from the visits of Raffles. Is engaged in transferring his bank, & arranging the rest of his property for management without his personal presence. Is seeing Caleb Garth on this subject.

Hence Caleb is going to Stone Court on business. Overtakes Raffles who is ill.
takes him up in his gig. Raffles tells Caleb everything about Bulstrode.
(Raffles has also told Bambridge) page 60 /

(36)

1 That Raffles should tell the whole story of Bulstrode to Caleb Garth; that Caleb should remain silent on the subject even to his wife.
That Raffles should tell Bulstrode how Caleb knew all — but no one else than Caleb.
That Bulstrode sounds Caleb, who tells him his reasons for never disclosing
Caleb calls on Bulstrode tells him that Raffles is at Stone Court & in need of a doctor. Also declines to act further for Bulstrode.
Bulstrode calls in Lydgate.
Gives orders to the woman who sits up with Raffles, to administer opium & alcohol
Gives Lydgate the thousand pounds
Mr Farebrother, not knowing comes with help.
[Lydgate's anguish. Rosamond's repulsion] VIII.
Scene of outburst at a Vestry meeting in which Mr Hawley tells Bulstrode that he is known.
[Lydgate pours out to Dorothea about his misery, & she comforts him. VIII]

(37)
Conclusion of Part VII.

The discussion at Dollop's a type of what was going on in all Middlemarch circles.
The fact of his betrayal bursts upon Bulstrode at a Vestry meeting:
Returns home finds Mrs. Bulstrode partly informed: on Lydgate
The news reaches Lowick & Freshitt

Curtain follows on Dorothea's arrival

Query: connexion of Will's return[22] **page 61 /**

(38)

Course of Part VII.

1 Mr Farebrother makes advances to Lydgate — refused.
2 Lydgate trying to get rid of his house: Rosd. thwarts him
3 Difficulties increase Sir Godwin's letter comes
4 Lydgate goes to the billiard room. Fred Vincy is there: Mr Farebrother comes to fetch him.
5 Fred Vincy & he walk together
6 Lydgate begins to think of applying to Bulstrode. Bulstrode's efforts to free himself & wish to quit Middlemarch — business with Caleb Garth.
7. Lydgate sounds Bulstrode
8 Caleb Garth picks up Raffles. Takes him to Stone Court. Raffles tells him the secrets
9 Caleb calls on Bulstrode, who tells him Raffles is there & declines further transactions. Bulstrode suspects the reasons. Caleb reassures him as to secrecy. Execution in Lydgate's house
10 Bulstrode having called in Lydgate, neglects his orders, & causes Raffles to take alcohol etc.
11 Bulstrode calls on Lydgate & gives him £1000 or £500 (?)
12 Lydgate out of his difficulties. Scandal. Outburst of Mr Hawley against Bulstrode

(39)

Conditions

Return of Will Ladislaw: reasons for his return. Time at which it happens.
What becomes of Bulstrode's arrangements as to property, especially Stone Court?
How Fred & Mary get married.

About Dorothea's money, over & above her own 700 a year.

Times

The death of Raffles about 21st. March page 62 /
Bambridge's return 26th.
Meeting on Sanitary Reform, April 10th.
Return of Will Ladislaw

(40)

Part VIII

1 Dorothea & Lydgate
2 Dorothea goes to deliver a letter at Lydgate's
Finds Will Ladislaw there. Suspicions confirmed by their emotion.

---

1 Reasons why Dorothea does not immediately have her interview with Lydgate.
3 Mrs Bulstrode made aware of the Facts about her husband. [Their final arrangements. Fred Vincy]
Lydgate's misery [*written in above:*2] & gloom.) Rosamond's repulsion.
Will Ladislaw's arrival & its causes
3 Lydgate's outpouring to Dorothea. She takes the money to free him, & finds Will Ladislaw with Dorothea.[23] She goes away with the impression that they are lovers. Her emotions of jealousy: making her more distinctly aware of her love.
Her struggle to overcome her selfish feeling. She goes again to R.
Will's outburst to Rosamond after Dorothea is gone away: cutting to the quick.

When Dorothea comes again to Rosamond with love, Rosamond is wrought upon to tell her that Will loves Dorothea alone.

(41)

Dorothea's motive in going to Rosamond.

(42)[24]

Part VIII

1 Dorothea wants to help Lydgate & is checked
2 Lydgate's first anguish under the sense of his position
3 Mrs Bulstrode learns her sorrow page 63 /
4 Rosamond's behavior & Lydgate's towards her

5 Lydgate tells Dorothea
6 Dorothea goes to see Rosamond & take (the £1000) money for Lydgate. Finds Will with Rosamond.
7 Will's outburst of bitterness against R.
8 Dorothea's anguish & struggles. She goes to Rosamond again who tells her about Will's truth.
9 Will's interview with Dorothea: Reconciliation
10 The Garths & Fred Vincy.
11 Dorothea tells her uncle & the Chettams that she is going to marry Will
12 Mr Brooke will be father at the wedding but as a corrective proposes to cut off the entail

Finale **page 64 /**

NOTES TO QUARRY TWO

(Notebook reversed)

1 Miscellaneous dates, probably from the *Annual Register.*

2 *Annual Register* probably used here also, but the data were available in many books. The author's statements add details.

3 Page 2 is the verso of page 1. The right-hand pages are ordinarily numbered with odd numbers, the left with even; but occasionally a page is left blank and this rule is upset, e.g., page 11 is the verso of 10, and page 27 is a verso.

4 The "letter on Hospitals" was written by Mrs. Richard Congreve, whose father, Dr. Bury, had attended Robert Evans in his last illness.

5 Votes of the directors of the Middlemarch Infirmary cast in the choice of a chaplain.

6 Many situations in the novel are timed to correspond with stages of the First Reform Bill; here the author gives her own timetable for important happenings in her story.

7 Page 5 begins the listing of chapters with titles. Note that chapters 11 and 12, here listed in Part I, are transferred to Part II. The lack of paging here suggests the author's indecision about the proper place for these chapters.

8 Note the changed wording of the chapter headings. The paging for these chapters, omitted on page 5, is given here.

9 The difficulty of weaving in the Fred Vincy strands is seen on pages 6, 7, and 8 of *Quarry II.* The chapters listed as 19–21 were first included in Part II, but finally formed the opening chapters of Part III, numbered 22, 23, and 24. The original chapter 20 of Part II (see *Quarry II*, p. 6) is split into two chapters, 20 and 21. The original 21 becomes 22 and concludes Part II.

[10] Page 7, the verso of page 6, is a fair copy of page 8. The Vincy material is here logically and naturally interwoven with the Dorothea-Casaubon strand.

[11] Page 8 shows the process of working out the structure of Part III. Compare with page 7. "Dorothea Married," the original title of III, was crossed out and "Waiting for Death" substituted.

[12] The heading "Motives" covers a variety of details dealing with plot and characterization.

13. The first rough estimate of the number of pages in Part IV, "pp. 150–170," is crossed out and "pp. 164" substituted.

[14] Here the "Motives (in general)" is followed by a further elaboration of Part V, previously dealt with chapter by chapter on page 12.

[15] The first item has already been listed on page 10 as "Mr Casaubon in prospect of death." The numbers to the left of the items are correct; the others are crossed. Note that with the renumbering of what was to have been the first chapter of Part V (originally 42, here 43) the chapters in the *Quarry* now correspond to those in the published text.

[16] On page 25 the important events of the Reform Bill period are narrated rather than merely listed. The probable source, again, is the *Annual Register.*

[17] See note 3.

[18] Page 29 works out in much greater detail the material outlined and then put into narrative form on pages 26 and 28.

[19] The first four lines on page 34 continue the "Sketch" on page 32. The seven items below deal with Part VII. page 65 /

[20] The author began here to use square brackets as well as parentheses.

[21] Pages 35 and 36 deal with the complications of Part VII.

[22] The "Query" which concludes page 37 emphasizes the author's difficulty in fitting in Will's comings and goings.

[23] One of George Eliot's rare slips occurs when she writes "Dorothea" for "Rosamond" in the eighth line from the bottom.

[24] The numbered, clear list of chapters in Part VIII given on page 42 should be compared with page 15.

In the MS notebook, *Quarry II* shows many crossings-out, vertical, horizontal, and oblique. It seems neither possible nor important to reproduce these in print. page 66 /

ÉMILE ZOLA

L'Assommoir (1877)

Author's Sketch*

[*Zola first indicates the general idea, the ruling thought which is to rule his novel.*]

The novel should do this: show the poor people's quarter and explain through their milieu the customs of the poor, as for example, drunkenness, the breakdown of the family, fights, submission to all the shame and misery arising from the very conditions of the workman's existence, hard work, promiscuity, indifference, etc. In a word, a very exact picture of the life of the people with its foulness, its loose life, its vulgar language, and this picture having as background — without presenting a thesis — the particular soil in which all these things grow. Do not flatter the worker, nor blacken his character. An absolutely exact reality. At the end the moral standing out inevitably. A good worker to play the opposite part, or rather no, don't fall into the *Manual*. A frightful picture which will carry its own moral lesson.

* ". . . I use my reasoning power," says Zola. "I argue with myself, I write monologues word for word just as they occur to me and so that read by another they would appear very strange. So-and-so does this or that; what would be the natural result of such an action? Would such-and-such an act affect my character? Assuredly. It is therefore logical that this other character would react in a given way. Then some other character may intervene, at a certain point; someone whom I have discovered in my researches and who seem absolutely to belong to the setting. . . . I examine the immediate consequences of the slightest incident. . . . I work as does a commissary of police. . . ."

Reprinted, by permission, from *Zola and His Time*, by Matthew Josephson (New York: The Macaulay Company, 1928).

[*Then he talks to himself about his principal character, whose story he retraces.*]

My Gervaise Macquart is to be the heroine. I make of her the woman of the people, the wife of a workman. It is her story I tell. This is her story. She quits Plassans to go to Paris with her lover Lantier, by whom she has two children: Claude and Etienne. She leaves in 1850. At that time she is twenty-two years old. Claude is eight and Etienne four.

Lantier, a tanner, abandons her three months after her arrival in Paris, where she has taken up her work as laundress again: he marries some one else, probably. She goes to Coupeau, a roofer, who marries her. She has a daughter by him right away, Anna, in 1851. I free her of Claude when he is about ten or twelve. I leave her only Etienne and Anna. At the opening of the story, Anna must be at least fourteen and Etienne eighteen years old. The drama will then take place toward 1865. I shall relate previously the life of Gervaise.

As my framework I shall probably be able to take the life of a page 528 / woman of the people. I take Gervaise at Paris, twenty-two years old (in 1850) and I follow her until 1869, when she is forty-one. I make her pass through all the crises and shame imaginable. Finally I kill her in a tragedy.

[*If the reader will now turn to Zola's completed work, he will perceive that Gervaise is not "killed in a tragedy." Zola's first instinct is to have something sensational happen to end her. The after-thought, however, wins the day: to have nothing exaggerated; to have Gervaise descend gradually and pass from life as naturally as an old tree which has been beset by the elements, and little by little is brought to the ground. Such a solution (in the 1870's) is the more original, after all the romantic and melodramatic balderdash we have been getting; it is in the Naturalistic mood.*]

To begin with, then, I shall have the following phases of existence:

Arrival in Paris in 1850 — abandoned by Lantier, Gervaise remains alone with two children, one eight, the other four years old. (The scene of the abandonment, the children, etc.)

The meeting with Coupeau, somewhere; typical; (Coupeau knows that she lived with Lantier). The marriage (typical also). The early days of the family. The first adjustments.

The success of Gervaise, who finally establishes herself. A little laundry shop beside her former mistress. The rival's jealousy leading to a tragic dénouement. [*This idea changed.*]

Life in the little shop. Coupeau no longer works. The workwoman.

Reappearance of Lantier. Details on tanners (La Bièvre Quarter). Extraordinary life of the lover in the family. Coupeau broken down, drinking. Lantier explaining: "The children are mine, no? I can come and embrace them, can't I?" Or better still, Coupeau brings him. An old friend. Then, little by little, the two men begin to live off Gervaise. Show her resisting at first, then letting herself go little by little.

Then follows the slow ruin of the little shop. Gervaise is obliged to go to work again for other people, after having lost her clientèle one by one. Coupeau pawns other people's laundry, etc. When Gervaise works out, sordid misery, days without bread.

There is the drama to end on. I make Gervaise die tragically, or rather I show her dying at forty-one, exhausted with work and misery.

Gervaise must be a sympathetic figure. Formerly at Plassans, her mother made her drink anisette, and she became pregnant by Lantier at fourteen. Explain these beginnings. She is by temperament yielding and passionate; that will do as a fault. As for drunkenness, she drank because her mother used to drink. But at bottom she is a sodden beast, devoted like her mother. She is an exact reproduction of "Fine" (her page 529 / mother) at the moment of conception (later, even, I have her grow fat like her mother). She is lame, slightly, do not forget. Then, at Paris, I have a new Gervaise. She drinks no longer, she loves Lantier, she devotes herself to her children. With all that, she must have a decided character or I shall be too dull. At first, as I said, a sodden beast for work; then, a tender nature, an excellent woman, whom education might have developed, but who is lost. Each of her qualities turn against her; work breaks her down, her tenderness leads her to extraordinary weaknesses. One can give her material longings by giving her an ideal. In the beginning, she says:

"I should like a little corner where I might be happy, see my children well settled. Eat bread every day, not be beaten. Die at home, etc." On the whole give her those modest desires that will never be realized.

I cannot escape from the banality of the intrigue save by the size and truth of my pictures of the people. Nothing exceeds that in importance. As long as I am taking the bestial, drab, filthy side of life, I must give it in great relief. The subject is poor. I must therefore give it such versimilitude that it will be a miracle of exactness.

[*What of his dual nature, as Flaubert had observed, he must goad himself all the time to be a Naturalist, to struggle for such exactness as will astound the reader. This is undoubtedly a cardinal principle of Naturalism, as distinguished from the realism of a Flaubert, or of the forgotten Champfleury. It is the reason for the greater attraction he exerted upon Huysmans and Maupassant.*

He now ponders over the secondary characters who are to fill out the picture.]

The secondary characters must help me complicate the story.

These characters are:

Bijard, his daughter and the two children. Bijard, bad workman, painter, perhaps (to be found).

Goujet, a smith (give him a mother). Muscular effort, a handsome fellow, a trifle somber, loving Gervaise. Use him at the end; good workman.

Lorilleux, Parisian workman, engaged in very fine work, seated all day long. Nasty. Married Mme. Lorilleux, sister of Coupeau.

An old workman (*Père Bru*) seventy years old, a drama.

Then women.

Gervaise's mistress, Mme. Fauconnier, with her employees, Eugénie, Lise, etc.

A widow (elder sister of Coupeau), working at something or other.

The janitor of the house. page 530 /

Coupeau's mother, incapable of working any longer, whom Gervaise takes in and who dies (death among the workers).

I shall make most of these people live in the same house. Some, however, outside; that will give me a thread to follow. I must add a fruiterer, a coal merchant, and a few other small retailers. Very definite characters, Bijard, Goujet, Lorilleux.

[*He warns himself further:*]

If I take as title "The Simple Life of Gervaise Macquart," the character of the book must have exactly that simplicity; a story of magisterial nudity, day to day reality, going in a straight line, no complications, very few scenes and those extremely commonplace, absolutely nothing romantic nor affected. Facts placed side by side, but giving the *entire life of the people.*

In the house live the following persons: Gervaise, Coupeau, Lantier, Coupeau's mother, Anna, the Lorilleux, the Bijards, Goujet and his mother, the aged workman (Bazouge), the janitress (Mme. Boche), a wine merchant.

The following persons live elsewhere: the laundress, Mme. Fauconnier, the elder sister of Coupeau, a widow, Mme. Levat: a grocer, whose husband is a policeman, the coal vender.

[*Only now does Zola devote himself to the intrigue that is to link these characters together and explain the milieu.*]

This is how the episodes could be arranged. My first scene in a washing-house. The abandonment of Gervaise dramatized with the aid of some of the other characters.

The first meeting of Gervaise and Coupeau; Coupeau to be a friend of Lantier. He brings Gervaise to see his family, the Lorilleux. That is where I shall describe the house where all the characters live (especially the Lorilleux). . . . A word about Bijard; little Josephine must be very young. . . .

Gervaise has a shop in the laundry, in the place of some shopkeeper who has left. She takes the mother of Coupeau with her. Then the return of Lantier. Quarrels, escapades, parties. The whole family at a meal.

Show the three men, Lantier, Coupeau and Goujet around Gervaise. When Gervaise is cleaned up, show the death of Mme. Coupeau. The whole family chipping in for the burial. Important episode. Return to Bijard. . . .

Misery of Gervaise. She goes to see Coupeau at the hospital. Her presentiment that she will die there. She leaves the shop. Winter; unemployment, the pawn-shop.

A drama between the three men? page 531 /
Third picture of the Bijards. Death of the little girl, exhausted. The end of Gervaise; Lantier goes away, Goujet, etc. . . .

[*The whole drama is as yet quite vague in the first "sketch" for L'Assommoir. None of the threads are bound up; none of the events have the* inevitability *that he wishes to give them. He is worrying now about how to give it all a unified and overwhelming movement. And then the idea comes to him: "I must show the whole world trying to bring about her ruin, consciously or unconsciously."*]

The drama at the end must be considered above all. I must use all the characters in it, above all her relatives, the Poissons and the Boches. Gervaise must remain the principal, the central character, and I must show the whole world trying to bring about her ruin, consciously or unconsciously.

Debts are necessary at first. In order to feed herself and her idle husband in addition, she has to borrow on all sides — from the butcher, the baker, the coal-merchant, the grocer, etc. Then pushed to her limit, I can show her descending to street-walking. Finally, to make the drama more terrible, I can have her made pregnant again (she thinks of suicide).

A banal drama among the people, some scene of brutal jealousy that finishes with a play of knives. So; there might be a battle between Lantier, Coupeau, and Goujet, pushed on one another by the other characters. . . .

[*Zola thinks of various lurid resolutions: Gervaise, enceinte, will discover her old lover* in flagrante, *cast vitriol on him and the other woman, and die herself of a kick in the stomach! Such a dénouement would make a good case for Zola as a "repressed" sadist. But Zola is a "balanced" neurotic. He sees that an episode of this kind would have a rather "classical" character. And then how would he keep Gervaise "sympathetic"? He relents then, and gropes for a more "banal" solution, while hoping to keep it powerful and full of relief. . . .*]

But I wish to keep the simplicity of facts themselves, stay in the main current of common life, while remaining dramatic and very touching. . . .

[*He considers shifting the character of various personages, for reasons of utility: Gervaise must have a rival, the big Adèle, with whom she will have the famous fight in the public laundry, in the very first chapter, and with whom Lantier runs away. But then in order to keep Adèle a rival throughout the book, he decides to have her sister the inamorata of Lantier, and Adèle merely fighting Gervaise over her sister. In this way the person who evokes Gervaise's opposition remains in the quarter* **page 532 /** *while Lantier runs away and disappears with the other woman. The opening scene of the fight in the public laundry between the two women, occurring by chance, soon becomes a tremendous episode and symbolic of the lonely fight of Gervaise against the whole world about her.*

Zola now turns to politics. The bavardage among the workers. He distributes political opinions. Lantier, the villain, has the most radical opinions of all; he is a fake. But still there is a vast discontent among the people. Workingmen give their harassed women children, one upon another!]

Later on in another novel I must study this whole situation in a more complete manner. [*Germinal*, 1885.] But the novel of Gervaise must deal chiefly with the morals of the common people.

[*This is the end of the first, crude "Sketch." Nothing is as yet in its proportion, nothing is in its place, when we refer to the finished text of the novel. The plot suggested above is still to be abandoned in favor of another, which shapes itself in the "Plan" or Scenario of the individual chapters.*

Zola now goes on to elaborate the characters. Each of them is distinguished by a salient, a dominant trait. His psychology is broad or coarse rather than delicate. His portfolios are like a police record, containing all but the thumb-print. These people are seldom complex; they are always a single impulse, a single force of resistance or sympathy. They must be this, in view of the deductive method with which Zola works from the general group to the individual. He lists some thirty-five characters, be-

ginning with Gervaise, and moving through the principal and secondary characters.]

Gervaise, born in 1828, twenty-two years old now. Limps slightly, owing to brutalities her mother had borne from drunken husband. Tall, with a pleasant round face; her infirmity is almost a grace. At fourteen she has her first child through Lantier. They escape to Paris together. Three months later, when she is abandoned, she has two children, Claude and Etienne. She goes to work courageously. In short, she is to be an average person, who would have made an excellent wife; she takes life seriously, loves her children, asks only not to be beaten, etc. By heredity, she is much like her mother, a beast of toil, devoted; some natural weaknesses; she is like a thing thrown into the air, to fall by chance head or tail. *Her environment will determine her lot.*

[*The other charcters are studied in more or less detail in the same wise. Bits of action are attached to them. Their possible rôles are demarcated. It is a terribly important part of the preparation. But there is no* page 533 / *space here for all of it, and the studies and descriptions of* milieux *are even more characteristic.*]

THE ENVIRONMENT

[*Zola believed with Taine that man could not be separated from his social environment; that he left his imprint, "upon his external life, his house, his furniture, his business, his gestures, his speech." To express all, one must explain the "multitude of effects, and at the same time one must assemble the whole multitude of causes." And so Zola arrived at his theory that description in the novel must represent "the state of environment which determines and completes the man."*

He therefore wanders about the quarter he has selected for his study, which is to be the determining environment of his subjects.

Here is a street, such as he is seeking:]

La rue Neuve-de-la-Goutte-d'Or. The street slopes downhill from about the middle of its length; narrow; sidewalks missing in places; gutters always running soapy water.

From the end, on the side of the rue de la Goutte d'Or, descending. At the right, dark shops, rope makers, coopers, to the left, dry-goods, musty grocers; (shops shut and pasted up with advertisements). Then in the middle, the houses become lower, a single story, stinking water. There, to the right, the washing-house; body of the building small, dominated by three large cyclinders and a zinc reservoir; the steam machine to the right, the office to the left, the entrance and the passage to the washing-house in the middle; above, the drying room with its shutters. After the washing-house, a beautiful red-brick house, a tree (acacia) extending its branches into the street; the gaiety of the street. Across the way a factory of seltzer water; and beyond that, a livery stable, Louise. Then, at the end of the street along the exterior boulevard, four or five laundresses, of whom one has a handsome shop. Opposite, little shops, a barber with brass bowl hanging outside. The low houses are painted yellow, green, red, blue, fences, etc.

[*Here is even the big grimy house, in which he will lodge all his characters, such a tenement as the one in which he himself lived as a youth, next door to an undertaker:*]

Rue de la Goutte d'Or. Toward the rue des Poissoniers, thickly populated; in the other direction, provincial. My big house (between two little ones) is near the rue des Poissoniers, five or six houses away. It is eleven windows across and six stories high; all black, in one block, no sculpture; windows with black shutters crumbling, and with pieces missing. page 534 / The door in the middle, immense, arched. At the right, a huge wine shop with a room for the workmen; at the left the coal vender's shop, painted, a parrafin shop and the shop that Gervaise will have and where there is now a fruit vendor. Entering through the passage, the gutters flow with water; in the middle, a great square court, enclosed; the janitor to the right (the tap is beside the lodge). The four sides with their six stories; bare, pierced by black windows without shutters. Below, shops all about, carpenters, a locksmith, a dyeing establishment always sending out tinted water. Four staircases, A B C D, one for each side of the building. Within, long corridors on each floor, with uniform doors painted yellow. In front, in the flats with shutters, live people who pass for rich. In the court, none but workmen; wash hanging on lines. There is a sunny side and a side where the sun never shines, darker and damper. The court is paved; the place around the tap is damp. The raw daylight falls into the court.

Opposite the house, a blacksmith's shop; a large gray wall without a window, a gaping door in the middle, shows a court filled with wagons, buggies, their shafts in the air. There is also a forge; one can hear the rumbling of the bellows and see the glow of the furnace; on the wall, horseshoes painted black, arranged in the form of a pan. To the right and left of the door, little booths, holes with a painted front; a junk-shop; "*à la bonne friture*" — a watchmaker (We repair clocks and watches); cuckoo clocks going in back of the hole, in the window; watches in silver cases; before the little counter, full of tiny utensils and delicate things under glass, a gentleman in a frock coat, well dressed, who works continuously. (The image of fragile things, in the midst of the noise and movement of the life of the people.)

[*He stops to regard people passing him in the street, takes out his notebook and writes:*]

THE PEOPLE ON THE BOULEVARD

Many women bare-headed; some with caps, many with net bags; vestees, aprons, loose skirts hanging straight. A band of children with runny noses, some of them clean, many of them dirty. Games, skip rope, etc. Women seated with infants in their arms, nursing. Clean working-girls, almost coquettes; baskets, packages, knitted bags. Workers in smocks, blouses, jackets; some carrying tools, others with swinging arms; some carry children. Women shopping for dinner. Carriages, vans returning empty. Omnibuses and cabs later. . . .

Man with a ladder. Children playing in a pile of sand. Women, hatless, running home to dinner, their baskets on their arms; little girls page 535 / with loaves of bread. Men talking aloud to others, walking fast. Workmen. Women with children. Men with working tools; in jacket and cap, smoking or not, running or stopping. Masons in wagons. Carts, barrels, plaster not emptied out, trucks. Paris lighting its gas-lamps. The sky. Hands in pockets. . . . Men alone or in groups. Painters with their paint-pots. Men dragging carts along by means of straps over their shoulders. Belts.

[*Voluminous descriptions of streets, shops and houses follow.*

And now Zola devotes himself to the study of the trades; for this is an integral part of the "environment." He takes precise notes on the labors of the laundress, the goldsmith, the cooper, the blacksmith. There is moreover a quantity of notes on special questions, such as "Alcoholism," which enter into his domain. Thus the illness and death of Coupeau are the "textual reproduction of clinical observations made at the Ste. Anne Hospital in Paris." "It is above all the doctors whom I have abused," he wrote. "I have never treated a scientific question or discussed a disease without putting the whole faculty to work for me."—Emile Zola, Les Droits du Romancier, op. cit.]

ALCOHOLISM

First indications in Coupeau. Merry tipsiness at first, good appetite, indistinct nightmares. Mucous discharge, loss of appetite, loss of sleep; slight trembling of the hands, itching, etc. Sticking sensation all over the skin, especially on the hands and feet, abnormal feeling of cold and warmth, cramps; weakness of the legs and trembling of the hands. Heaviness and slowness of the head. Occasional blindness, rumbling in the ears, extreme surprise, vertigo.

First illness. Swelling. He is sent to Sainte-Anne. Alcoholic delirium, short and rapid; his hands alone tremble. At the end of two or three days, he laughs at his nightmares; but fear conquers him in the evening, when night falls and he is put to bed. Sleep builds him up, abstinence cures him.

Finally, the great crisis, the big scene preceding death. Place the time at night, the disease strengthened by excessive drinking. The whole delirium tremens. . . .

Injection into the eyes, sweat, alteration of features. Fever of 104°. Disordered movements, very serious. Trembling of face and entire body accompanied by jumps, shudders, and twitching muscles, even during sleep. Suffering of the marrow, when a hand is placed on the body. Continued and generalized labor of the body. Wavy movement under the skin. Finally weakening of the muscles, beginning of paralysis. The body soaked with alcohol.

Four days of cries and trembling. The straightjacket. Padded cell. page 536 / Portrait of the victim to be used; at first whirrings, ringings and whistlings in the ears, confused rings, bells, cries, tumultuous voices. The sight is troubled, dimmed, pictures seen in a cloud. Sparks, flames, shadows, animals, devils that grow larger and smaller, changing color. Talkative, incoherent, diffuse; he believes the physicians are working against him. He smells rats, sulphur; food seems to contain vitriol, the tea smells of whiskey or wine. Mad, agitated crying, bawling, perspiring. He believes himself covered with vermin, animals under his skin, worms that he tries to shake off. He also believes himself tied in iron bands and tries to escape from them; he feels a cold wet thing creeping along his thighs. . . . Gervaise is present at the agony. Finally the trembling spreads over the entire body. Stiffness of the neck, the face in a grimace, both eyes turned to the right, a little foam on his lips. He can no longer stand upright, he seats himself on the bed. During sleep, his feet, which stretch beyond the mattress tremble, rhythmically, a little before death. Picture of Coupeau dead regarded by Gervaise.

[*From* "Le Sublime," *a novel of the working classes, he, in fact, lifts several paragraphs almost word for word, chiefly those of political discussion among workingmen; above all he adopts the argot which Poulot has used, and amplifies it by use of a slang dictionary*, Dictionnaire de la langue verte, *by Alfred Delvau. He even makes up a little slang lexicon for his own immediate use; Massis has set down a list of some* 800 *colloquial expressions which Zola used not only in the dialogue of* L'Assommoir *but in his own description or comment. The whole book is permeated with argot.*]

THE PLANS

[*The work of documentation over, Zola now labors with great patience and determination over his plan, which he organizes out of the material in the Sketch and the Characters.*

He divides the matter of the novel into a certain number of chapters, and writes a "Summary" for each chapter, detailed but still very brief, of the action which is to take place.

Thereafter he develops from these brief outlines his "Detailed plans," or "Analytical Plans," which resemble greatly the scenario of a play, or of a motion picture. Even these very last plans have two stages. They are not blue prints from which a building is cold-bloodedly erected. Everything is remodeled or altered as he goes in accordance with new exigencies or suggestions. Thus the original scheme of L'Assommoir *in* 21 *chapters is altered to* 13. *There was a "primitive" scenario and a "definitive" one.*

It will be noted, for instance, in the following "Summary" plan, that page 537 / *Zola still thinks he is going to have a good deal of political talk in this novel, that he is still fascinated by the grave-digger, Bazouge, and means to have him play a considerable part, that he has Coupeau take to drink without any particular motive as yet; whereas, in the last analysis, he tones down the rôle of the grave-digger to a very delicate suggestion of the proximity of death, he later has Coupeau become severely injured and lose his ambition during the long convalescence, and drops political matter, to a great extent, entirely out of the book.*

Some interesting ideas have occurred to him in the meantime; the idea of a melodramatic fight among the men, with knife-play, has been dropped in favor of the much more human incident of Coupeau, husband, becoming a friend of the former lover of Gervaise, Lantier, and their all living together in a ménage á trois! *Truer and more original solution, leading to an inevitable débâcle on the part of the woman.*]

PLAN IN BRIEF

Chapters of 20 pages, average uneven in size, the shortest ten pages, the longest 30 pages.

The style in full flight.

The novel is to be the degeneration of Gervaise and Coupeau, the latter entraining the former, in the workers' quarter. Explain the customs of the people, their vices, their degeneration, the moral and physical ugliness induced by the milieu, by the conditions imposed on the worker in our society.

I. 1850, May. The abandonment. Scene in the wash-house. Return home. Mme. Fauconnier, Mme. Boche, Adèle Poisson. (The quarter in the morning.)

II. Meeting of Coupeau and Gervaise. At the wine merchant's

(Colombe). (She wants to have nothing to do with him.) They come together. The Lorilleux, their portrait, their interior, their work. Bazouge (grave-digger) met with in the hallway. (The quarter at eleven o'clock P.M.)

III. 1850, 29th June. The marriage of Coupeau and Gervaise. Politics.

IV. Three first years of the couple together; birth of Anna. Coupeau's accident. Gervaise caring for him. The Goujets brought in here.

V. Bring in somewhere, the Gingerbread Fair, meeting with the Goujets. Acquaintance. Goujet finding Gervaise reasonable. The house-hold gets on nicely. Politics. (*This chapter suppressed altogether later.*)

VI. 1855. Renting of the shop. The street. Father Bru. The Boches. Picture of them and their home. The Lorilleux angry. Coupeau begins to debauch himself. The café gains in influence. Gervaise slightly gourmand. Her courage. The work done by laundresses. Adèle reappears. page 538 / The proprietor, Marescot. A coal dealer, on the other side of the door. The other dealers. A word about Bazouge.

VII. First episode in the home of Bijard. Mme. Bijard works for Gervaise. Gervaise worries lest Coupeau become like Bijard.

VIII. Goujet at work. The forge.

IX. Gervaise's birthday. *Make her downfall very gradual.* Quarrel with the Lorilleux made up. *The street.* Adèle and her husband. Gervaise already slipping. The Boches. Politics. Bazouge invited. Happy still, no desire for death. Father Bru.

X. Lantier returns. All the characters mixed up. Coupeau speaks of settling accounts with Lantier. They go to Colombe's cafe. Coupeau brings Lantier home. The rearrangement of the house.

XI. Lantier installed. The worker dressed up. Politics. The shop consumed. The two men at Colombe's. Anna, her bad education. Quarrels with Mme. Coupeau. Goujet in love; his proposals. An escapade of Coupeau. Lantier takes Gervaise again; she submits. There the cafe-concert, or perhaps in another chapter.

XII. Pillage of the shop. Adèle Poisson on good terms with Gervaise and spying on the shop. Gervaise trying to reëstablish herself. Second Bijard episode.

XIII. Burial of Mme. Coupeau. The shop is completely eaten up, dirty. All the characters, Mme. Lérat, the Lorilleux, etc. The lease is given over. The Boches. Bazouge. Father Bru.

XIV. Gervaise in a tiny lodging. The quarter in the evening. (The boulevard as it is.) First days. She goes back to work for Mme. Fauconnier. She supports her husband. Anna's first communion. Anna as a child. . . . A conversation between the women on their husbands.

XV. . . . First hard winter to go through. Second Bijard episode (flat next to Gervaise). The proprietor Marescot. Gervaise going to find Coupeau at the cafe and sitting down with him. A new stage in her fall. The pawn-shop. Sensation of misery. A word about Father Bru. A rascality of Coupeau's that might be concerned with linen to be cleaned. Coupeau at the hospital.

XV. A country picnic with the Goujets, which does Gervaise some good.

VI. Anna working at making artificial flowers, insolent with her parents, filthy words. She walks about the streets with other young people. The shop where the flowers are made. Mme. Lérat. (The working day, the hours.) Anna at a public dance, searched for by her father.

XVII. 67. Lantier in the home of the Poissons. (They attempt to throw Gervaise out.) He consumes the sweet-shop. Their home life. Adèle triumphant. (The spanking.) Politics. The policeman (his little boxes). A Sunday: the quarter including the Boulevard Ornano. page 539 /

XVIII. Frightful winter. A single scene, broad, terrible. No bread. Debts. The Lorilleux refuse to lend a franc. Coupeau disappears, escapade. Anna has run away. Gervaise near prostitution, almost pushed to it by Coupeau. She gets drunk like him. Goujet meets her soliciting. (Father Bru. Bazouge. Gervaise longs for him.)

XIX. Third Bijard episode. Death of Lalie.

XX. The climax. Coupeau, Lantier, Goujet, the Lorilleux.

XXI. The final degradation of Gervaise. Her death. The last word of Bazouge.

[*Many of the indications for chapter divisions are as yet inadequate. The veritable climax, or progression, seems as yet undecided in the mind of the writer. It will form itself later, as*

Zola makes his "plan in detail," out of the return of Lantier, Gervaise Coupeau's first lover, to her present household. This event, combined with Coupeau's prodigious drinking, is surely calculated to bring on her ruin.

I am able to cite here only three chapters from the plan in detail, using only the "definitive" project, and dropping the "primitive" form of these synopses. In any event, the manuscript notes do not contain all of the "primitive" scenarios, which indicate a slightly more intermediary stage; some of these were lost either by Zola or his heirs.

The "definitive" chapters which I cite are clearly more logical and restrained than the intermediary stage. The action is more crystallized; for instance, Chapter III "primitive" is about one-fourth as long or complete in its directions as Chapter II "definitive," which describes the marriage of Gervaise. In fact the marriage swells beyond all the proportions for it, and in its final form, stands out as a supremely humorous piece.

Again, Chapter VIII, "definitive," is a condensation of Chapter X and XII "primitive." Here the return of Lantier is described. He installs himself complacently, by easy stages, at the Coupeaus. He pays nothing. Seeing that Gervaise suffers from her drunken spouse, he makes approaches to her. She resists. Lonely, she permits him to take her to a café-concert one evening. Returning, she refuses to enter his room, adjoining hers; but her husband, arrived from a terrific bout, has rendered the whole bed-room so foul that she has no place to sleep, except with the boarder, Lantier! The turning point. *This determining episode is of course not discovered until the "definitive plan" is made.*]

PLAN IN DETAIL

CHAPTER I

Begin with a description of the room. Show Gervaise and the children in the hotel room. Lantier is there or arrives; he returns after having **page 540 /** spent the night out: a rapid picture of him. Fix the time of the scene. Arrival of Lantier and Gervaise in Paris, February, the beginning of the month; three months later; therefore May 1, 1850. The boulevard in the morning (short). The 1700 francs are spent. Lantier has only three francs left over from a party the night before, the few gifts he has made to Gervaise are at the pawn-shop. Reproaches. Given to understand that he prepares for flight, the trunk. Gervaise reproaches him, but gently; the two children. Lantier bored. He sends her to the pawn-shop with her last silk dress, anything to get some money; he has evidently spent the night with the woman he means to go away with. He comes back to get his clothes. Then Gervaise goes to do her washing; she is going to work for Mme. Fauconnier. Adèle and her sister indicated. The things Gervaise is to carry to the washing house; Lantier retains his shirts; the children's clothes she leaves at home; she is to return to prepare the lunch. In this part do not give complete details about the facts preceding their arrival and stay in Paris; that will do for the conversation between Gervaise and Mme. Boche, in the washing house. Show Coupeau before the arrival of Lantier. He appears only at the door. "The old man isn't there?" — "No, M. Coupeau," and she tries to smile. He comes to speak to her about work; that will do.

As Gervaise is going to the washing-house, she meets Mme. Boche, who is going there also. Mme. Boche is a concierge in the street where I shall place my house, but at another number. They go along together (a word about the street, not much, the description later.)

The washing-house. Description: the women, perhaps Mme. Bijard? Noise, odor, light, the individual places, arrange the setting. Mme. Boche and Gervaise are side by side; the conversation during the washing — (how they wash the wash); other women mixing in the conversation. Mme. Boche knows some scandal, her lodging is opposite Mme. Fauconnier's; she has seen Lantier at the home of Adèle and her sister; the sisters live together; the little one is a metal polisher, Adèle is a seamstress (or something else), no family. . . . Adèle comes to wash her little bundle, but she comes mainly to spy. She comes before the arrival of the children, sets to work, grins at Gervaise; it is then that Mme. Boche gives a few details in a veiled manner.

Arrival of the children with the key: "Well, where's papa?" He has left in a carriage (and a woman?). Gervaise, paling, continues to wash, damp, soak. Then the battle; pails of water thrown; the big Adèle and Gervaise taking each other by the hair, then using the beaters. Something very energetic and very dramatic, exaggerated. Finally Gervaise, wounded, her blood running, goes away, holding her two children by the hand. The room cleaned up, a second description, with the trunk gone, inventory, nothing more. **page 541 /**

CHAPTER II

May, 1850. The rue des Poissonniers first (the exterior boulevard as it was then with the old slaughter-houses).

A week later, Gervaise and Coupeau together in the street. They meet each other while walking, at the end of the day. He has been permitted to come and wait for her as she leaves Mme. Fauconnier's; the two children are there. Then, in passing, "Look, there is the house where my sister lives. I eat there, but they have no room for me to sleep." The house, description in a few words. From there, they go to the boulevard. (Picture of the boulevard at the end of the working day, very complete.) Their conversation, Coupeau is in love, he wants to sleep with Gervaise, but she doesn't want to. What's the use? She must be serious. At that point, excuse her for the anisette that her mother made her drink (when Coupeau offers her something to drink) and for having had a child at fourteen years (when he presses her). By temperament tender and sympathetic, she is warm and passionate, but not very voluptuous; very reasonable, she dreams of working; her mother, "Fine" in her, story of her family, the physiological question.

However, he offers her something and she accepts. At the door of a cafe on some big street (at Colombe's, short description of the shop). Coupeau; his family, his story (see his portrait). Description of the crowd; popular love-making under these conditions. Coupeau very nice. And then, the ideal of Gervaise: not to be beaten, to work, to eat, "to die in my bed, to bring up my children well," everything that she will not have. The children playing. Then the visit to the Lorilleux, giving me a chance to describe the inside of the house. The marriage is considered. Coupeau, almost decided, making experiments, however. He takes her one evening to the Lorilleux, after dinner. He comes for her after supper. The house lighted up; the evening, picture of the Lorilleux; disagreeable about some incident with regard to a marriage. Place them well.

Finally, on the stairs, make her meet Bazouge. Make the appearance of the grave-digger coincide with a word about happiness. Fright of Gervaise: "You will go the same way all the same." The appearance of Bazouge in the middle of laughter; keep him for the wedding if necessary. The Lorilleux on good terms with Bazouge, he tells them stories of grave-diggers. The house when they leave it, early in the evening; Gervaise turns around, looks at it; how it is at that hour.

CHAPTER III

(Gervaise very sweet and Coupeau very gay during the whole of the chapter. Filled with short descriptions.) page 542 /

I pass rapidly by the account of the mairie and the church. (Begin with very short explanations.) Gervaise did not want a wedding, but Coupeau insists. One cannot get married so, they will all eat a bite together, a picnic, some friends and the family. They won't be foolish, and so he brings her around. (The question of money: bargaining for a cheap mass. Lorilleux furnishes the wedding-ring. Gervaise takes care of her own costume, the children, whatever they need to dress them properly.) The dinner is ordered at a wine-shop on the boulevard de la Chapelle (a name) at five francs a head, everything included. There is a little place for dancing in a narrow garden behind the wine-shop. (Coupeau invites Mes-Bottes.)

The day before, it has been decided that to fill up the afternoon, they would go for a walk out towards Saint-Denis. They could even take the train there. The rendez-vous is given at the wine-shop where they are to have dinner. Not everybody is to go to the mass and to the church.

At the mairie and at the church. The bride and groom (costume of Gervaise and Coupeau), the witnesses: Lorilleux and Boche (for Gervaise), M. Madinier and Bibi-la-Grillade (for Coupeau), Madame Coupeau. The two children stay with Mme. Boche, who is only coming in the evening. Madame Lorilleux refuses to come to the mairie or the church.

The meeting at the wine-shop. (They have a bite; Coupeau pays; "That's my treat.") Arrange everybody. Mes Bottes does not appear, he has gone to Saint-Denis; I shall show him in the evening, coming back. It is then that the storm breaks. The women are annoyed, it is impossible to go to the country. They cannot be gay, but they must not be bores.

Only sketch the characters and place them. Someone suggests

going to the Museum. (How they go.) Gervaise has never been to see it. So they go, not everybody: Gervaise, Coupeau, Lorilleux, Boche, Mlle. Remanjou, M. Madinier, Bibi-la-Grillade, Mme. Lérat, Mme. Fauconnier, Mme. Lorilleux, Mme. Bougron and her husband. The attitude of these people; at four o'clock they have to leave. A conversation between the Lorilleux against Gervaise; give the dramatic side. ("This Gervaise has no family . . ." pauper, the wedding ring.) Divide the characters into two camps. Paris, the summertime, the rain. The Lorilleux explain the money question: Coupeau has had to borrow a hundred francs of them.

They are embarrassed; they still have three hours. Then they walk along the quays (busy them with all sorts of things). They cross the Tuileries, come to the Place Vendôme, climb up the column (Paris in the rain), etc., and return for dinner. Coupeau scared of the Lorilleux. (Conversation about the future: Gervaise and Coupeau.)

The dinner. The children and Mme. Boche (the little ones dressed up for the wedding). Gervaise embraces the children when she comes. page 543 / "Have you been good?" (The Lorilleux smirk.) Mes Bottes arrives when everybody is at table. The dinner; how everyone is seated. Conversation, at this point, on politics. Lorilleux conservative, his story; Coupeau skeptic and jokester: farce. All the characters. Relapse to drunkenness, but slight, gradually, on such a day, however, it is permitted to drink a little. A word for everyone according to his character, the children. Lorilleux speaks of his work (jewelers used to carry a sword). Conversation on the future.

However, the room gives on a dance floor. They have promised not to become too gay; but after dinner, pipes are lit, liqueurs are ordered, some want to sing; only the others prefer to go downstairs and dance, just a little, not much (avoiding the encores).

Then they leave the guests there. Madame Boche takes the two children. Coupeau and Gervaise have not yet been able to rent a place; they return to Gervaise's room at the Hotel Boncoeur. The Lorilleux accompany them, then they accompany the Lorilleux home. Episode with Bazouge at the door; Bazouge very drunk; he speaks of his dead, he frightens Gervaise, who has been very gay up to now. A typical word from him: "You will pass on just the same, little one, and perhaps you'll be just as glad to be carried away. We let a lot of people out of their misery." (Less philosophical.)

That night they go to bed without a cent.

[*Having made his plans in their final form, Zola would depart from them very slightly. When he begins to write, he must know in what direction he is going. He has a horror of pausing in uncertainty. For the mass of detail which he desires to accumulate in his books there must be organization, else he would remain tongue-tied forever. His style is vigorous; almost impersonal, save in its reflections by choice of material, he moves forward steadily, making few changes, without looking back over his shoulder. The* mot juste *does not trouble him. He never hesitates because all his material has resolved itself in his mind in a final form. The preparatory stage has absorbed by far the greater part of the year which he devotes to his novel.*

Zola appears a terribly methodical man. Is it his documentation that furnishes the greatness of L'Assommoir? *We know, on the contrary, that his observation was highly arbitrary; that he got facts from sources often which were very suspect. As to his plans, they are neither* experimental *nor scientific. Poor plans! What if he had stopped at them only? It is the realization of these "documents" and of these "plans" which is the curious and impressive fact. To document himself, to observe on the field, was clearly a foilble of his, a trick that stirred him to greater* page 544 / *artistic deeds, a fashion that gave him the feeling that he was keeping abreast of modern science. In reality, no matter how much he observes, he* invents *more. His action, in* L'Assommoir, *is a "scientific experiment carried along in the full flight of the imagination." Hence the superiority of* L'Assommoir *to* Pot-Bouille, *for instance, in which imagination is almost nil, in which he is dully carrying out the theory of the "experimental novel" propounded post-factum.*

The social novel, roman de moeurs, *as Zola conceived it, involved the mastery of a great many facts, a great deal of historical or rational knowledge even, in order to arrive at the proper judgments. (These judgments once disproved, the novel too must disappear, in ratio to its lack of artistic character.) At any rate Zola must needs find a method of organizing this vast material so that it could be fused into a literary form. Even Zola's superior engineering could not always achieve this end as witness* La Débâcle, *a series of historical episodes, exact, but at the loss of all literary unity.*

Zola willed to leave us his plans and notes, as a military hero would leave us his charts and maps of successful campaigns.

The problem, the mystery, nevertheless, remains of the creative effort which puffs breath into these figures of a plan, and energy or drama into these movements of a scenario. Most of us having such plans all set up would probably abandon the effort of carrying them out. We know even that Zola was a romantic, a lyrical temperament, capable of great emotivity. It is as a counterfoil to the "flood of ideas which would surge into his mind and choke all activity" that he no doubt erected his whole system. He understood and guarded himself superbly; he understod also, that he would not be dismayed by his "plans"; that he possessed the indomitable will to carry them out.] page 545 /

GUY de MAUPASSANT

Pierre et Jean (1888)

Author's Preface: Of "The Novel"

I do not intend in these pages to put in a plea for this little novel. On the contrary, the ideas I shall try to set forth will rather involve a criticism of the class of psychological analysis which I have undertaken in *Pierre and Jean.* I propose to treat of novels in general.

I am not the only writer who finds himself taken to task in the same terms each time he brings out a new book. Among many laudatory phrases, I invariably meet with this observation, penned by the same critics: "The greatest fault of this book is that it is not, strictly speaking, a novel."

The same form might be adopted in reply:

"The greatest fault of the writer who does me the honour to review me is that he is not a critic."

For what are, in fact, the essential characteristics of a critic?

It is necessary that, without preconceived notions, prejudices of "School," or partisanship for page xli / any class of artists, he should appreciate, distinguish, and explain the most antagonistic tendencies and the most dissimilar temperaments, recognising and accepting the most varied efforts of art.

Now the Critic who, after reading *Manon Lescaut*, *Paul and Virginia*, *Don Quixote*, *Les Liaisons dangereuses*, *Werther*, *Elective Affinities (Wahlverwandschaften)*, *Clarissa Harlowe*, *Émile*, *Candide*, *Cinq-Mars*, *René*, *Les Trois Mousquetaires*, *Mauprat*, *Le Père Goriot*, *La Cousine Bette*, *Colomba*, *Le Rouge et le Noir*, *Mademoiselle de Maupin*, *Notre-Dame de Paris*,

---

Reprinted from *Pierre & Jean*, translated by Clara Dell (New York: P. F. Collier & Son, 1902).

Salammbo, *Madame Bovary*, *Adolphe*, *M. de Camors*, *l'Assommoir*, *Sapho*, etc., still can be so bold as to write "This or that is, or is not, a novel," seems to me to be gifted with a perspicacity strangely akin to incompetence. Such a critic commonly understands by a novel a more or less improbable narrative of adventure, elaborated after the fashion of a piece for the stage, in three acts, of which the first contains the exposition, the second the action, and the third the catastrophe or *dénouement*.

And this method of construction is perfectly admissible, but on condition that all others are accepted on equal terms.

Are there any rules for the making of a novel, which, if we neglect, the tale must be called by page xlii / another name? If *Don Quixote* is a novel, then is *Le Rouge et le Noir* a novel? If *Monte Christo* is a novel, is *l'Assommoir?* Can any conclusive comparison be drawn between Goethe's *Elective Affinities*, *The Three Mousqueteers*, by Dumas, Flaubert's *Madame Bovary*, *M. de Camors*, by Octave Feuillet, and *Germinal*, by Zola? Which of them all is The Novel? What are these famous rules? Where did they originate? Who laid them down? And in virtue of what principle, of whose authority, and of what reasoning?

And yet, as it would appear, these critics know in some positive and indisputable way what constitutes a novel, and what distinguishes it from other tales which are not novels. What this amounts to is that without being producers themselves they are enrolled under a School, and that, like the writers of novels, they reject all work which is conceived and executed outside the pale of their æsthetics. An intelligent critic ought, on the contrary, to seek out everything which least resembles the novels already written, and urge young authors as much as possible to try fresh paths.

All writers, Victor Hugo as much as M. Zola, have insistently claimed the absolute and incontrovertible right to compose — that is to say, to imagine or observe — in accordance with their in- page xliii / dividual conception of originality, and that is a special manner of thinking, seeing, understanding, and judging. Now the critic who assumes that "the novel" can be defined in conformity with the ideas he has based on the novels he prefers, and that certain immutable rules of construction can be laid down, will always find himself at war with the artistic temperament of a writer who introduces a new manner of work. A critic really worthy of the name ought to be an analyst, devoid of preferences or passions; like an expert in pictures, he should simply estimate the artistic value of the object of art submitted to him. His intelligence, open to everything, must so far supersede his individuality as to leave him free to discover and praise books which as a man he may not like, but which as a judge he must duly appreciate.

But critics, for the most part, are only readers; whence it comes that they almost always find fault with us on wrong grounds, or compliment us without reserve or measure.

The reader, who looks for no more in a book than that it should satisfy the natural tendencies of his own mind, wants the writer to respond to his predominant taste, and he invariably praises a work or a passage which appeals to his imagina- page xliv / tion, whether idealistic, gay, licentious, melancholy, dreamy or positive, as "striking" or "well written."

The public as a whole is composed of various groups, whose cry to us writers is:

"Comfort me."

"Amuse me."

"Touch me."

"Make me dream."

"Make me laugh."

"Make me shudder."

"Make me weep."

"Make me think."

And only a few chosen spirits say to the artist:

"Give me something fine in any form which may suit you best, according to your own temperament."

The artist makes the attempt; succeeds or fails.

The critic ought to judge the result only in relation to the nature of the attempt; he has no right to concern himself about tendencies. This has been said a thousand times already; it will always need repeating.

Thus, after a succession of literary schools which have given us deformed, superhuman, poeti- page xlv / cal, pathetic, charming or magnificent pictures of life, a realistic or naturalistic school has arisen, which asserts that it shows us the truth, the whole truth, and nothing but the truth.

All these theories of art must be recognised as of equal interest, and we must judge the works which are their outcome solely from the point of view of artistic value, with an *a priori* acceptance of the general notions which gave birth to each. To dispute the author's right to produce a poetical work or a realistic work, is to endeavour to coerce his temperament, to take exception to his originality, to forbid his using the eyes and wits bestowed on him by Nature. To blame him for seeing things as beautiful or ugly, as mean or epic, as gracious or sinister, is to reproach him for not being made on this or that pattern, and for having eyes which do not see exactly as ours see.

Let him be free by all means to conceive of things as he pleases, provided he is an artist. Let us rise to poetic heights to judge an idealist, and then prove to him that his dream is commonplace, ordinary, not mad or magnificent enough. But if we judge a materialistic writer, let us show him wherein the truth of life differs from the truth in his book.

It is self-evident that schools so widely differ- page xlvi / ent must have adopted diametrically opposite processes in composition.

The novelist who transforms truth — immutable, uncompromising, and displeasing as it is — to extract from it an exceptional and delightful plot, must necessarily manipulate events without an exaggerated respect for probability, moulding them to his will, dressing and arranging them so as to attract, excite, or affect the reader. The scheme of his romance is no more than a series of ingenious combinations, skilfully leading to the issue. The incidents are planned and graduated up to the culminating point and effect of the conclusion, which is the crowning and fatal result, satisfying the curiosity aroused from the first, closing the interest, and ending the story so completely that we have no further wish to know what happened on the morrow to the most engaging actors in it.

The novelist who, on the other hand, proposes to give us an accurate picture of life, must carefully eschew any concatenation of events which might seem exceptional. His aim is not to tell a story to amuse us, or to appeal to our feelings, but to compel us to reflect, and to understand the occult and deeper meaning of events. By dint of seeing and meditating he has come to regard the page xlvii / world, facts, men, and things in a way peculiar to himself, which is the outcome of the sum total of his studious observation. It is this personal view of the world which he strives to communicate to us by reproducing it in a book. To make the spectacle of life as moving to us as it has been to him, he must bring it before our eyes with scrupulous exactitude. Hence he must construct his work with such skill, it must be so artful under so simple a guise, that it is impossible to detect and sketch the plan, or discern the writer's purpose.

Instead of manipulating an adventure and working it out in such a way as to make it interesting to the last, he will take his actor or actors at a certain period of their lives, and lead them by natural stages to the next. In this way he will show either how men's minds are modified by the influence of their environment, or how their passions and sentiments are evolved; how they love or hate, how they struggle in every sphere of society, and how their interests clash — social interests, pecuniary interests, family interests, political interests. The skill of his plan will not consist in emotional power or charm, in an attractive opening or a stirring catastrophe, but in the happy grouping of small but constant facts from which the final purpose of the work may be **page xlviii /** discerned. If within three hundred pages he depicts ten years of a life so as to show what its individual and characteristic significance may have been in the midst of all the other human beings which surrounded it, he ought to know how to eliminate from among the numberless trivial incidents of daily life all which do not serve his end, and how to set in a special light all those which might have remained invisible to less clear-sighted observers, and which give his book calibre and value as a whole.

It is intelligible that this method of construction, so unlike the old manner which was patent to all, must often mislead the critics, and that they will not all detect the subtle and secret wires — almost invisibly fine — which certain modern artists use instead of the one string formerly known as the "plot."

In a word, while the novelist of yesterday preferred to relate the crises of life, the acute phases of the mind and heart, the novelist of to-day writes the history of the heart, soul and intellect in their normal condition. To achieve the effect he aims at — that is to say, the sense of simple reality, and to point the artistic lesson he endeavours to draw from it — that is to say, a revelation of what his contemporary man is before his **page xlix /** very eyes, he must bring forward no facts that are not irrefragible and invariable.

But even when we place ourselves at the same point of view as these realistic artists, we may discuss and dispute their theory, which seems to be comprehensively stated in these words: "The whole Truth and nothing but the Truth." Since the end they have in view is to bring out the philosophy of certain constant and current facts, they must often correct events in favour of probability and to the detriment of truth; for

"Le vrai peut quelquefois, n'être pas le vraisemblable." (Truth may sometimes not seem probable.)

The realist, if he is an artist, will endeavour not to show us a commonplace photograph of life, but to give us a presentment of it which shall be more complete, more striking, more cogent than reality itself. To tell everything is out of the question; it would require at least a volume for each day to enumerate the endless, insignificant incidents which crowd our existence. A choice must be made — and this is the first blow to the theory of "the whole truth."

Life, moreover, is composed of the most dissimilar things, the most unforeseen, the most contradictory, the most incongruous; it is merciless, page l / without sequence or connection, full of inexplicable, illogical, and contradictory catastrophes, such as can only be classed as miscellaneous facts. This is why the artist, having chosen his subject, can only select such characteristic details as are of use to it, from this life overladen with chances and trifles, and reject everything else, everything by the way.

To give an instance from among a thousand. The number of persons who, every day, meet with an accidental death, all over the world, is very considerable. But how can we bring a tile on to the head of an important character, or fling him under the wheels of a vehicle in the middle of a story, under the pretext that accident must have its due?

Again, in life there is no difference of foreground and distance, and events are sometimes hurried on, sometimes left to linger indefinitely. Art, on the contrary, consists in the employment of foresight, and elaboration in arranging skilful and ingenious transitions, in setting essential events in a strong light, simply by the craft of composition, and giving all else the degree of relief, in proportion to their importance, requisite to produce a convincing sense of the special truth to be conveyed.

"Truth" in such work consists in producing a page li /

complete illusion by following the common logic of facts and not by transcribing them pell-mell, as they succeed each other.

Whence I conclude that the higher order of Realists should rather call themselves Illusionists.

How childish it is, indeed, to believe in this reality, since to each of us the truth is in his own mind, his own organs! Our own eyes and ears, taste and smell, create as many different truths as there are human beings on earth. And our brains, duly and differently informed by those organs, apprehend, analyze, and decide as differently as if each of us were a being of an alien race. Each of us, then, has simply his own illusion of the world—poetical, sentimental, cheerful, melancholy, foul, or gloomy, according to his nature. And the writer has no other mission than faithfully to reproduce this illusion, with all the elaborations of art which he may have learned and have at his command. The illusion of beauty—which is merely a conventional term invented by man! The illusion of ugliness—which is a matter of varying opinion! The illusion of truth—never immutable! The illusion of depravity—which fascinates so many minds! All the great artists are those who can make other men see their own particular illusion.

Then we must not be wroth with any theory, **page lii /** since each is simply the outcome, in generalizations, of a special temperament analyzing itself.

Two of these theories have more particularly been the subject of discussion, and set up in opposition to each other instead of being admitted on an equal footing: that of the purely analytical novel, and that of the objective novel.

The partisans of analysis require the writer to devote himself to indicating the smallest evolutions of a soul, and all the most secret motives of our every action, giving but a quite secondary importance to the act and fact in itself. It is but the goal, a simple milestone, the excuse for the book. According to them, these works, at once exact and visionary, in which imagination merges into observation, are to be written after the fashion in which a philosopher composes a treatise on psychology, seeking out causes in their remotest origin, telling the why and wherefore of every impulse, and detecting every reaction of the soul's movements under the promptings of interest, passion, or instinct.

The partisans of objectivity—odious word—aiming, on the

contrary, at giving us an exact presentment of all that happens in life, carefully avoid all complicated explanations, all disquisitions on motive, and confine themselves to let persons page liii / and events pass before our eyes. In their opinion, psychology should be concealed in the book, as it is in reality, under the facts of existence.

The novel as conceived of on these lines gains in interest; there is more movement in the narrative, more colour, more of the stir of life.

Hence, instead of giving long explanations of the state of mind of an actor in the tale, the objective writer tries to discover the action or gesture which that state of mind must inevitably lead to in that personage, under certain given circumstances. And he makes him so demean himself from one end of the volume to the other, that all his actions, all his movements shall be the expression of his inmost nature, of all his thoughts, and all his impulses or hesitancies. Thus they conceal psychology instead of flaunting it; they use it as the skeleton of the work, just as the invisible bony frame-work is the skeleton of the human body. The artist who paints our portrait does not display our bones.

To me it seems that the novel executed on this principle gains also in sincerity. It is, in the first place, more probable, for the persons we see moving about us do not divulge to us the motives from which they act.

We must also take into account the fact that, page liv / even if by close observation of men and women we can so exactly ascertain their characters as to predict their behaviour under almost any circumstances, if we can say decisively: "Such a man, of such a temperament, in such a case, will do this or that;" yet it does not follow that we could lay a finger, one by one, on all the secret evolutions of his mind — which is not our own; all the mysterious pleadings of his instincts — which are not the same as ours; all the mingled promptings of his nature — in which the organs, nerves, blood, and flesh are different from ours.

However great the genius of the gentle, delicate man, guileless of passions and devoted to science and work, he never can so completely transfuse himself into the body of a dashing, sensual, and violent man, of exuberant vitality, torn by every desire or even by every vice, as to understand and delineate the inmost impulses and sensations of a being so unlike himself, even though he may very adequately foresee and relate all the actions of his life.

In short, the man who writes pure psychology can do no more than put himself in the place of all his puppets in the various situations in which he places them. It is impossible that he should change his organs, which are the sole intermediary **page lv /** between external life and ourselves, which constrain us by their perceptions, circumscribe our sensibilities, and create in each of us a soul essentially dissimilar to all those about us. Our purview and knowledge of the world, and our ideas of life, are acquired by the aid of our senses, and we cannot help transferring them, in some degree, to all the personages whose secret and unknown nature we propose to reveal. Thus, it is always ourselves that we disclose in the body of a king or an assassin, a robber or an honest man, a courtesan, a nun, a young girl, or a coarse market-woman; for we are compelled to put the problem in this personal form: "If *I* were a king, a murderer, a prostitute, a nun, or a market-woman, what should *I* do, what should *I* think, how should *I* act?" We can only vary our character by altering the age, the sex, the social position, and all the circumstances of life, of that *ego* which nature has in fact inclosed in an insurmountable barrier of organs of sense. Skill consists in not betraying this *ego* to the reader, under the various masks which we employ to cover it.

Still, though on the point of absolute exactitude, pure psychological analysis is impregnable, it can nevertheless produce works of art as fine as any other method of work.

Here, for instance, we have the *Symbolists.* **page lvi /** And why not? Their artistic dream is a worthy one; and they have this especially interesting feature: that they know and proclaim the extreme difficulty of art.

And, indeed, a man must be very daring or foolish to write at all nowadays. And so many and such various masters of the craft, of such multifarious genius, what remains to be done that has not been done, or what to say that has not been said? Which of us all can boast of having written a page, a phrase, which is not to be found — or something very like it — in some other book? When we read, we who are so soaked in (French) literature that our whole body seems as it were a mere compound of words, do we ever light on a line, a thought, which is not familiar to us, or of which we have not had at least some vague forecast?

The man who only tries to amuse his public by familiar methods, writes confidently, in his candid mediocrity, works intended only for the ignorant and idle crowd. But those who are conscious of the weight of centuries of past literature, whom nothing satisfies, whom everything disgusts because they dream of something better, to whom the bloom is off everything, and who always are impressed with the uselessness, the commonness of their own achievements — these come to regard page lvii / literary art as a thing unattainable and mysterious, scarcely to be detected save in a few pages by the greatest masters.

A score of phrases suddenly discovered thrill us to the heart like a startling revelation; but the lines which follow are just like all other verse, the further flow of prose is like all other prose.

Men of genius, no doubt, escape this anguish and torment because they bear within themselves an irresistible creative power. They do not sit in judgment on themselves. The rest of us, who are no more than persevering and conscious workers, can only contend against invincible discouragement by unremitting effort.

Two men by their simple and lucid teaching gave me the strength to try again and again: Louis Bouilhet and Gustave Flaubert.

If I here speak of myself in connection with them, it is because their counsels, as summed up in a few lines, may prove useful to some young writers who may be less self-confident than most are when they make their *début* in print. Bouilhet, whom I first came to know somewhat intimately about two years before I gained the friendship of Flaubert, by dint of telling me that a hundred lines — or less — if they are without a flaw and contain the very essence of the talent and originality page lviii / of even a second-rate man, are enough to establish an artist's reputation, made me understand that persistent toil and a thorough knowledge of the craft, might, in some happy hour of lucidity, power, and enthusiasm, by the fortunate occurrence of a subject in perfect concord with the tendency of our mind, lead to the production of a single work, short but as perfect as we can make it. Then I learned to see that the best-known writers have hardly ever left us more than one such volume; and that needful above all else is the good fortune which leads us to hit upon and discern, amid the multifarious matter which offers itself for selection, the subject which will absorb all our faculties, all that is of worth in us, all our artistic power.

At a later date, Flaubert, whom I had occasionally met, took a fancy to me. I ventured to show him a few attempts. He read them kindly and replied: "I cannot tell whether you will have any talent. What you have brought me proves a certain intelligence; but never forget this, young man: talent — as Chateaubriand* says — is nothing but long patience. Go and work."

I worked; and I often went to see him, feeling that he liked me, for he had taken to calling me, in jest, his disciple. For seven years I wrote page lix / verses, I wrote tales, I even wrote a villainous play. Nothing of all this remains. The master read it all; then, the next Sunday while we breakfasted together, he would give me his criticisms, driving into me by degrees two or three principles which sum up the drift of his long and patient exhortations: "If you have any originality," said he, "you must above all things bring it out; if you have not you must acquire it."

Talent is long patience.

Everything you want to express must be considered so long, and so attentively, as to enable you to find some aspect of it which no one has yet seen and expressed. There is an unexplored side to everything, because we are wont never to use our eyes but with the memory of what others before us have thought of the things we see. The smallest thing has something unknown in it; we must find it. To describe a blazing fire, a tree in a plain, we must stand face to face with that fire or that tree, till to us they are wholly unlike any other fire or tree. Thus we may become original.

Then, having established the truth that there are not in the whole world two grains of sand, two flies, two hands, or two noses absolutely alike, he would make me describe in a few sentences page lx / some person or object, in such a way as to define it exactly, and distinguish it from every other of the same race or species.

"When you pass a grocer sitting in his doorway," he would say, "a porter smoking his pipe, or a cab-stand, show me that grocer and that porter, their attitude and their whole physical aspect, including, as indicated by the skill of the portrait, their whole

* The idea did not originate with Chateaubriand.

moral nature, in such a way that I could never mistake them for any other grocer or porter; and by a single word give me to understand wherein one cab-horse differs from fifty others before or behind it."

I have explained his notions of style at greater length in another place; they bear a marked relation to the theory of observation I have just laid down. Whatever the thing we wish to say, there is but one word to express it, but one verb to give it movement, but one adjective to qualify it. We must seek till we find this noun, this verb and this adjective, and never be content with getting very near it, never allow ourselves to play tricks, even happy ones, or have recourse to sleights of language to avoid a difficulty. The subtlest things may be rendered and suggested by applying the hint conveyed in Boileau's line:

"D'un mot mis en sa place enseigna le pou- page lxi / voir."
"He taught the power of a word put in the right place."

There is no need for an eccentric vocabulary to formulate every shade of thought — the complicated, multifarious, and outlandish words which are put upon us nowadays in the name of artistic writing; but every modification of the value of a word by the place it fills must be distinguished with extreme clearness. Give us fewer nouns, verbs, and adjectives, with almost inscrutable shades of meaning, and let us have a greater variety of phrases, more variously constructed, ingeniously divided, full of sonority and learned rhythm. Let us strive to be admirable in style, rather than curious in collecting rare words.

It is in fact more difficult to bend a sentence to one's will and make it express everything — even what it does not say, to fill it full of implications of covert and inexplicit suggestions, than to invent new expressions, or seek out in old and forgotten books all those which have fallen into disuse and lost their meaning, so that to us they are as a dead language.

The French tongue, to be sure, is a pure stream, which affected writers never have and never can trouble. Each age has flung into the limpid waters its pretentious archaisms and euphu- page lxii / isms, but nothing has remained on the surface to perpetuate these futile attempts and impotent efforts. It is the nature of the language to be clear, logical, and vigorous. It does not lend itself to weakness, obscurity, or corruption.

Those who describe without duly heeding abstract terms, those who make rain and hail fall on the *cleanliness* of the window-panes, may throw stones at the simplicity of their brothers of the pen. The stones may indeed hit their brothers, who have a body, but will never hurt simplicity — which has none.

GUY DE MAUPASSANT.

LA GUILLETTE, ÉTRETAT, *September, 1887.* page lxiii /

JOSEPH CONRAD

The Nigger of the "Narcissus" (*1898*)

Author's Preface

A work that aspires, however humbly, to the condition of art should carry its justification in every line. And art itself may be defined as a single-minded attempt to render the highest kind of justice to the visible universe, by bringing to light the truth, manifold and one, underlying its every aspect. It is an attempt to find in its forms, in its colors, in its light, in its shadows, in the aspects of matter and in the facts of life, what of each is fundamental, what is enduring and essential — their one illuminating and convincing quality — the very truth of their existence. The artist, then, like the thinker or the scientist, seeks the truth and makes his appeal. Impressed by the aspect of the world the thinker plunges into ideas, the scientist into facts — whence, presently, emerging they make their appeal to those qualities of our being that fit us best for the hazardous enterprise of living. They speak authoritatively to our common sense, to our intelligence, to our desire of peace or to our desire of unrest; not seldom to our prejudices, sometimes to our fears, often to our egoism — but always to our credulity. And their words are heard with reverence, for their concern is with weighty matters: with the cultivation of our minds and the proper care of our bodies, with the attainment of our ambitions, with the perfection of the means and the glorification of our precious aims.

It is otherwise with the artist.

Confronted by the same enigmatical spectacle the artist **page 49 /** descends within himself, and in that lonely region of stress

---

Reprinted, by permission, from *Conrad's Prefaces* (London: J. M. Dent & Sons, Ltd., 1937).

and strife, if he be deserving and fortunate, he finds the terms of his appeal. His appeal is made to our less obvious capacities: to that part of our nature which, because of the warlike conditions of existence, is necessarily kept out of sight within the more resisting and hard qualities — like the vulnerable body within a steel armor. His appeal is less loud, more profound, less distinct, more stirring — and sooner forgotten. Yet its effect endures forever. The changing wisdom of successive generations discards ideas, questions facts, demolishes theories. But the artist appeals to that part of our being which is not dependent on wisdom: to that in us which is a gift and not an acquisition — and, therefore, more permanently enduring. He speaks to our capacity for delight and wonder, to the sense of mystery surrounding our lives; to our sense of pity, and beauty, and pain; to the latent feeling of fellowship with all creation — and to the subtle but invincible conviction of solidarity that knits together the loneliness of innumerable hearts, to the solidarity in dreams, in joy, in sorrow, in aspirations, in illusions, in hope, in fear, which binds men to each other, which binds together all humanity — the dead to the living and the living to the unborn.

It is only some such train of thought, or rather of feeling, that can in a measure explain the aim of the attempt, made in the tale which follows, to present an unrestful episode in the obscure lives of a few individuals out of all the disregarded multitude of the bewildered, the simple and the voiceless. For, if any part of truth dwells in the belief confessed above, it becomes evident that there is not a place of splendor or a dark corner of **page 50 /** the earth that does not deserve if only a passing glance of wonder and pity. The motive then, may be held to justify the matter of the work; but this preface, which is simply an avowal of endeavor, cannot end here — for the avowal is not yet complete.

Fiction — if it at all aspires to be art — appeals to temperament. And in truth it must be, like painting, like music, like all art, the appeal of one temperament to all the other innumerable temperaments whose subtle and resistless power endows passing events with their true meaning, and creates the moral, the emotional, atmosphere of the place and time. Such an appeal to be effective must be an impression conveyed through the senses; and, in fact, it cannot be made in any other way, because temperament, whether individual or collective, is not amenable to persuasion. All art, therefore, appeals primarily to the senses, and the artistic aim when expressing itself in written words must also make its appeal through the senses, if its high desire is to reach the secret spring of responsive emotions. It must strenuously aspire to the plasticity of sculpture, to the color of painting, and to the magic suggestiveness of music — which is the art of arts. And it is only through complete, unswerving devotion to the perfect blending of form and substance; it is only through an unremitting never-discouraged care for the shape and ring of sentences that an approach can be made to plasticity, to color, and that the light of magic suggestiveness may be brought to play for an evanescent instant over the commonplace surface of words: of the old, old words, worn thin, defaced by ages of careless usage.

The sincere endeavor to accomplish that creative task, to go as far on that road as his strength will carry him, to **page 51 /** go undeterred by faltering, weariness or reproach, is the only valid justification for the worker in prose. And if his conscience is clear, his answer to those who in the fullness of a wisdom which looks for immediate profit, demand specifically to be edified, consoled, amused; who demand to be promptly improved, or encouraged, or frightened, or shocked, or charmed, must run thus: My task which I am trying to achieve is, by the power of the written word to make you hear, to make you feel — it is, before all, to make you see. That — and no more, and it is everything. If I succeed, you shall find there according to your deserts: encouragement, consolation, fear, charm — all you demand — and, perhaps, also that glimpse of truth for which you have forgotten to ask.

To snatch in a moment of courage, from the remorseless rush of time, a passing phase of life, is only the beginning of the task. The task approached in tenderness and faith is to hold up unquestioningly, without choice and without fear, the rescued fragment before all eyes in the light of a sincere mood. It is to show its vibration, its color, its form; and through its movement, its form, and its color, reveal the substance of its truth — disclose its inspiring secret: the stress and passion within the core of each convincing moment. In a singleminded attempt of that kind, if one be deserving and fortunate, one may perchance attain to such clearness of sincerity that at last the presented vision of regret or pity, of terror or mirth, shall awaken in the hearts of the beholders that feeling of unavoidable solidarity; of the solidarity in mysterious origin, in toil, in joy, in hope, in uncertain fate, which binds men to each other and all mankind to the visible world. **page 52 /**

It is evident that he who, rightly or wrongly, holds by the convictions expressed above cannot be faithful to any one of the temporary formulas of his craft. The enduring part of them—the truth which each only imperfectly veils—should abide with him as the most precious of his possessions, but they all: Realism, Romanticism, Naturalism, even the unofficial sentimentalism (which like the poor, is exceedingly difficult to get rid of), all these gods must, after a short period of fellowship, abandon him—even on the very threshold of the temple—to the stammerings of his conscience and to the outspoken consciousness of the difficulties of his work. In that uneasy solitude the supreme cry of Art for Art itself loses the exciting ring of its apparent immorality. It sounds far off. It has ceased to be a cry, and is heard only as a whisper, often incomprehensible, but at times and faintly encouraging.

Sometimes, stretched at ease in the shade of a roadside tree, we watch the motions of a laborer in a distant field, and, after a time, begin to wonder languidly as to what the fellow may be at. We watch the movements of his body, the waving of his arms, we see him bend down, stand up, hesitate, begin again. It may add to the charm of an idle hour to be told the purpose of his exertions. If we know he is trying to lift a stone, to dig a ditch, to uproot a stump, we look with a more real interest at his efforts; we are disposed to condone the jar of his agitation upon the restfulness of the landscape; and even, if in a brotherly frame of mind, we may bring ourselves to forgive his failure. We understood his object, and after all, the fellow has tried, and perhaps he had not the strength—and perhaps he had **page 53 /** not the knowledge. We forgive, go on our way—and forget.

And so it is with the workman of art. Art is long and life is short, and success is very far off. And thus, doubtful of strength to travel so far, we talk a little about the aim—the aim of art, which, like life itself, is inspiring, difficult—obscured by mists. It is not in the clear logic of a triumphant conclusion; it is not in the unveiling of one of those heartless secrets which are called the Laws of Nature. It is not less great, but only more difficult.

To arrest, for the space of a breath, the hands busy about the work of the earth, and compel men entranced by the sight of distant goals to glance for a moment at the surrounding vision of form and color, of sunshine and shadows; to make them pause for a look, for a sigh, for a smile — such is the aim, difficult and evanescent, and reserved only for a very few to achieve. But sometimes, by the deserving and the fortunate, even that task is accomplished. And when it is accomplished — behold! — all the truth of life is there: a moment of vision, a sigh, a smile — and the return to an eternal rest. page 54 /

Nostromo (1904)

Author's Reminiscences

. . . .

No ditch or wall encompassed my abode. The window was open; the door too stood open to that best friend of my work, the warm, still sunshine of the wide fields. They lay around me infinitely helpful, but truth to say I had not known for weeks whether the sun shone upon the earth and whether the stars above still moved on their appointed courses. I was just then giving up some days of my allotted span to the last chapters of the novel "Nostromo," a tale of an imaginary (but true) seaboard, which is still mentioned now and again, and indeed kindly, sometimes in connection with the word "failure" and sometimes in conjunction with the word "astonishing." I have no opinion on this dis-

---

Reprinted, by permission, from *A Personal Record: Some Reminiscences,* by Joseph Conrad (New York: Doubleday, Page & Company, 1923).

crepancy. It's the sort of difference that can never be settled. All I know, is that, for twenty months, neglecting the common joys of life that fall to the lot of the humblest on this earth, I had, like the prophet of old, "wrestled with the Lord" for my creation, for the headlands of the coast, for the darkness of the Placid Gulf, the light on the snows, the clouds on the sky, and for the breath of life that had to be blown into the shapes of men and women, of Latin and Saxon, of Jew and Gentile. These are, perhaps, strong words, but it is difficult to characterise otherwise the intimacy and the strain of a creative effort in which mind and will and conscience are engaged to the full, hour after hour, day after day, away from the world, and to the exclusion of all that makes life really lovable and gentle — something for which a material parallel can only be found in the page 98 / everlasting sombre stress of the westward winter passage round Cape Horn. For that too is the wrestling of men with the might of their Creator, in a great isolation from the world, without the amenities and consolations of life, a lonely struggle under a sense of over-matched littleness, for no reward that could be adequate, but for the mere winning of a longitude. Yet a certain longitude, once won, cannot be disputed. The sun and the stars and the shape of your earth are the witnesses of your gain; whereas a handful of pages, no matter how much you have made them your own, are at best but an obscure and questionable spoil. Here they are. "Failure" — "Astonishing": take your choice; or perhaps both, or neither — a mere rustle and flutter of pieces of paper settling down in the night, and undistinguishable, like the snowflakes of a great drift destined to melt away in sunshine.

"How do you do?"

It was the greeting of the general's daughter. I had heard nothing — no rustle, no footsteps. I had felt only a moment before a sort of premonition of evil; I had the sense of an inauspicious presence — just that much warning and no more; and then came the sound of the voice and the jar as of a terrible fall from a great height — a fall, let us say, from the highest of the clouds floating in gentle procession over the fields in the faint westerly air of that July afternoon. I picked myself up quickly, of course; in other words, I jumped up from my chair stunned and dazed, every nerve quivering with the pain of being uprooted out of one world and flung down into another — perfectly civil.

"Oh! How do you do? Won't you sit down?"

That's what I said. This horrible but, I assure you, perfectly true reminiscence tells you more than a whole volume of confessions *à la* Jean Jacques Rousseau would page 99 / do. Observe! I didn't howl at her, or start upsetting furniture, or throw myself on the floor and kick, or allow myself to hint in any other way at the appalling magnitude of the disaster. The whole world of Costaguana (the country, you may remember, of my seaboard tale), men, women, headlands, houses, mountains, town, *campo* (there was not a single brick, stone, or grain of sand of its soil I had not placed in position with my own hands); all the history, geography, politics, finance; the wealth of Charles Gould's silver-mine, and the splendour of the magnificent Capataz de Cargadores, whose name, cried out in the night (Dr. Monygham heard it pass over his head — in Linda Viola's voice), dominated even after death the dark gulf containing his conquests of treasure and love — all that had come down crashing about my ears. I felt I could never pick up the pieces — and in that very moment I was saying, "Won't you sit down?"

The sea is strong medicine. Behold what the quarterdeck training even in a merchant ship will do! This episode should give you a new view of the English and Scots seamen (a much-caricatured folk) who had the last say in the formation of my character. One is nothing if not modest, but in this disaster I think I have done some honour to their simple teaching. "Won't you sit down?" Very fair; very fair indeed. She sat down. Her amused glance strayed all over the room. There were pages of MS. on the table and under the table, a batch of typed copy on a chair, single leaves had fluttered away into distant corners; there were there living pages, pages scored and wounded, dead pages that would be burnt at the end of the day — the litter of a cruel battlefield, of a long, long and desperate fray. Long! I suppose I went to bed sometimes, and got up the same number of times. Yes, I suppose I slept, and page 100 / ate the food put before me, and talked connectedly to my household on suitable occasions. But I had never been aware of the even flow of daily life, made easy and noiseless for me by a silent, watchful, tireless affection. Indeed, it seemed to me that I had been sitting at that table surrounded by the litter of a desperate fray for days and nights on end. It seemed so, because of the intense weariness of

which that interruption had made me aware — the awful disenchantment of a mind realising suddenly the futility of an enormous task, joined to a bodily fatigue such as no ordinary amount of fairly heavy physical labour could ever account for. I have carried bags of wheat on my back, bent almost double under a ship's deck-beams, from six in the morning till six in the evening (with an hour and a half off for meals), so I ought to know. . . .
page 101 /

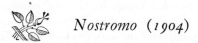

Nostromo (1904)

Author's Preface

"Nostromo" is the most anxiously meditated of the longer novels which belong to the period following upon the publication of the "Typhoon" volume of short stories.

I don't mean to say that I became then conscious of any impending change in my mentality and in my attitude towards the tasks of my writing life. And perhaps there was never any change, except in that mysterious, extraneous thing which has nothing to do with the theories of art; a subtle change in the nature of the inspiration; a phenomenon for which I can not in any way be held responsible. What, however, did cause me some concern was that after finishing the last story of the "Typhoon" volume it seemed somehow that there was nothing more in the world to write about.

This so strangely negative but disturbing mood lasted some little time; and then, as with many of my longer stories, the first hint for "Nostromo" came to me in the shape of a vagrant anecdote completely destitute of valuable details.

As a matter of fact in 1875 or '6, when very young, in the

Reprinted, by permission, from *Conrad's Prefaces* (London: J. M. Dent & Sons, Ltd., 1937).

West Indies or rather in the Gulf of Mexico, for my contacts with land were short, few, and fleeting, I heard the story of some man who was supposed to have stolen single-handed a whole lighter-full of silver, somewhere on the Tierra Firme seaboard during the troubles of a revolution.

On the face of it this was something of a feat. But page 85 / I heard no details, and having no particular interest in crime *qua* crime I was not likely to keep that one in my mind. And I forgot it till twenty-six or seven years afterwards I came upon the very thing in a shabby volume picked up outside a second-hand bookshop. It was the life story of an American seaman written by himself with the assistance of a journalist. In the course of his wanderings that American sailor worked for some months on board a schooner, the master and owner of which was the thief of whom I had heard in my very young days. I have no doubt of that because there could hardly have been two exploits of that peculiar kind in the same part of the world and both connected with a South American revolution.

The fellow had actually managed to steal a lighter with silver, and this, it seems, only because he was implicitly trusted by his employers, who must have been singularly poor judges of character. In the sailor's story he is represented as an unmitigated rascal, a small cheat, stupidly ferocious, morose, of mean appearance and altogether unworthy of the greatness this opportunity had thrust upon him. What was interesting was that he would boast of it openly.

He used to say: "People think I make a lot of money in this schooner of mine. But that is nothing. I don't care for that. Now and then I go away quietly and lift a bar of silver. I must get rich slowly — you understand."

There was also another curious point about the man. Once in the course of some quarrel the sailor threatened him: "What's to prevent me reporting ashore what you have told me about that silver?"

The cynical ruffian was not alarmed in the least. He actually laughed. "You fool, if you dare talk like that page 86 / on shore about me you will get a knife stuck in your back. Every man, woman and child in that port is my friend. And who's to prove the lighter wasn't sunk? I didn't show you where the silver is hidden. Did I? So you know nothing. And suppose I lied? Eh?"

Ultimately the sailor, disgusted with the sordid meanness of that impenitent thief, deserted from the schooner. The whole episode takes about three pages of his autobiography. Nothing to speak of; but as I looked them over, the curious confirmation of the few casual words heard in my early youth evoked the memories of that distant time when everything was so fresh, so surprising, so venturesome, so interesting; bits of strange coasts under the stars, shadows of hills in the sunshine, men's passions in the dusk, gossip half-forgotten, faces grown dim. . . . Perhaps, perhaps, there still was in the world something to write about. Yet I did not see anything at first in the mere story. A rascal steals a large parcel of a valuable commodity — so people say. It's either true or untrue; and in any case it has no value in itself. To invent a circumstantial account of the robbery did not appeal to me, because my talents not running that way I did not think that the game was worth the candle. It was only when it dawned upon me that the purloiner of the treasure need not necessarily be a confirmed rogue, that he could be even a man of character, an actor and possibly a victim in the changing scenes of a revolution, it was only then that I had the first vision of a twilight country which was to become the province of Sulaco, with its high shadowy Sierra and its misty Campo for mute witnesses of events flowing from the passions of men short-sighted in good and evil. page 87 /

Such are in very truth the obscure origins of "Nostromo" — the book. From that moment, I suppose, it had to be. Yet even then I hesitated, as if warned by the instinct of self-preservation from venturing on a distant and toilsome journey into a land full of intrigues and revolutions. But it had to be done.

It took the best part of the years 1903–4 to do; with many intervals of renewed hesitation, lest I should lose myself in the ever-enlarging vistas opening before me as I progressed deeper in my knowledge of the country. Often, also, when I had thought myself to a standstill over the tangled-up affairs of the Republic, I would, figuratively speaking, pack my bag, rush away from Sulaco for a change of air and write a few pages of the "Mirror of the Sea." But generally, as I've said before, my sojourn on the Continent of Latin America, famed for its hospitality, lasted for about two years. On my return I found (speaking somewhat in the style of Captain Gulliver) my family all well, my wife heartily glad to learn that the fuss was all over, and our small boy considerably grown during my absence.

My principal authority for the history of Costaguana is, of course, my venerated friend, the late Don José Avellanos, Minister to the Courts of England and Spain, etc., etc., in his impartial and eloquent "History of Fifty Years of Misrule." That work was never published — the reader will discover why — and I am in fact the only person in the world possessed of its contents. I have mastered them in not a few hours of earnest meditation, and I hope that my accuracy will be trusted. In justice to myself, and to allay the fears of prospective readers, I beg to point out that the few historical allusions are never dragged in **page 88 /** for the sake of parading my unique erudition, but that each of them is closely related to actuality; either throwing a light on the nature of current events or affecting directly the fortunes of the people of whom I speak.

As to their own histories I have tried to set them down, Aristocracy and People, men and women, Latin and Anglo-Saxon, bandit and politician, with as cool a hand as was possible in the heat and clash of my own conflicting emotions. And after all this is also the story of their conflicts. It is for the reader to say how far they are deserving of interest in their actions and in the secret purposes of their hearts revealed in the bitter necessities of the time. I confess that, for me, that time is the time of firm friendships and unforgotten hospitalities. And in my gratitude I must mention here Mrs. Gould, "the first lady of Sulaco," whom we may safely leave to the secret devotion of Dr. Monygham, and Charles Gould, the Idealist-creator of Material Interests whom we must leave to his Mine — from which there is no escape in this world.

About Nostromo, the second of the two racially and socially contrasted men, both captured by the silver of the San Tomé Mine, I feel bound to say something more.

I did not hesitate to make that central figure an Italian. First of all the thing is perfectly credible: Italians were swarming into the Occidental Province at the time, as anybody who will read further can see; and secondly, there was no one who could stand so well by the side of Giorgio Viola the Garibaldino, the Idealist of the old, humanitarian revolutions. For myself I needed there a Man of the People as free as possible from his class-conventions and all settled modes of thinking. This is not page 89 / a side snarl at conventions. My reasons were not moral but artistic. Had he been an Anglo-Saxon he would have tried to get into local politics. But Nostromo does not aspire to be a leader in a personal game. He does not want to raise himself above the mass. He is content to feel himself a power — within the People.

But mainly Nostromo is what he is because I received the inspiration for him in my early days from a Mediterranean sailor. Those who have read certain pages of mine will see at once what I mean when I say that Dominic, the padrone of the *Tremolino*, might under given circumstances have been a Nostromo. At any rate Dominic would have understood the younger man perfectly — if scornfully. He and I were engaged together in a rather absurd adventure, but the absurdity does not matter. It is a real satisfaction to think that in my very young days there must, after all, have been something in me worthy to command that man's half-bitter fidelity, his half-ironic devotion. Many of Nostromo's speeches I have heard first in Dominic's voice. His hand on the tiller and his fearless eyes roaming the horizon from within the monkish hood shadowing his face, he would utter the usual exordium of his remorseless wisdom: "Vous autres gentilhommes!" in a caustic tone that hangs on my ear yet. Like Nostromo! "You hombres finos!" Very much like Nostromo. But Dominic the Corsican nursed a certain pride of ancestry from which my Nostromo is free; for Nostromo's lineage had to be more ancient still. He is a man with the weight of countless generations behind him and no parentage to boast of. . . . Like the People.

In his firm grip on the earth he inherits, in his improvidence and generosity, in his lavishness with his gifts, page 90 / in his manly vanity, in the obscure sense of his greatness and in his faithful devotion with something despairing as well as desperate in its impulses, he is a Man of the People, their very own unenvious force, disdaining to lead but ruling from within. Years afterwards, grown older as the famous Captain Fidanza, with a stake in the country, going about his many affairs followed by respectful glances in the modernized streets of Sulaco, calling on the widow of the cargador, attending the Lodge, listening in unmoved silence to anarchist speeches at the meeting, the enigmatical patron of the new revolutionary agitation, the trusted, the wealthy comrade Fidanza with the knowledge of his moral ruin locked up in his breast, he remains essentially a Man of the People. In his mingled love and scorn of life and in the bewildered conviction of having been betrayed, of dying betrayed he hardly knows by what or by whom, he is still of the People, their undoubted Great Man — with a private history of his own.

One more figure of those stirring times I would like to mention: and that is Antonia Avellanos — the "beautiful Antonia." Whether she is a possible variation of Latin-American girlhood I wouldn't dare to affirm. But, for me, she *is*. Always a little in the background by the side of her father (my venerated friend) I hope she has yet relief enough to make intelligible what I am going to say. Of all the people who had seen with me the birth of the Occidental Republic, she is the only one who has kept in my memory the aspect of continued life. Antonia the Aristocrat and Nostromo the Man of the People are the artisans of the New Era, the true creators of the New State; he by his legendary and daring feat, she, like a woman, simply by the force of what she is: the only being page 91 / capable of inspiring a sincere passion in the heart of a trifler.

If anything could induce me to revisit Sulaco (I should hate to see all these changes) it would be Antonia. And the true reason for that — why not be frank about it? — the true reason is that I have modelled her on my first love. How we, a band of tallish schoolboys, the chums of her two brothers, how we used to look up to that girl just out of the schoolroom herself, as the standard-bearer of a faith to which we all were born but which she alone knew how to hold aloft with an unflinching hope! She had perhaps more glow and less serenity in her soul than Antonia, but she was an uncompromising Puritan of patriotism with no taint of the slightest worldliness in her thoughts. I was not the only one in love with her; but it was I who had to hear oftenest her scathing criticism of my levities — very much like poor Decoud — or stand the brunt of her austere, unanswerable invective. She did not quite understand — but never mind. That afternoon when I came in, a shrinking yet defiant sinner, to say the final good-bye I received a hand-squeeze that made my heart leap and saw a tear that took my breath away. She was softened at the last as though she had suddenly perceived (we were such children still!) that I was really going away for good, going very far away — even as far as Sulaco, lying unknown, hidden from our eyes in the darkness of the Placid Gulf.

That's why I long sometimes for another glimpse of the "beautiful Antonia" (or can it be the Other?) moving in the dimness of the great cathedral, saying a short prayer at the tomb of the first and last Cardinal-Archbishop of Sulaco, standing absorbed in filial devotion before the page 92 / monument of Don José Avellanos, and, with a lingering, tender, faithful glance at the medallion-memorial to Martin Decoud, going out serenely into the sunshine of the Plaza with her upright carriage and her white head; a relic of the past disregarded by men awaiting impatiently the Dawns of other New Eras, the coming of more Revolutions.

But this is the idlest of dreams; for I did understand perfectly well at the time that the moment the breath left the body of the Magnificent Capataz, the Man of the People, freed at last from the toils of love and wealth, there was nothing more for me to do in Sulaco.

J. C.

October, 1917. page 93 /

The Secret Agent (1907)

AUTHOR'S PREFACE

The origin of *The Secret Agent:* subject, treatment, artistic purpose, and every other motive that may induce an author to take up his pen, can, I believe, be traced to a period of mental and emotional reaction.

The actual facts are that I began this book impulsively and

Reprinted, by permission, from *Conrad's Prefaces* (London: J. M. Dent & Sons, Ltd., 1937).

wrote it continuously. When in due course it was bound and delivered to the public gaze I found myself reproved for having produced it at all. Some of the admonitions were severe, others had a sorrowful note. I have not got them textually before me but I remember perfectly the general argument, which was very simple; and also my surprise at its nature. All this sounds a very old story now! And yet it is not such a long time ago. I must conclude that I had still preserved much of my pristine innocence in the year 1907. It seems to me now that even an artless person might have foreseen that some criticisms would be based on the ground of sordid surroundings and the moral squalor of the tale.

That of course is a serious objection. It was not universal. In fact it seems ungracious to remember so little reproof amongst so much intelligent and sympathetic appreciation; and I trust that the readers of this Preface will not hasten to put it down to wounded vanity or a natural disposition to ingratitude. I suggest that a charitable heart could very well ascribe my choice to natural modesty. Yet it isn't exactly modesty that makes me select reproof for the illustration of my case. No, it page 103 / isn't exactly modesty. I am not at all certain that I am modest; but those who have read so far through my work will credit me with enough decency, tact, *savoir-faire*, what you will, to prevent me from making a song for my own glory out of the words of other people. No! The true motive of my selection lies in quite a different trait. I have always had a propensity to justify my action. Not to defend. To justify. Not to insist that I was right but simply to explain that there was no perverse intention, no secret scorn for the natural sensibilities of mankind at the bottom of my impulses.

That kind of weakness is dangerous only so far that it exposes one to the risk of becoming a bore; for the world generally is not interested in the motives of any overt act but in its consequences. Man may smile and smile but he is not an investigating animal. He loves the obvious. He shrinks from explanations. Yet I will go on with mine. It's obvious that I need not have written that book. I was under no necessity to deal with that subject; using the word subject both in the sense of the tale itself and in the larger one of a special manifestation in the life of mankind. This I fully admit. But the thought of elaborating mere ugliness in order to shock, or even simply to surprise my readers by a change of front, has never entered my head. In making this statement I expect to be believed, not only on the evidence of my general character but also for the reason, which anybody can see, that the whole treatment of the tale, its inspiring indignation and underlying pity and contempt, prove my detachment from the squalor and sordidness which lie simply in the outward circumstances of the setting.

The inception of *The Secret Agent* followed immediately **page 104 /** on a two years' period of intense absorption in the task of writing that remote novel, *Nostromo*, with its far-off Latin-American atmosphere; and the profoundly personal *Mirror of the Sea*. The first an intense creative effort on what I suppose will always remain my largest canvas, the second an unreserved attempt to unveil for a moment the profounder intimacies of the sea and the formative influences of nearly half my lifetime. It was a period, too, in which my sense of the truth of things was attended by a very intense imaginative and emotional readiness which, all genuine and faithful to facts as it was, yet made me feel (the task once done) as if I were left behind, aimless amongst mere husks of sensations and lost in a world of other, of inferior, values.

I don't know whether I really felt that I wanted a change, change in my imagination, in my vision, and in my mental attitude. I rather think that a change in the fundamental mood had already stolen over me unawares. I don't remember anything definite happening. With *The Mirror of the Sea* finished in the full consciousness that I had dealt honestly with myself and my readers in every line of that book, I gave myself up to a not unhappy pause. Then, while I was yet standing still, as it were, and certainly not thinking of going out of my way to look for anything ugly, the subject of *The Secret Agent*—I mean the tale—came to me in the shape of a few words uttered by a friend in a casual conversation about anarchists or rather anarchist activities; how brought about I don't remember now.

I remember, however, remarking on the criminal futility of the whole thing, doctrine, action, mentality; and on the contemptible aspect of the half-crazy pose as of a **page 105 /** brazen cheat exploiting the poignant miseries and passionate credulities of a mankind always so tragically eager for self-destruction. That was what made for me its philosophical pretences so unpardonable. Presently, passing to particular instances, we recalled the already old story of the attempt to blow up the Greenwich Observatory; a blood-stained inanity of so fatuous a kind that it was impossible to fathom its origin by any reasonable or even unreasonable process of thought. For perverse unreason has its own logical processes. But that outrage could not be laid hold of mentally in any sort of way, so that one remained faced by the fact of a man blown to bits for nothing even most remotely resembling an idea, anarchistic or other. As to the outer wall of the Observatory it did not show as much as the faintest crack.

I pointed all this out to my friend, who remained silent for a while and then remarked in his characteristically casual and omniscient manner: 'Oh, that fellow was half an idiot. His sister committed suicide afterwards.' These were absolutely the only words that passed between us; for extreme surprise at this unexpected piece of information kept me dumb for a moment and he began at once to talk of something else. It never occurred to me later to ask how he arrived at his knowledge. I am sure that if he had seen once in his life the back of an anarchist that must have been the whole extent of his connection with the underworld. He was, however, a man who liked to talk with all sorts of people, and he may have gathered those illuminating facts at second or third hand, from a crossing-sweeper, from a retired police officer, from some vague man in his club, or even, perhaps, from a Minister of State met at some public or private reception.
page 106 /

Of the illuminating quality there could be no doubt whatever. One felt like walking out of a forest on to a plain — there was not much to see but one had plenty of light. No, there was not much to see and, frankly, for a considerable time I didn't even attempt to perceive anything. It was only the illuminating impression that remained. It remained satisfactory but in a passive way. Then, about a week later, I came upon a book which as far as I know had never attained any prominence, the rather summary recollections of an Assistant Commissioner of Police, an obviously able man with a strong religious strain in his character who was appointed to his post at the time of the dynamite outrages in London, away back in the eighties. The book was fairly interesting, very discreet of course; and I have by now forgotten the bulk of its contents. It contained no revelations, it ran over the surface agreeably, and that was all. I won't even try to explain why I should have been arrested by a little passage of about seven lines, in which the author (I believe his name was Anderson) reproduced a short dialogue held in the lobby of the House of Commons after some unexpected anarchist outrage, with the Home Secretary. I think it was Sir William Harcourt then. He was very much irritated and the official was very apologetic. The phrase, amongst the three which passed between them, that struck me most was Sir W. Harcourt's angry sally: 'All that's very well. But your idea of secrecy over there seems to consist of keeping the Home Secretary in the dark.' Characteristic enough of Sir W. Harcourt's temper but not much in itself. There must have been, however, some sort of atmosphere in the whole incident because all of a sudden I felt myself stimulated. And page 107 / then ensued in my mind what a student of chemistry would best understand from the analogy of the addition of the tiniest little drop of the right kind, precipitating the process of crystallization in a test-tube containing some colourless solution.

It was at first for me a mental change, disturbing a quieted-down imagination, in which strange forms, sharp in outline but imperfectly apprehended, appeared and claimed attention as crystals will do by their bizarre and unexpected shapes. One fell to musing before the phenomenon — even of the past: of South America, a continent of crude sunshine and brutal revolutions, of the sea, the vast expanse of salt waters, the mirror of heaven's frowns and smiles, the reflector of the world's light. Then the vision of an enormous town presented itself, of a monstrous town more populous than some continents and in its man-made might as if indifferent to heaven's frowns and smiles; a cruel devourer of the world's light. There was room enough there to place any story, depth enough there for any passion, variety enough there for any setting, darkness enough to bury five millions of lives.

Irresistibly the town became the background for the ensuing period of deep and tentative meditations. Endless vistas opened before me in various directions. It would take years to find the right way! It seemed to take years! . . . Slowly the dawning conviction of Mrs. Verloc's maternal passion grew up to a flame between me and that background, tingeing it with its secret ardour and receiving from it in exchange some of its own sombre colouring. At last the story of Winnie Verloc stood out complete from the days of her childhood to the end, unproportioned as yet, with everything still on the first page 108 / plan, as it were; but ready now to be dealt with. It was a matter of about three days.

This book is *that* story, reduced to manageable proportions, its whole course suggested and centred round the absurd cruelty of the Greenwich Park explosion. I had there a task I will not say arduous but of the most absorbing difficulty. But it had to be done. It was a necessity. The figures grouped about Mrs. Verloc and related directly or indirectly to her tragic suspicion that 'life doesn't stand much looking into,' are the outcome of that very necessity. Personally I have never had any doubt of the reality of Mrs. Verloc's story; but it had to be disengaged from its obscurity in that immense town, it had to be made credible, I don't mean so much as to her soul but as to her surroundings, not so much as to her psychology but as to her humanity. For the surroundings hints were not lacking. I had to fight hard to keep at arm's length the memories of my solitary and nocturnal walks all over London in my early days, lest they should rush in and overwhelm each page of the story as these emerged one after another from a mood as serious in feeling and thought as any in which I ever wrote a line. In that respect I really think that *The Secret Agent* is a perfectly genuine piece of work. Even the purely artistic purpose, that of applying an ironic method to a subject of that kind, was formulated with deliberation and in the earnest belief that ironic treatment alone would enable me to say all I felt I would have to say in scorn as well as in pity. It is one of the minor satisfactions of my writing life that having taken that resolve I did manage, it seems to me, to carry it right through to the end. As to the personages whom the absolute necessity of the case — Mrs. Verloc's page 109 / case — brings out in front of the London background, from them, too, I obtained those little satisfactions which really count for so much against the mass of oppressive doubts that haunt so persistently every attempt at creative work. For instance, of Mr. Vladimir himself (who was fair game for a caricatural presentation) I was gratified to hear that an experienced man of the world had said 'that Conrad must have been in touch with that sphere or else has an excellent intuition of things,' because Mr. Vladimir was 'not only possible in detail but quite right in essentials.' Then a visitor from America informed me that all sorts of revolutionary refugees in New York would have it that the book was written by somebody who knew a lot about them. This seemed to me a very high compliment, considering that, as a matter of hard fact, I had seen even less of their kind than the omniscient friend who gave me the first suggestion for the novel. I have no doubt, however, that there had been moments during the writing of the book when I was an extreme revolutionist, I won't say more convinced than they but certainly cherishing a more concentrated purpose than any of them had ever done in the whole course of his life. I don't say this to boast. I was simply attending to my business. In the matter of all my books I have always attended to my business. I have attended to it with complete self-surrender. And this statement, too, is not a boast. I could not have done otherwise. It would have bored me too much to make believe.

The suggestions for certain personages of the tale, both law-abiding and lawless, came from various sources which, perhaps, here and there, some reader may have recognized. They are not very recondite. But I am not page 110 / concerned here to legitimize any of those people, and even as to my general view of the moral reactions as between the criminal and the police all I will venture to say is that it seems to me to be at least arguable.

The twelve years that have elapsed since the publication of the book have not changed my attitude. I do not regret having written it. Lately, circumstances, which have nothing to do with the general tenor of this preface, have compelled me to strip this tale of the literary robe of indignant scorn it had cost me so much to fit on it decently, years ago. I have been forced, so to speak, to look upon its bare bones. I confess that it makes a grisly skeleton. But still I will submit that telling Winnie Verloc's story to its anarchistic end of utter desolation, madness, and despair, and telling it as I have told it here, I have not intended to commit a gratuitous outrage on the feelings of mankind.

1920. J. C. page 111 /

HENRY JAMES

The Wings of the Dove (1902)

Author's Notebooks: Notebook IV

3 November 1894 — 15 October 1895[1]

34 De Vere Gardens, W., November 3d, 1894.

Isn't perhaps something to be made of the idea that came to me some time ago and that I have not hitherto made any note of — the little idea of the situation of some young creature (it seems to me preferably a woman, but of this I'm not sure), who, at 20, on the threshold of life that has seemed boundless, is suddenly condemned to death (by consumption, heart-disease, or whatever) by the voice of the physician? She learns that she has but a short time to live, and she rebels, she is terrified, she cries out in her anguish, her tragic young despair. She is in love with life, her dreams of it have been immense, and she clings to it with passion, with supplication. 'I don't want to die — I won't, oh, let me live; oh, save me!' She is equally pathetic in her doom and in her horror of it. If she only could live just a little; just a little more — just a little longer. She is like a creature dragged shrieking to the guillotine — to the shambles. The idea of a young man who meets her, who, knowing her fate, is terribly touched by her, and who conceives the idea of saving her as far as he can — little as that may be. She has known nothing, has seen nothing, it

[1] Three sheets, two of them written on on both sides, and one, written on on one side, have been torn out at the beginning of this notebook.

Reprinted, by permission, from *The Notebooks of Henry James*, edited by F. O. Matthiessen and Kenneth B. Murdock (New York: Oxford University Press, 1947).

was all beginning to come to her. Even a respite, with one hour of joy, of what other people, of what happy people, know: even this would come to her as a rescue, as a blessing. The young man, in his pity, wishes he could make her taste of happiness, give her something that it breaks her heart to go without having known. That 'something' can only be — of course — the chance to love and to be loved. He is not in love with her, he only deeply pities her: he has imagination enough to know what she feels. His impulse of kindness, of indulgence to her. She will live at the most but her little hour — so what does it matter? But the young man is entangled with another woman, committed, pledged, 'engaged' to one — and it is in that that a little story seems to reside. I see him as having somehow to risk something, to lose something, to sacrifice something in order to be kind to her, and page 169 / to do it without a reward, for the poor girl, even if he loved her, has no life to give him in return: no life and no personal, no physical surrender, for it seems to me that one must represent her as too ill for *that* particular case. It has bothered me in thinking of the little picture — this idea of the physical possession, the brief physical, passional rapture which at first appeared essential to it; bothered me on account of the ugliness, the incongruity, the nastiness, *en somme*, of the man's 'having' a sick girl: also on account of something rather pitifully obvious and vulgar in the presentation of such a remedy for her despair — and such a remedy only. 'Oh, she's dying without having had it? Give it to her and let her die' — that strikes me as sufficiently second-rate. Doesn't a greater prettiness, as well as a better chance for a story, abide in her being already too ill for that, and in his being able merely to show her some delicacy of kindness, let her think that they might have loved each other *ad infinitum* if it hadn't been too late. That, however, is a detail: what some dim vision of a little dramatic situation seems to attach to is the relation that this encounter places him in to the woman to whom he is *otherwise* attached and committed and whom he has never doubted (any more than this person herself has) that he loves. It appears inevitably, or necessarily, preliminary that his encounter with the tragic girl shall be *through* the other woman: I mean that *she* shall know all about her too (they may be relatives — brought together after an absence or for the first time) and shall be a close witness of the story. If I were writing for a French public the whole thing would be simple — the elder, the 'other,' woman would simply be the mistress of the young man, and it would be a question of his taking on the dying girl for a time — having a temporary liaison with her. But one can do so little with English adultery — it is so much less inevitable, and so much more ugly in all its hiding and lying side. It is so undermined by our immemorial tradition of original freedom of choice, and by our practically universal acceptance of divorce. At any rate in this case, the anecdote, which I don't, by the way, at all yet *see*, is probably more dramatic, in truth, on some basis of marriage being in question, marriage with the other woman, or even with both! The little action hovers before me as abiding, somehow, in the particular complication that his attitude (to the girl) engenders for the man, a complication culminating in some sacrifice for him, or some great loss, or disaster. The difficulty is that the beauty of the thing is precisely in his not being in love with the girl — in the disinterestedness of his conduct. She is in love with him — that is it: she has been already so before she is condemned. He *knows* it, he learns it at the same time that he learns — as *she* has learnt — that her illness will carry her off. Say that she swims into his ken as the cousin page 170 / — newly introduced — of the woman he is engaged to. Say he *is* definitely engaged to this elder girl and has been engaged some time, but that there is some serious obstacle to their marrying soon. It is what is called a long engagement. They are obliged to wait, to delay, to have patience. He has no income and she no fortune, or there is some insurmountable opposition on the part of her father. Her father, her family, have reasons for disliking the young man; the father is infirm, she has to be with him to the end, he will do nothing for them, etc., etc. Or say they have simply no means — which indeed has the drawback of not being very creditable to the hero. From the moment a young man engages himself he ought to have means: if he hasn't he oughtn't to engage himself. The little story *que j'entrevois* here suddenly seems to remind me of Ed. About's *Germaine*, read long years ago and but dimly remembered. But I don't care for that. If the young couple have at any rate, and for whatever reason, to *wait* (say for her, or for *his*, father's death) I get what is essential. *Ecco*. They are waiting. The young man in these circumstances encounters the dying girl as a friend or relation of his fiancée. *She* has money — *she* is rich. She is in love with him — she is tragic and touching. He takes his betrothed, his fiancée, fully into his confidence about her and says, 'Don't be jealous if I'm kind to her — you see *why* it is.' The fiancée is generous, she also is magnanimous — she is full of pity too. She gives him rope — she says, 'Oh yes, poor thing: be kind to her.' It goes further than she quite likes; but still she holds out — she is so sure of her lover. The poor child *is* — most visibly — dying: what, therefore, does it matter? She can last but a little; and she's so in love! But they are weary of their waiting, the two fiancés — and it is their own prospects that are of prime importance to them. It becomes very clear that the dying girl would marry the young man on the spot if she could.

November 7th, 1894. I dropped the foregoing the other day — I was pressed for time and it was taking me too far. There are difficulties in it — and what I meant was really only to throw out a feeler. I had asked myself if there was anything in the idea of the man's *agreeing with his fiancée that he shall marry the poor girl in order to come into her money and in the certitude that she will die and leave the money to him* — on which basis (his becoming a widower with property) they themselves will at last be able to marry. Then the sequel to that? — I can scarcely imagine any — I doubt if I can — that isn't ugly and vulgar: I mean vulgarly ugly. This would be the case with the girl's not, after all, dying — and that's not what I want, or mean. Moreover if she's as much in love with the young man as I conceive her, she would leave him the money without any question of marriage. I seem to get hold **page 171 /** of the tail of a pretty idea in making that happiness, that life, that snatched experience the girl longs for, BE, *in fact,* some rapturous act of that sort — some act of generosity, of passionate beneficence, of pure sacrifice, to the man she loves. This would obviate all 'marriage' between *them,* and everything so vulgar as an 'engagement,' and, removing the poor creature's yearning from the class of egotistic pleasures, the dream of being possessed and possessing, etc., make it something fine and strange. I think I see something good in *that* solution — it seems dimly to come to me. I think I see the thing beginning with the 2 girls — *who must not love each other.* This idea would require that the dying girl, whom family or personal circumstances have brought into relation with the other, should not be fond of her, should have some reason to dislike her, to do *her* at least no benefit or service. One may see the story begin with them — the two together; brought a little nearer by the younger girl's illness and trouble — so that the *other* is the FIRST witness of her despair and has the FIRST knowledge of her doom. The poor girl breaks out to her, raves, can't help it. The elder girl is privately, secretly engaged to the young man, and the other hasn't seen him when the doom aforesaid is pronounced. She sees him and she loves him — he becomes witness of her state and, as I have noted, immensely pities her. It is with a vision of what she could do for *him* that she renewedly pleads for life. *Then* she learns, discovers — or rather she doesn't discover at first — that the 2 others — her relative and the young man — are engaged. I seem to see what passes between the young man and his fiancée on the subject. The fiancée has a plan — she suddenly has a vision of what may happen. She forbids her lover to tell the girl they are engaged. Her plan is that he shall give himself to her for the time, be 'nice' to her, respond, express, devote himself to her, let her love him and behave as if he loved her. She foresees that, under these circumstances, the girl will become capable of some act of immense generosity — generosity by which her own life, her own prospect of marriage will profit — and without her really losing anything in the meanwhile. She therefore *checks* her lover's impulse, and he rather mystifiedly and bewilderedly assents. He 'reads her game' at last — she doesn't formally communicate it to him. She knows the girl dislikes her — say she has jilted the girl's brother, who has afterwards died. At any rate there is a *reason* for the dislike — and she, the elder woman, knows it. So much as this the latter tells her lover — for she has, after all, to *give* him a reason — explain to *him*, too, the dislike. In fact, in giving it, she virtually communicates her idea. 'Play a certain game — and you'll have money from her. But if she knows the money is to help you to marry me, you *won't* have it; never in the world!' My idea is that the poor (that is the rich) girl shall, page 172 / at last, know this — learn this. *How* does she learn it? From the inexorable father? From the jilted brother (if he be *not* dead)? From the man (some other man, that is) whom the inexorable father *does* want her (i.e., want the elder girl) to marry; and who, disgusted with her, turns, in a spirit both vindictive and mercenary, to the rich little invalid?

I seem to see, a little, THAT. I seem to see a penniless peer, whom my elder girl refuses. Her father will help her if she does that — if she makes the snobbish alliance. Her merit, her virtue is that she *won't* make it, and it is by this sacrifice that she holds her lover — *en le faisant valoir* — and makes him enter, as it were, into her scheme. Lord X. is a poor creature and has *nothing* but his title. The girl's sacrifice is a sacrifice of that — but of nothing else. If Lord X. goes, then, rebuffed, mercenarily and vindictively to the dying girl and tells her the other woman's 'game' (that is, her presumed, divined, engagement, from which she little by little, piece by piece, or in a vivid flash of divination, *constructs* the engagement, I seem to get almost a little 3-act play — with the main part for a young actress. I get, at any rate, a distinct and rather dramatic *action*, don't I? — *Voyons un peu.* The poor dying girl has an immense shock from her new knowledge — but her passion, after a little, is splendidly proof against it. She rallies to it — to her passion, her yearning just to taste, briefly, of life *that* way — and becomes capable of still clinging to her generosity. She clings, she clings. But the young man learns from her that she *knows* — knows of his existing tie. This enables him to measure her devotion, her beauty of soul — and it produces a tremendous effect upon him. He becomes ashamed of his tacit assent to his fiancée's idea — conceives a horror of it. In that horror he draws close to the dying girl. He tells his prospective bride that she knows — and yet how she seems determined to behave. 'So much the better!' says the prospective bride. My story pure and simple, very crudely and briefly, appears to be that the girl dies, leaving money — a good deal of money — to the man she has so hopelessly and generously loved, and whom it has become her idea of causing to contribute to her one surpreme experience *by* thus helping, thus, at any cost, testifying to a pure devotion to. Then the young man is left with the money face to face with his fiancée. It is what now happens between them that constitutes the climax, the denouement of the story. She is eager, ready to marry now, but he has really fallen in love with the dead girl. Something in the other woman's whole attitude in the matter — in the 'game' he consented in a manner to become the instrument of: something in all this revolts him and puts him off. In the light of how exquisite the dead girl was he sees how little exquisite is the living. He's in distress <about> what to do — he hangs

fire — he asks himself to what extent he can do himself vio- page
173 / lence. This change, this regret and revulsion, this deep commotion, his betrothed perceives, and she presently charges him with his infidelity, with failing her now, when they've reached, as it were, their goal. Does he want to keep the money for himself? There is a very painful, almost violent scene between them. (How it all — or am I detached? — seems to map itself out as a little 3-act play!) They *break*, in a word — he says, 'Be it so!' — as the woman gives him, in her resentment and jealousy (of the other's memory, now) an *opening* to break — by offering to let him off. But he offers her the money and she *takes* it. Then vindictively, in spite, *with* the money and with her father's restored countenance, she marries Lord X., while he lives poor and single and faithful — faithful to the image of the dead. Of course in the case of a play that one might entertain any hope of having acted, this denouement would have to be altered. The action would be the same up <to> the point of the girl's apparently impending death — and the donation of money would be before the EVENT. The rupture between the two fiancés would take place also before — he would buy her off with the money, the same way — and the hero would go back to the poor girl as her very own. Under this delight she would revive and cleave to him, and the curtain would fall on their embrace, as it were, and the *possibility* of their marriage and of her living. Lord X. and the betrothed's flunkeyizing father would be characters, and there would have to be a confidant of the hero's *evolution*, his emotions. I seem to see a vivid figure, and perhaps, for the hero, THAT figure — i.e., the 'confidant' — in the dying girl's *homme d'affaires*. I seem to see her perhaps as an American and this personage, the *homme d'affaires*, as a good American comedy-type. His wife would be the elderly woman. I seem to see Nice or Mentone — or Cairo — or Corfu — designated as the scene of the action, at least in the 1st act, and the gatherability of the people on some common ground, the salon of an hotel or the garden of the same. x x x x x

[*In a manner comparable to his preliminary outline for* The Golden Bowl, *James thought his way here into the situation that he was to develop several years later in* The Wings of the Dove

(1902). *But again the emotional possibilities were to be deepened and enriched by his final handling. He was writing the above at about the time* Guy Domville *went into rehearsal, which probably accounts for his thinking in terms of a possible play. But by now his bitter experience with the current standards of the stage made him take it for granted that he would have to sacrifice much of his essential theme for the sake of a happy ending.*

In view of the fact that Milly Theale became his quintessential ex- **page 174 /** *pression of the American girl, 'the heiress of all the ages,' it is interesting to note that he began to think of her 'perhaps as an American' only in the final sentences of this outline. He opened his preface with the statement that* The Wings of the Dove *'represents to my memory a very old — if I shouldn't perhaps rather say a very young — motive; I can scarce remember the time when the situation on which this long-drawn ficition mainly rests was not vividly present to me.' In this case he was to bring to his sketched outline not the kind of immediate observation that suddenly made a young man on the next bench into Owen Wingrave, but rather the stored-up accumulation of one of the primary emotional experiences of his youth. In presenting Milly Theale he drew — to a more penetrating extent than with any of his other characters — upon someone he had known, upon his cousin Minny Temple. This vivid brilliant girl who had died of tuberculosis at twenty-four was to remain for him 'the supreme case of a taste for life as life.' He was to end his* Notes of a Son and Brother (1914) *with a chapter dealing with her, and so say that in her death William and he had felt together the end of their own youth. The extent to which James' image of the American girl, in Isabel Archer as well as in Milly Theale, depended upon Minny Temple may be read in that commemoration, and also in several of James' letters.*

His remembrance of Minny's thirst for life helped him solve one of the problems of his story, the problem — which he came back to in the preface — of presenting a sick heroine. James knew that it is 'by the act of living' that characters appeal, and he created a heroine less tenuous than the outline might suggest. She has made no such high-pitched renunciation of love. James probed the deep connection between love and the will to live, and when Milly learns of the relation between Merton Densher and Kate

Croy, she does not 'rally to it.' Instead, she 'turns her face to the wall.' Her generosity to Densher remains, but she had wanted something more than to immolate herself in sacrificial devotion. Just as James wrote about Minny on the final page of Notes of a Son and Brother: *'Death, at last, was dreadful to her; she would have given anything to live.'*

His matching of the forces arrayed against Milly also became more affecting, especially in the kind of character he created in Kate Croy. She possesses finally a terrifying force of will, but she is by no means wholly brutal. There is no dislike posited between her and Milly, no introduction of a jilted brother. James gave the bulk of his opening book to accounting for her later actions as a result of her impoverished background, in particular through her natural desire to escape her flashy **page 175 /** *sordid father. Lionel Croy is very different from the character in the outline; the role of social ambition is taken over by Kate's Aunt Maud. Kate becomes ruthless as she is swept along by the forces she has set in motion, but she is never a 'vindictive' villainess. The question whether she accepts Densher's offer of the money is, as so often in James, left to the reader to decide — on the basis of the impression produced by her whole character. But there is no possibility of her marrying Lord Mark 'in spite.' Densher is transformed by the action in the way suggested, but James did not give him a confidant, and as a result the handling of the denouement, with Milly dying offstage, is the most indirect that even James ever attempted.*

When he recurred to the theme for his only other discussion of it in these notebooks, in the following February, Guy Domville *had failed, and James was no longer encumbered with thoughts of how to make his material suit the theater. When he finally brought it to expression, he had moved as far from the plays of Scribe as from any reminiscences of a plot of Edmond About's. His accumulated resources of pity and terror enabled him to produce his principal tragedy.*] **page 176 /**

. . . .

34 D. V. G. W., February 14th, 1895.

I have been reading over the long note — the 1st in this book — I made some time since on the subject of the dying girl who wants to live — to live and love, etc.; and am greatly struck with all it contains. It is there, the story; strongly, richly there; a thing, surely, of great potential interest and beauty and of a strong, firm artistic *ossature*. It is *full* — the scheme; and one has only to stir it up *à pleines mains*. I allude to my final sketch of it — the idea of the rupture at last between the 2 fiancés: his giving her the money and her taking it and marrying Lord X. . . . **page 187 /**

The Wings of the Dove (1902)

Author's Preface

The Wings of the Dove, published in 1902, represents to my memory a very old — if I shouldn't perhaps rather say a very young — motive; I can scarce remember the time when the situation on which this long-drawn fiction mainly rests was not vividly present to me. The idea, reduced to its essence, is that of a young person conscious of a great capacity for life, but early stricken and doomed, condemned to die under short respite, while also enamoured of the world; aware moreover of the condemnation and passionately desiring to "put in" before extinction as many of the finer vibrations as possible, and so achieve, however briefly and brokenly, the sense of having lived. Long had I turned it over, standing off from it, yet coming back to it; convinced of what might be done with it, yet seeing the theme as formidable. The image so figured would be, at best, but half the matter; the rest would be all the picture of the struggle involved, the adventure brought about, the gain recorded or the loss incurred, the precious experience somehow compassed. These things, I had from the first felt, would require much working-out; that in-

Reprinted, by permission, from *The Wings of the Dove* (New York: Charles Scribner's Sons, 1909).

deed was the case with most things worth working at all; yet there are subjects and subjects, and this one seemed particularly to bristle. It was formed, I judged, to make the wary adventurer walk round and round it — it had in fact a charm that invited and mystified alike that attention; not being somehow what one thought of as a "frank" subject, after the fashion of some, with its elements well in view and its whole character in its face. It stood there with secrets and compartments, with possible treacheries and traps; it might have a great deal to give, but would probably ask for equal services in return, and would collect this debt to the last shilling. It involved, to begin with, the placing in the strongest light a person infirm and ill — a case sure to prove difficult and to require page v / much handling; though giving perhaps, with other matters, one of those chances for good taste, possibly even for the play of the very best in the world, that are not only always to be invoked and cultivated, but that are absolutely to be jumped at from the moment they make a sign.

Yes then, the case prescribed for its central figure a sick young woman, at the whole course of whose disintegration and the whole ordeal of whose consciousness one would have quite honestly to assist. The expression of her state and that of one's intimate relation to it might therefore well need to be discreet and ingenious; a reflexion that fortunately grew and grew, however, in proportion as I focussed my image — roundabout which, as it persisted, I repeat, the interesting possibilities and the attaching wonderments, not to say the insoluble mysteries, thickened apace. Why had one to look so straight in the face and so closely to cross-question that idea of making one's protagonist "sick"? — as if to be menaced with death or danger hadn't been from time immemorial, for heroine or hero, the very shortest of all cuts to the interesting state. Why should a figure be disqualified for a central position by the particular circumstance that might most quicken, that might crown with a fine intensity, its liability to many accidents, its consciousness of all relations? This circumstance, true enough, might disqualify it for many activities — even though we should have imputed to it the unsurpassable activity of passionate, of inspired resistance. This last fact was the real issue, for the way grew straight from the moment one recognised that the poet essentially *can't* be concerned with the act of dying. Let him deal with the sickest of the sick, it is still by the act of living that they appeal to him, and appeal the more as the conditions plot against them and prescribe the battle. The process of life gives way fighting, and often may so shine out on the lost ground as in no other connexion. One had had moreover, as a various chronicler, one's secondary physical weaklings and failures, one's accessory invalids — introduced with a complacency that made light of criticism. To Ralph Touchett in *The Portrait of a Lady*, page vi / for instance, his deplorable state of health was not only no drawback; I had clearly been right in counting it, for any happy effect he should produce, a positive good mark, a direct aid to pleasantness and vividness. The reason of this moreover could never in the world have been his fact of sex; since men, among the mortally affiicted, suffer on the whole more overtly and more grossly than women, and resist with a ruder, an inferior strategy. I had thus to take *that* anomaly for what it is worth, and I give it here but as one of the ambiguities amid which my subject ended by making itself at home and seating itself quite in confidencc.

With the clearness I have just noted, accordingly, the last thing in the world it proposed to itself was to be the record predominantly of a collapse. I don't mean to say that my offered victim was not present to my imagination, constantly, as dragged by a greater force than any she herself could exert; she had been given me from far back as contesting every inch of the road, as catching at every object the grasp of which might make for delay, as clutching these things to the last moment of her strength. Such an attitude and such movements, the passion they expressed and the success they in fact represented, what were they in truth but the soul of drama? — which is the portrayal, as we know, of a catastrophe determined in spite of oppositions. My young woman would *herself* be the opposition — to the catastrophe announced by the associated Fates, powers conspiring to a sinister end and, with their command of means, finally achieving it, yet in such straits really to *stifle* the sacred spark that, obviously, a creature so animated, an adversary so subtle, couldn't but be felt worthy, under whatever weaknesses, of the foreground and the limelight. She would meanwhile wish, moreover, all along, to live for particular things, she would found her struggle on particular human interests, which would inevitably determine, in respect to her, the attitude of other persons, persons affected in such a manner as to make them part of the action. If her impulse to wrest from her shrinking hour still as much of the fruit of life as possible, if this longing can take effect page vii / only by the aid of others, their participation (appealed to, entangled and coerced as they find themselves) becomes their drama too — that of their promoting her illusion, under her importunity, for reasons, for interests and advantages, from motives and points of view, of their own. Some of these promptings, evidently, would be of the highest order — others doubtless mightn't; but they would make up together, for her, contributively, her sum of experience, represent to her somehow, in good faith or in bad, what she should have *known*. Somehow, too, at such a rate, one would see the persons subject to them drawn in as by some pool of a Lorelei — see them terrified and tempted and charmed; bribed away, it may even be, from more prescribed and natural orbits, inheriting from their connexion with her strange difficulties and still stranger opportunities, confronted with rare questions and called upon for new discriminations. Thus the scheme of her situation would, in a comprehensive way, see itself constituted; the rest of the interest would be in the number and nature of the particulars. Strong among these, naturally, the need that life should, apart from her infirmity, present itself to our young woman as quite dazzlingly liveable, and that if the great pang for her is in what she must give up we shall appreciate it the more from the sight of all she has.

One would see her then as possessed of all things, all but the single most precious assurance; freedom and money and a mobile mind and personal charm, the power to interest and attach; attributes, each one, enhancing the value of a future. From the moment his imagination began to deal with her at close quarters, in fact, nothing could more engage her designer than to work out the detail of her perfect rightness for her part; nothing above all more solicit him than to recognise fifty reasons for her national and social status. She should be the last fine flower — blooming alone, for the fullest attestation of her freedom — of an "old" New York stem; the happy congruities thus preserved for her being matters, however, that I may not now go into, and this even though the fine association that shall yet elsewhere page viii / await me is of a sort, at the best, rather to defy than to encourage exact expression. There goes with it, for the heroine of *The*

Wings of the Dove, a strong and special implication of liberty, liberty of action, of choice, of appreciation, of contact — proceeding from sources that provide better for large independence, I think, than any other conditions in the world — and this would be in particular what we should feel ourselves deeply concerned with. I had from far back mentally projected a certain sort of young American as more the "heir of all the ages" than any other young person whatever (and precisely on those grounds I have just glanced at but to pass them by for the moment); so that here was a chance to confer on some such figure a supremely touching value. To be the heir of all the ages only to know yourself, as that consciousness should deepen, balked of your inheritance, would be to play the part, it struck me, or at least to arrive at the type, in the light on the whole the most becoming. Otherwise, truly, what a perilous part to play *out* — what a suspicion of "swagger" in positively attempting it! So at least I could reason — so I even think I *had* to — to keep my subject to a decent compactness. For already, from an early stage, it had begun richly to people itself; the difficulty was to see whom the situation I had primarily projected might, by this, that or the other turn, *not* draw in. My business was to watch its turns as the fond parent watches a child perched, for its first riding-lesson, in the saddle; yet its interest, I had all the while to recall, was just in its making, on such a scale, for developments.

What one had discerned, at all events, from an early stage, was that a young person so devoted and exposed, a creature with her security hanging so by a hair, couldn't but fall somehow into some abysmal trap — this being, dramatically speaking, what such a situation most naturally implied and imposed. Didn't the truth and a great part of the interest also reside in the appearance that she would constitute for others (given her passionate yearning to live while she might) a complication as great as any they might **page xi /** constitute for herself? — which is what I mean when I speak of such matters as "natural." They would be as natural, these tragic, pathetic, ironic, these indeed for the most part sinister, liabilities, to her living associates, as they could be to herself as prime subject. If her story was to consist, as it could so little help doing, of her being let in, as we say, for this, that and the other irreducible anxiety, how could she not have put a premium on the acquisition, by any close sharer of her life, of a consciousness similarly embarrassed? I have named the Rhinemaiden, but our young friend's existence would create rather, all round her, very much that whirlpool movement of the waters produced by the sinking of a big vessel or the failure of a great business; when we figure to ourselves the strong narrowing eddies, the immense force of suction, the general engulfment that, for any neighboring object, makes immersion inevitable. I need scarce say, however, that in spite of these communities of doom I saw the main dramatic complication much more prepared *for* my vessel of sensibility than by her — the work of other hands (though with her own imbrued too, after all, in the measure of their never not being, in some direction, generous and extravagant, and thereby provoking).

The great point was, at all events, that if in a predicament she was to be, accordingly, it would be of the essence to create the predicament promptly and build it up solidly, so that it should have for us as much as possible its ominous air of awaiting her. That reflexion I found, betimes, not less inspiring than urgent; one begins so, in such a business, by looking about for one's compositional key, unable as one can only be to move till one has found it. To start without it is to pretend to enter the train and, still more, to remain in one's seat, without a ticket. Well — in the steady light and for the continued charm of these verifications — I had secured my ticket over the tolerably long line laid down for *The Wings of the Dove* from the moment I had noted that there could be no full presentation of Milly Theale as *engaged* with elements amid which she was to draw her breath in such pain, should not the elements have been, with page x / all solicitude, duly prefigured. If one had seen that her stricken state was but half her case, the correlative half being the state of others as affected by her (they too should have a "case," bless them, quite as much as she!) then I was free to choose, as it were, the half with which I should begin. If, as I had fondly noted, the little world determined for her was to "bristle" — I delighted in the term! — with meanings, so, by the same token, could I but make my medal hang free, its obverse and its reverse, its face and its back, would beautifully become optional for the spectator. I somehow wanted them correspondingly embossed, wanted them inscribed and figured with an equal salience; yet it was none the less visibly my "key," as I have said, that though my regenerate young New Yorker, and what might depend on her, should form my centre, my circumference was every whit as treatable. Therefore I must trust myself to know when to proceed from the one and when from the other. Preparatively and, as it were, yearningly — given the whole ground — one began, in the event, with the outer ring, approaching the centre thus by narrowing circumvallations. There, full-blown, accordingly, from one hour to the other, rose one's process — for which there remained all the while so many amusing formulae.

The medal *did* hang free — I felt this perfectly, I remember, from the moment I had comfortably laid the ground provided in my first Book, ground from which Milly is superficially so absent. I scarce remember perhaps a case — I like even with this public grossness to insist on it — in which the curiosity of "beginning far back," as far back as possible, and even of going, to the same tune, far "behind," that is behind the face of the subject, was to assert itself with less scruple. The free hand, in this connexion, was above all agreeable — the hand the freedom of which I owed to the fact that the work had ignominiously failed, in advance, of all power to see itself "serialised." This failure had repeatedly waited, for me, upon shorter fictions; but the considerable production we here discuss was (as *The Golden Bowl* was to be, two or three years later) born, not otherwise than page xi / a little bewilderedly, into a world of periodicals and editors, of roaring "successes" in fine, amid which it was wellnigh unnotedly to lose itself. There is fortunately something bracing, ever, in the alpine chill, that of some high icy *arête*, shed by the cold editorial shoulder; sour grapes may at moments fairly intoxicate and the storyteller worth his salt rejoice to feel again how many accommodations he can practise. Those addressed to "conditions of publication" have in a degree their interesting, or at least their provoking, side; but their charm is qualified by the fact that the prescriptions here spring from a soil often wholly alien to the ground of the work itself. They are almost always the fruit of another air altogether and conceived in a light liable to represent *within* the circle of the work itself little else than darkness. Still, when not too blighting, they often operate as a tax on ingenuity — that ingenuity of the expert craftsman which likes to be taxed very much to the same tune to which a well-bred horse likes to be saddled. The best and finest ingenuities, nevertheless, with all respect to that truth, are apt to be, not one's compromises, but one's fullest conformities, and I well remember, in the case before us, the pleasure of feeling my divisions, my proportions and general rhythm, rest all on permanent rather than in any degree on momentary proprieties. It was enough for my alternations, thus, that they were good in themselves; it was in fact so much for them that I really think any further account of the constitution of the book reduces itself to a just notation of the law they followed.

There was the "fun," to begin with, of establishing one's successive centres — of fixing them so exactly that the portions of the subject commanded by them as by happy points of view, and accordingly treated from them, would constitute, so to speak, sufficiently solid *blocks* of wrought material, squared to the sharp edge, as to have weight and mass and carrying power; to make for construction, that is, to conduce to effect and to provide for beauty. Such a block, obviously, is the whole preliminary presentation of Kate Croy, which, from the first, I recall, absolutely declined to page xii / enact itself save in terms of amplitude. Terms of amplitude, terms of atmosphere, those terms, and those terms only, in which images assert their fullness and roundness, their power to revolve, so that they have sides and backs, parts in the shade as true as parts in the sun — these were plainly to be my conditions, right and left, and I was so far from overrating the amount of expression the whole thing, as I saw and felt it, would require, that to retrace the way at present is, alas, more than anything else, but to mark the gaps and the lapses, to miss, one by one, the intentions that, with the best will in the world, were not to fructify. I have just said that the process of the general attempt is described from the moment the "blocks" are numbered, and that would be a true enough picture of my plan. Yet one's plan, alas, is one thing and one's result another; so that I am perhaps nearer the point in saying that this last strikes me at present as most characterised by the happy features that *were*, under my first and most blest illusion, to have contributed to it. I meet them all, as I renew acquaintance, I mourn for them all as I remount the stream, the absent values, the palpable voids, the missing links, the mocking shadows, that reflect, taken together, the early bloom of one's good faith. Such cases are of course far from abnormal — so far from it that some acute mind ought surely to have worked out by this time the "law" of the degree in which the artist's energy fairly depends on his fallibility. How much and how often, and in what connexions and with what almost infinite variety, must he be a dupe, that of his prime object, to be at all measurably a master, that of his actual substitute for it—or in other words at all appreciably to exist? He places, after an earnest survey, the piers of his bridge—he has at least sounded deep enough, heaven knows, for their brave position; yet the bridge spans the stream, after the fact, in apparently complete independence of these properties, the principal grace of the original design. *They* were an illusion, for their necessary hour; but the span itself, whether of a single arch or of many, seems by the oddest chance in the world to be a reality; since, actually, the rueful builder, passing under it, page xiii / sees figures and hears sounds above: he makes out, with his heart in his throat, that it bears and is positively being "used."

The building-up of Kate Croy's consciousness to the capacity for the load little by little to be laid on it was, by way of example, to have been a matter of as many hundred close-packed bricks as there are actually poor dozens. The image of her so compromised and compromising father was all effectively to have pervaded her life, was in a certain particular way to have tampered with her spring; by which I mean that the shame and the irritation and the depression, the general poisonous influence of him, were to have been *shown*, with a truth beyond the compass even of one's most emphasised "word of honour" for it, to do these things. But where do we find him, at this time of day, save in a beggarly scene or two which scarce arrives at the dignity of functional reference? He but "looks in," poor beautiful dazzling damning apparition that he was to have been; he sees his place so taken, his company so little missed, that, cocking again that fine form of hat which has yielded him for so long his one effective cover, he turns away with a whistle of indifference that nobly misrepresents the deepest disappointment of his life. One's poor word of honour has *had* to pass muster for the show. Every one, in short, was to have enjoyed so much better a chance that, like stars of the theatre condescending to oblige, they have had to take small parts, to content themselves with minor identities, in order to come on at all. I haven't the heart now, I confess, to adduce the detail of so many lapsed importances; the explanation of most of which, after all, I take to have been in the crudity of a truth beating full upon me through these reconsiderations, the odd inveteracy with which picture, at almost any turn, is jealous of drama, and drama (though on the whole with a greater patience, I think) suspicious of picture. Between them, no doubt, they do much for the theme; yet each baffles insidiously the other's ideal and eats around the edges of its position; each is too ready to say "I can take the thing for 'done' only when done in *my* way." page xiv / The residuum of comfort for the witness of these broils is of course meanwhile in the convenient reflexion, invented for him in the twilight of time and the infancy of art by the Angel, not to say by the Demon, of Compromise, that nothing is so easy to "do" as not to be thankful for almost any stray help in its getting done. It wasn't, after this fashion, by making good one's dream of Lionel Croy that my structure was to stand on its feet — any more than it was by letting him go that I was irretrievably lamenting. The who and the what, the how and the why, the whence and the whither of Merton Densher, these, no less, were quantities and attributes that should have danced about him with the antique grace of nymphs and fauns circling round a bland Hermes and crowning him with flowers. One's main anxiety, for each one's agents, is that the air of each shall be *given*; but what does the whole thing become, after all, as one goes, but a series of sad places at which the hand of generosity has been cautioned and stayed? The young man's situation, personal, professional, social, was to have been so decanted for us that we should get all the taste; we were to have been penetrated with Mrs. Lowder, by the same token, saturated with her presence, her "personality," and felt all her weight in the scale. We were to have revelled in Mrs. Stringham, my heroine's attendant friend, her fairly choral Bostonian, a subject for innumerable touches, and in an extended and above all an *animated* reflexion of Milly Theale's experience of English society; just as the strength and sense of the situation in Venice, for our gathered friends, was to have come to us in a deeper draught out of a larger cup, and just as the pattern of Densher's final position and fullest consciousness there was to have been marked in fine stitches, all silk and gold, all pink and silver, that have had to remain, alas, but entwined upon the reel.

It isn't, no doubt, however — to recover, after all, our critical balance — that the pattern didn't, for each compartment, get itself somehow wrought, and that we mightn't thus, piece by piece, opportunity offering, trace it over and page xv / study it.

The thing has doubtless, as a whole, the advantage that each piece is true to its pattern, and that while it pretends to make no simple statement it yet never lets go its scheme of clearness. Applications of this scheme are continuous and exemplary enough, though I scarce leave myself room to glance at them. The clearness is obtained in Book First — or otherwise, as I have said, in the first "piece," each Book having its subordinate and contributive pattern — through the associated consciousness of my two prime young persons, for whom I early recognised that I should have to consent, under stress, to a practical *fusion* of consciousness. It is into the young woman's "ken" that Merton Densher is represented as swimming; but her mind is not here, rigorously, the one reflector. There are occasions when it plays this part, just as there are others when his plays it, and an intelligible plan consists naturally not a little in fixing such occasions and making them, on one side and the other, sufficient to themselves. Do I sometimes in fact forfeit the advantage of that distinctness? Do I ever abandon one centre for another after the former has been postulated? From the moment we proceed by "centres" — and I have never, I confess, embraced the logic of any superior process — they must *be*, each, as a basis, selected and fixed; after which it is that, in the high interest of economy of treatment, they determine and rule. There is no economy of treatment without an adopted, a related point of view, and though I understand, under certain degrees of pressure, a represented community of vision between several parties to the action when it makes for concentration, I understand no breaking-up of the register, no sacrifice of the recording consistency, that doesn't rather scatter and weaken. In this truth resides the secret of the discriminated occasion — that aspect of the subject which we have our noted choice of treating either as picture or scenically, but which is apt, I think, to show its fullest worth in the Scene. Beautiful exceedingly, for that matter, those occasions or parts of an occasion when the boundary line between picture and scene bears a little the weight of the double pressure. page xvi /

Such would be the case, I can't but surmise, for the long passage that forms here before us the opening of Book Fourth, where all the offered life centres, to intensity, in the disclosure of Milly's single throbbing consciousness, but where, for a due rendering, everything has to be brought to a head. This passage, the view of her introduction to Mrs. Lowder's circle, has its mate, for illustration, later on in the book and at a crisis for which the occasion submits to another rule. My registers or "reflectors," as I so conveniently name them (burnished indeed as they generally are by the intelligence, the curiosity, the passion, the force of the moment, whatever it be, directing them), work, as we have seen, in arranged alternation; so that in the second connexion I here glance at it is Kate Croy who is, "for all she is worth," turned on. She is turned on largely at Venice, where the appearances, rich and obscure and portentous (another word I rejoice in) as they have by that time become and altogether exquisite as they remain, are treated almost wholly through her vision of them and Densher's (as to the lucid interplay of which conspiring and conflicting agents there would be a great deal to say). It is in Kate's consciousness that at the stage in question the drama is brought to a head, and the occasion on which, in the splendid saloon of poor Milly's hired palace, she takes the measure of her friend's festal evening, squares itself to the same synthetic firmness as the compact constructional block inserted by the scene at Lancaster Gate. Milly's situation ceases at a given moment to be "renderable" in terms closer than those supplied by Kate's intelligence, or, in a richer degree, by Densher's, or, for one fond hour, by poor Mrs. Stringham's (since to that sole brief futility is this last participant, crowned by my original plan with the quaintest functions, in fact reduced); just as Kate's relation with Densher and Densher's with Kate have ceased previously, and are then to cease again, to be projected for us, so far as Milly is concerned with them, on any more responsible plate than that of the latter's admirable anxiety. It is as if, for these aspects, the impersonal plate — in other words the poor author's com- page xvii / paratively cold affirmation or thin guarantee — had felt itself a figure of attestation at once too gross and too bloodless, likely to affect us as an abuse of privilege when not as an abuse of knowledge.

Heaven forbid, we say to ourselves during almost the whole Venetian climax, heaven forbid we should "know" anything more of our ravaged sister than what Densher darkly pieces together, or than what Kate Croy pays, heroically, it must be owned, at the hour of her visit alone to Densher's lodging, for her superior handling and her dire profanation of. For we have time, while this passage lasts, to turn round critically; we have time to recognise intentions and proprieties; we have time to catch glimpses of an economy of composition, as I put it, interesting in itself: all in spite of the author's scarce more than half-dissimulated despair at the inveterate displacement of his general centre. *The Wings of the Dove* happens to offer perhaps the most striking example I may cite (though with public penance for it already performed) of my regular failure to keep the appointed halves of my whole equal. Here the makeshift middle — for which the best I can say is that it's always rueful and never impudent — reigns with even more than its customary contrition, though passing itself off perhaps too with more than its usual craft. Nowhere, I seem to recall, had the need of dissimulation been felt so as anguish; nowhere had I condemned a luckless theme to complete its revolution burdened with the accumulation of its difficulties, the difficulties that grow with a theme's development in quarters so cramped. Of course, as every novelist knows, it is difficulty that inspires; only, for that perfection of charm, it must have been difficulty inherent and congenital, and not difficulty "caught" by the wrong frequentations. The latter half, that is the false and deformed half, of *The Wings* would verily, I think, form a signal object-lesson for a literary critic bent on improving his occasion to the profit of the budding artist. This whole corner of the picture bristles with "dodges" — such as he should feel himself all committed to recognise and page xviii / denounce — for disguising the reduced scale of the exhibition, for foreshortening at any cost, for imparting to patches the value of presences, for dressing objects in an *air* as of the dimensions they can't possibly have. Thus he would have his free hand for pointing out what a tangled web we weave when — well, when, through our mislaying or otherwise trifling with our blest pair of compasses, we have to produce the illusion of mass without the illusion of extent. *There* is a job quite to the measure of most of our monitors — and with the interest for them well enhanced by the preliminary cunning quest for the spot where deformity has begun.

I recognise meanwhile, throughout the long earlier reach of the book, not only no deformities but, I think, a positively close and felicitous application of method, the preserved consistencies of which, often illusive, but never really lapsing, it would be of a certain diversion, and might be of some profit, to follow. The author's accepted task at the outset has been to suggest with force the nature of the tie formed between the two young persons first introduced — to give the full impression of its peculiar worried and baffled, yet clinging and confident, ardour. The picture constituted, so far as may be, is that of a pair of natures wellnigh consumed by a sense of their intimate affinity and congruity, the reciprocity of their desire, and thus passionately impatient of barriers and delays, yet with qualities of intelligence and character that they are meanwhile extraordinarily able to draw upon for the enrichment of their relation, the extension of their prospect and the support of their "game." They are far from a common couple, Merton Densher and Kate Croy, as befits the remarkable fashion in which fortune was to waylay and opportunity was to distinguish them — the whole strange truth of their response to which opening involves also, in its order, no vulgar art of exhibition; but what they have most to tell us is that, all unconsciously and with the best faith in the world, all by mere force of the terms of their superior passion combined with their superior diplomacy, they are laying a trap for the great page xix / innocence to come. If I like, as I have confessed, the "portentous" look, I was perhaps never to set so high a value on it as for all this prompt provision of forces unwittingly waiting to close round my eager heroine (to the eventual deep chill of her eagerness) as the result of her mere lifting of a latch. Infinitely interesting to have built up the relation of the others to the point at which its aching restlessness, its need to affirm itself otherwise than by an exasperated patience, meets as with instinctive relief and recognition the possibilities shining out of Milly Theale. Infinitely interesting to have prepared and organised, correspondingly, that young woman's precipitations and liabilities, to have constructed, for Drama essentially to take possession, the whole bright house of her exposure.

These references, however, reflect too little of the detail of the treatment imposed; such a detail as I for instance get hold of in the fact of Densher's interview with Mrs. Lowder before he goes to America. It forms, in this preliminary picture, the one patch not strictly seen over Kate Croy's shoulder; though it's notable that immediately after, at the first possible moment, we surrender again to our major convenience, as it happens to be at the time, that of our drawing breath through the young woman's lungs. Once more, in other words, before we know it, Densher's direct vision of the scene at Lancaster Gate is replaced by her apprehension, her contributive assimilation, of his experience: it melts back into that accumulation, which we have been, as it were, saving up. Does my apparent deviation here count accordingly as a muddle? — one of the muddles ever blooming so thick in any soil that fails to grow reasons and determinants. No, distinctly not; for I had definitely opened the door, as attention of perusal of the first two Books will show, to the subjective community of my young pair. (Attention of perusal, I thus confess by the way, is what I at every point, as well as here, absolutely invoke and take for granted; a truth I avail myself of this occasion to note once for all — in the interest of that variety of ideal reigning, I gather, in the connexion. The enjoyment of a page xx / work of art, the acceptance of an irresistible illusion, constituting, to my sense, our highest experience of "luxury," the luxury is not greatest, by my consequent measure, when the work asks for as little attention as possible. It is greatest, it is delightfully, divinely great, when we feel the surface, like the thick ice of the skater's pond, bear without cracking the strongest pressure we throw on it. The sound of the crack one may recognise, but never surely to call it a luxury.) That I had scarce availed myself of the privilege of seeing with Densher's eyes is another matter; the point is that I had intelligently marked my possible, my occasional need of it. So, at all events, the constructional "block" of the first two Books compactly forms itself. A new block, all of the squarest and not a little of the smoothest, begins with the Third — by which I mean of course a new mass of interest governed from a new centre. Here again I make prudent *provision* — to be sure to keep my centre strong. It dwells mainly, we at once see, in the depths of Milly Theale's "case," where, close beside it, however, we meet a supplementary reflector, that of the lucid even though so quivering spirit of her dedicated friend.

The more or less associated consciousness of the two women deals thus, unequally, with the next presented face of the subject — deals with it to the exclusion of the dealing of others; and if, for a highly particular moment, I allot to Mrs. Stringham the responsibility of the direct appeal to us, it is again, charming to relate, on behalf of that play of the portentous which I cherish so as a "value" and am accordingly for ever setting in motion. There is an hour of evening, on the alpine height, at which it becomes of the last importance that our young woman should testify eminently in this direction. But as I was to find it long since of a blest wisdom that no expense should be incurred or met, in any corner of picture of mine, without some concrete image of the account kept of it, that is of its being organically re-economised, so under that dispensation Mrs. Stringham has to register the transaction. Book Fifth is a new block mainly in its provision of a new set of occasions, page xxi / which readopt, for their order, the previous centre, Milly's now almost full-blown consciousness. At my game, with renewed zest, of driving portents home, I have by this time all the choice of those that are to brush that surface with a dark wing. They are used, to our profit, on an elastic but a definite system; by which I mean that having to sound here and there a little deep, as a test, for my basis of method, I find it everywhere obstinately present. It draws the "occasion" into tune and keeps it so, to repeat my tiresome term; my nearest approach to muddlement is to have sometimes — but not too often — to break my occasions small. Some of them succeed in remaining ample and in really aspiring then to the higher, the sustained lucidity. The whole actual centre of the work, resting on a misplaced pivot and lodged in Book Fifth, pretends to a long reach, or at any rate to the larger foreshortening — though bringing home to me, on reperusal, what I find striking, charming and curious, the author's instinct everywhere for the *indirect* presentation of his main image. I note how, again and again, I go but a little way with the direct — that is with the straight exhibition of Milly; it resorts for relief, this process, whenever it can, to some kinder, some merciful indirection: all as if to approach her circuitously, deal with her at second hand, as an unspotted princess is ever dealt with; the pressure all round her kept easy for her, the sounds, the movements regulated, the forms and ambiguities made charming. All of which proceeds, obviously, from her painter's tenderness of imagination about her, which reduces him to watching her, as it were, through the successive windows of other people's interest in her. So, if we talk of princesses, do the balconies opposite the palace gates, do the coigns of vantage and respect enjoyed for a fee, rake from afar the mystic figure in the gilded coach as it comes forth into the great *place*. But my use of windows and balconies is doubtless at best an extravagance by itself, and as to what there may be to note, of this and other supersubtleties, other arch-refinements, of tact and taste, of design and instinct, in *The Wings of the Dove*, I become conscious of overstepping my space **page xxii /** without having brought the full quantity to light. The failure leaves me with a burden of residuary comment of which I yet boldly hope elsewhere to discharge myself.

HENRY JAMES. **page xxii /**

ARNOLD BENNETT

The Old Wives' Tale (1908)

Author's Preface

In the autumn of 1903 I used to dine frequently in a restaurant in the Rue de Clichy, Paris. Here were, among others, two waitresses that attracted my attention. One was a beautiful, pale young girl, to whom I never spoke, for she was employed far away from the table which I affected. The other, a stout, middle-aged managing Breton woman, had sole command over my table and me, and gradually she began to assume such a maternal tone towards me that I saw I should be compelled to leave that restaurant. If I was absent for a couple of nights running she would reproach me sharply: "What! you are unfaithful to me?" Once, when I complained about some French beans, she informed me roundly that French beans were a subject which I did not understand. I then decided to be eternally unfaithful to her, and I abandoned the restaurant. A few nights before the final parting an old woman came into the restaurant to dine. She was fat, shapeless, ugly, and grotesque. She had a ridiculous voice, and ridiculous gestures. It was easy to see that she lived alone, and that in the long lapse of years she had developed the kind of peculiarity which induces guffaws among the thoughtless. She was burdened with a lot of small parcels, which she kept dropping. She chose one seat; and then, not liking it, chose another; and then another. In a few moments she had the whole restaurant laughing at her. That my middle-aged Breton should laugh was indifferent to me, but I was pained to see a coarse grimace of giggling on the pale face of the beautiful young waitress to whom I had never spoken.

"Preface to This Edition," by Arnold Bennett, reprinted by permission from *The Old Wives' Tale* (New York: Random House, n.d.).

I reflected, concerning the grotesque diner: "This woman was once young, slim, perhaps beautiful; certainly free from these ridiculous mannerisms. Very prob- page v / ably she is unconscious of her sigularities. Her case is a tragedy. One ought to be able to make a heartrending novel out of the history of a woman such as she." Every stout, ageing woman is not grotesque — far from it! — but there is an extreme pathos in the mere fact that every stout ageing woman was once a young girl with the unique charm of youth in her form and movements and in her mind. And the fact that the change from the young girl to the stout ageing woman is made up of an infinite number of infinitesimal changes, each unperceived by her, only intensifies the pathos.

It was at this instant that I was visited by the idea of writing the book which ultimately became "The Old Wives' Tale." Of course I felt that the woman who caused the ignoble mirth in the restaurant would not serve me as a type of heroine. For she was much too old and obviously unsympathetic. It is an absolute rule that the principal character of a novel must not be unsympathetic, and the whole modern tendency of realistic fiction is against oddness in a prominent figure. I knew that I must choose the sort of woman who would pass unnoticed in a crowd.

I put the idea aside for a long time, but it was never very distant from me. For several reasons it made a special appeal to me. I had always been a convinced admirer of Mrs. W. K. Clifford's most precious novel, "Aunt Anne," but I wanted to see in the story of an old woman many things that Mrs. W. K. Clifford had omitted from "Aunt Anne." Moreover, I had always revolted against the absurd youthfulness, the unfading youthfulness of the average heroine. And as a protest against this fashion, I was already, in 1903, planning a novel ("Leonora") of which the heroine was aged forty, and had daughters old enough to be in love. The reviewers, by the way, were staggered by my hardihood in offering a woman of forty as a subject of serious interest to the public. But I meant to go much farther than forty! Finally as a supreme reason, I had the example and the challenge of Guy de Maupassant's "Une Vie." In the page vi / nineties we used to regard "Une Vie" with mute awe, as being the summit of achievement in fiction. And I remember being very cross with Mr. Bernard Shaw because, having read "Une Vie" at the suggestion (I think) of Mr. William Archer, he failed to see in it anything very remarkable. Here I must confess that, in 1908, I read "Une Vie" again, and in spite of a natural anxiety to differ from Mr. Bernard Shaw, I was gravely disappointed with it. It is a fine novel, but decidedly inferior to "Pierre et Jean" or even "Fort Comme la Mort." To return to the year 1903. "Une Vie" relates the entire life history of a woman. I settled in the privacy of my own head that my book about the development of a young girl into a stout old lady must be the English "Une Vie." I have been accused of every fault except a lack of self-confidence, and in a few weeks I settled a further point, namely, that my book must "go one better" than "Une Vie," and that to this end it must be the life-history of two women instead of only one. Hence, "The Old Wives' Tale" has two heroines. Constance was the original; Sophia was created out of bravado, just to indicate that I declined to consider Guy de Maupassant as the last forerunner of the deluge. I was intimidated by the audacity of my project, but I had sworn to carry it out. For several years I looked it squarely in the face at intervals, and then walked away to write novels of smaller scope, of which I produced five or six. But I could not dally forever, and in the autumn of 1907 I actually began to write it, in a village near Fontainebleau, where I rented half a house from a retired railway servant. I calculated that it would be 200,000 words long (which it exactly proved to be), and I had a vague notion that no novel of such dimensions (except Richardson's) had ever been written before. So I counted the words in several famous Victorian novels, and discovered to my relief that the famous Victorian novels average 400,000 words apiece. I wrote the first part of the novel in six weeks. It was fairly easy to me, because, in the seventies, in the first decade of my life, I had lived in the actual draper's shop of the Baines's, page vii / and knew it as only a child could know it. Then I went to London on a visit. I tried to continue the book in a London hotel, but London was too distracting, and I put the thing away, and during January and February of 1908, I wrote "Buried Alive," which was published immediately, and was received with majestic indifference by the English public, an indifference which has persisted to this day.

I then returned to the Fontainebleau region and gave "The Old Wives' Tale" no rest till I finished it at the end of July, 1908. It was published in the autumn of the same year, and for six weeks afterward the English public steadily confirmed an opinion expressed by a certain person in whose judgment I had confidence, to the effect that the work was honest but dull, and that when it was not dull it had a regrettable tendency to facetiousness. My publishers, though brave fellows, were somewhat disheartened; however, the reception of the book gradually became less and less frigid.

With regard to the French portion of the story, it was not until I had written the first part that I saw from a study of my chronological basis that the Siege of Paris might be brought into the tale. The idea was seductive; but I hated, and still hate, the awful business of research; and I only knew the Paris of the Twentieth Century. Now I was aware that my railway servant and his wife had been living in Paris at the time of the war. I said to the old man, "By the way, you went through the Siege of Paris, didn't you?" He turned to his old wife and said, uncertainly, "The Siege of Paris? Yes, we did, didn't we?" The Siege of Paris had been only one incident among many in their lives. Of course, they remembered it well, though not vividly, and I gained much information from them. But the most useful thing which I gained from them was the perception, startling at first, that ordinary people went on living very ordinary lives in Paris during the siege, and that to the vast mass of the population the siege was not the dramatic, spectacular, thrilling, ecstatic affair that is described in history. Encouraged by this perception, I decided to include the siege in my scheme. I read page viii / Sarcey's diary of the siege aloud to my wife, and I looked at the pictures in Jules Claretie's popular work on the siege and the commune, and I glanced at the printed collection of official documents, and there my research ended.

It has been asserted that unless I had actually been present at a public execution, I could not have written the chapter in which Sophia was at the Auxerre solemnity. I have not been present at a public execution, as the whole of my information about public executions was derived from a series of articles on them which I read in the Paris *Matin*. Mr. Frank Harris, discussing my book in "Vanity Fair," said it was clear that I had not seen an execution, (or words to that effect), and he proceeded to give his own description of an execution. It was a brief but terribly convincing bit of writing, quite characteristic and quite worthy of the author of "Montes the Matador" and of a man who has been almost everywhere and seen almost everything. I comprehended how far short I had fallen of the truth! I wrote to Mr. Harris, regretting that his description had not been printed before I wrote mine, as I should assuredly have utilized it, and, of course, I admitted that I had never witnessed an execution. He simply replied: "Neither have I." This detail is worth preserving, for it is a reproof to that large body of readers, who, when a novelist has really carried conviction to them, assert off hand: "O, that must be autobiography!"

ARNOLD BENNETT page ix /

D. H. LAWRENCE

Sons and Lovers (1913)

Author's Letter

Postcard to Edward Garnett.

I was fearfully anxious to write a foreword to *Sons and Lovers*, and this is what I did. I am a fool — but it will amuse you.

I am glad you think my prospects so good. It is raining here. I wonder how that rheumatism of yours is. I'll write immediately.

Did Harold give you all your books back?

D. H. L.

Foreword to Sons and Lovers.

To Edward Garnett.

John, the beloved disciple, says, "The Word was made page 97 / Flesh." But why should he turn things round? The women simply go on bearing talkative sons, as an answer. "The Flesh was made Word."

For what was Christ? He was Word, or He became Word. What remains of Him? No flesh remains on earth, from Christ; perhaps some carpentry He shaped with His hands retains somewhere His flesh-print; and then His word, like His carpentry just the object that His flesh produced, is the rest. He is Word. And the Father was Flesh. For even if it were by the Holy Ghost His spirit were begotten, yet flesh cometh only out of flesh. So the Holy Ghost must either have been, or have borne from the Father, at least one grain of flesh. The Father was Flesh — and the Son, who in Himself was finite and had form, became Word.

Reprinted, by permission, from *The Letters of D. H. Lawrence*, edited by Aldous Huxley (New York: The Viking Press, 1932).

For form is the uttered Word, and the Son is the flesh as it utters the Word, but the unutterable Flesh is the Father.

And the Word is not spoken by the Father, who is Flesh, forever unquestioned and unanswerable, but by the Son. Adam was the first Christ: not the Word made Flesh, but the Flesh made word. Out of the Flesh cometh the Word, and the Word is finite, as a piece of carpentry, and hath an end. But the Flesh is infinite and has no end. Out of the Flesh cometh the Word, which blossoms for a moment and is no more. Out of the Flesh hath come every Word, and in the Flesh lies every Word that will be uttered. The Father is the Flesh, the eternal and unquestionable, the law-giver but not the law; whereas the Son is the mouth. And each law is a fabric that must crumble away, and the Word is a graven image that is worn down, and forsaken, like the Sphinx in the desert.

We are the Word, we are not the Flesh. The Flesh is beyond us. And when we love our neighbour as ourself, we love that word, our neighbour, and not that flesh. For that Flesh is not our neighbour, it is the Father, which is in Heaven, and forever beyond our knowledge. We are the Word, we know the Word, and the Word alone is ours. When we say "I," we mean "The Word I am." This flesh I am is beyond me.

So that if we love our neighbour, we love that Word, our neighbour, and we hate that Lie, our neighbour, which is a deformity. With that Flesh, our neighbour, We, the Word-**page 98 /** Utterer, have nothing to do. For the Son is not greater than the Father. And if we love and subserve that Flesh, our neighbour, which is the Father, it is only by denying and desecrating the Father in ourselves. For the Father is the Almighty. The Flesh will feel no pain that is not upon itself, and will know no hurt but its own destruction. But no man can destroy the Almighty, yet he can deny Him. And pain is a denial of the Father. If then we feel the pain and suffering of our neighbour's flesh, we are putting destruction upon our own flesh, which is to deny and make wrathful the Father. Which we have done. For in loving our neighbour, the Flesh, as ourself, we have said, "There is no Father, there is only the Word." For it is the Word hath charity, not the Flesh. And it is the Word that answereth the cry of the Word. But if the Word, hearing a cry, shall say, "My flesh is destroyed, the bone melteth away," that is to blaspheme the Father. For the Word is but fabric builded of the Flesh. And when the fabric is finished, then shall the Flesh enjoy it in its hour.

But we have said, "Within this fabric of the Word the Flesh is held." And so, the Son has usurped the Father. And so, the Father, which is the Flesh, withdraws from us, and the Word stands in ruins, as Nineveh and Egypt are dead words on the plains, whence the Flesh has withdrawn itself. For the lesser cannot contain the greater, nor the Son contain the Father, but he is of the Father.

And it is upon the head of that nation that shall deny the Father. For the Flesh will depart from that collective Word, the nation, and that great nation shall remain as a Word in ruin, its own monument.

For who shall say, "No child shall be borne of me and my wife. I, the Word, have said it"? And who shall say — "That woman whom my flesh, in its unquestionable sincerity, cleaveth toward, shall not come unto my flesh. But my Word shall come unto her. I, the Word have said it"? That is to usurp the flesh of my neighbour, and hold governance over it by the word. And who shall say, "That woman shall be Flesh of my Flesh. I, the Word, have said it"? For either the woman is Flesh of my Flesh, or she is not, and the Word altereth nothing, but can only submit or deny. **page 99 /**

And when we burned the heretic at the stake, then did we love that Word, our neighbour, and hate that lie, the heretic. But we did also deny the Father, and say, "There is only Word." And when we suffer in our flesh the pangs of those that hunger, then we do deny the Flesh, and say, it is not. For the Flesh suffereth not from the hunger of the neighbour, but only from its own hunger. But the Word loveth its neighbour, and shall answer to the cry of the Word, "It is just, what thou askest." For the Word hath neither passion nor pain, but lives and moves in equity. It has charity, which we call love. But only the Flesh has love, for that is the Father, and in love he begets us all, of love are we begotten. But it was spoken, "They shall be one Flesh." Thus did the Word usurp the Father, saying, "I unite you one flesh." Whereas the Word can but confirm. For the twain are one flesh, whether the Word speak or not. And if they be not one twain, then the Word can never make them so, for the Flesh is not contained in the Word, but the Word in the Flesh. But if a man shall say, "This woman is flesh of my flesh," let him see to it that he be not blaspheming the Father. For the woman is not flesh of his flesh, by the bidding of the Word; but it is of the Father. And if he take a woman, saying in the arrogance of the Word, "The flesh of that woman is goodly," then he has said, "The flesh of that woman is goodly as a servant unto the Word, which is me," and so hath blasphemed the Father, by which he has his being, and she hath her being. And the Flesh shall forsake these two, they shall be fabric of Word. And their race shall perish.

But if in my passion I slay my neighbour, it is no sin of mine, but it is his sin, for he should not have permitted me. But if my Word shall decide and decree that my neighbour die, then that is sin, for the Word destroyeth the Flesh, the Son blasphemeth the Father. And yet, if a man hath denied his Flesh, saying, "I, the Word, have dominion over the flesh of my neighbour," then shall the Flesh, his neighbour, slay him in self-defence. For a man may hire my Word, which is the utterance of my flesh, which is my work. But my Flesh is the Father, which is before the Son.

And so it was written: "The Word was made Flesh," then, **page 100 /** as corollary, "And of the Flesh was made Flesh-of-the-Flesh, woman." This is again backward, and because the Son, struggling to utter the Word, took for his God the accomplishment of his work, the Uttered Word. Out of his flesh the Word had to come, and the flesh was difficult and unfathomed, so it was called the servant. And the servant of the servant was woman. So the Son arranged it, because he took for his God his own work when it should be accomplished: as if a carpenter called the chair he struggled with but had not yet made, God. But the Chair is not a god, it is only a rigid image. So is the Word a rigid image, parallel of the chair. And so the end having been chosen for the beginning, the whole chronology is upside-down: the Word created Man, and Man lay down and gave birth to Woman. Whereas we know the Woman lay in travail, and gave birth to Man, who in his hour uttered his word.

It is as if a bit of apple-blossom stood for God in his Wonder, the apple was the Son, as being something more gross but still wonderful, while the pip that comes out of the apple, like Adam's rib, is the mere secondary produce, that is spat out, and which, if it falls to the ground, just happens to start the process of apple-tree going again. But the little pip that one spits out has in it all the blossom and apples, as well as all the tree, the leaves, the perfume, the drops of gum, and heaven knows what else that we never see, contained by miracle in its bit of white flesh: and the tree, the leaves, the flowers themselves, and the apple are only amplifications of this little seed, spent: which never has amplified itself enough, but can go on to other than just five-petalled flowers and little brown apples, if we did but know.

So we take the seed as the starting point in this cycle. The woman is the Flesh. She produces all the rest of the flesh, including the intermediary pieces called man — and these curious pieces called man are like stamens that can turn into exquisite-coloured petals. That is, they can beat out the stuff of their life thin, thin, thin, till it is a pink or a purple petal, or a thought, or a word. And when it is so beaten out that it ceases to be begetting stuff, of the Father, but is spread much wider, expanded and showy: then we say, "This is the Utmost!" — as everybody will agree that a rose is only a rose because of the page 101 / petals, and that the rose is the utmost of all that flow of life, called "Rose." But what is really "Rose" is only in that quivering, shimmering flesh of flesh which is the same, unchanged for ever, a constant stream, called if you like rodoplasm, the eternal, the unquestionable, the infinite of the Rose, the Flesh, the Father — which were more properly, the Mother.

So there is the Father — which should be called Mother — then the Son, who is the Utterer, and then the Word. And the Word is that of the Father which, through the Son, is tossed away. It is that part of the Flesh in the Son which is capable of spreading out thin and fine, losing its concentration and completeness, ceasing to be a begetter, and becoming only a vision, a flutter of petals, God rippling through the Son till he breaks in a laugh, called a blossom, that shines and is gone. The vision itself, the flutter of petals, the rose, the Father through the Son wasting himself in a moment of consciousness, consciousness of his own infinitude and gloriousness, a Rose, a Clapping of the Hands, a Spark of Joy thrown off from the Fire to die ruddy in mid-darkness, a Snip of Flame, the Holy Ghost, the Revelation. And so, the eternal Trinity.

And God the Father, the Inscrutable, the Unknowable, we

know in the Flesh, in Woman. She is the door for our in-going and our out-coming. In her we go back to the Father: but like the witnesses of the Transfiguration, blind and unconscious.

Yea, like bees in and out of a hive, we come backwards and forwards to our woman. And the Flowers of the World are Words, are Utterance — "Uttering glad leaves," Whitman said. And we are bees that go between, from the flowers home to the hive and the Queen; for she lies at the centre of the hive, and stands in the way of bees for God the Father, the Almighty, the Unknowable, the Creator. In her all things are born, both words and bees. She is the quick of all the change, the labour, the production.

And the bee, who is a Son, comes home to his Queen as to the Father, in service and humility, for suggestion, and renewal, and identification which is the height of his glory, for begetting. And again the bee goes forth to attend the flowers, the Word in his pride and masterfulness of new strength and new wisdom. And as he comes and goes, so shall man for ever come and go: **page 102 /** go to his work, his Uttering, wherein he is masterful and proud; come home to his woman, through whom is God the Father, and who is herself, whether she will have it or not, God the Father, before whom the man in his hour is full of reverence, and in whom he is glorified and hath the root of his pride.

But not only does he come and go: it is demanded of him that he come and go. It is the systole and diastole of the Heart, that shall be. The bee comes home to the hive, and the hive expels him to attend the flowers. The hive draws home the bee, the bee leaps off the threshold of the hive, with strength, and is gone. He carries home to the hive his essence, of flowers, his joy in the Word he has uttered, he flies forth again from the hive, carrying to the flowers the strength and vigour of his scrambling body, which is God Almighty in him. So he fetches and carries, carries and fetches.

So the man comes home to woman and to God, so God the Father receives his Son again, a man of the undying flesh; and so the man goes forth from the house of his woman, so God expels him forth to waste himself in utterance, in work, which is only God the Father realizing himself in a moment of forgetfulness. Thus the eternal working. And it is joy enough to see it, without asking why. For it is as if the Father took delight in seeing himself for a moment unworking, for a moment wasting himself that he might know himself. For every petalled flower, which alone is a Flower, is a work of productiveness. It is a moment of joy, of saying, "I am I." And every table or chair a man makes is a self-same waste of his life, a fixing into stiffness and deadness of a moment of himself, for the sake of the glad cry: "This is I — I am I." And this glad cry, when we know, is the Holy Ghost, the Comforter.

So, God Eternal, the Father, continues, doing we know not what, not why: we only know He is. And again and again comes the exclamation of joy, or of pain which is joy — like Galileo and Shakespeare and Darwin — which announces "I am I."

And in the woman is the eternal continuance, and from the man, in the human race, comes the exclamation of joy and astonishment at new self-revelation, revelation of that which is Woman to a man.

Now every woman, according to her kind, demands that a **page 103 /** man shall come home to her with joy and weariness of the work he has done during the day: that he shall then while he is with her, be re-born of her; that in the morning he shall go forth with his new strength.

But if the man does not come home to a woman, leaving her to take account of him, but is a stranger to her; if when he enters her house, he does not become simply her man of flesh, entered into her house as if it were her greater body, to be warmed, and restored, and nourished, from the store the day has given her, then she shall expel him from her house, as a drone. It is as inevitable as the working of the bees, as that a stick shall go down stream.

For in the flesh of the woman does God exact Himself. And out of the flesh of the woman does He demand: "Carry this of Me forth to utterance." And if the man deny, or be too weak, then shall the woman find another man, of greater strength. And if, because of the Word, which is the Law, she do not find another man, nor he another woman, then shall they both be destroyed. For he, to get that rest, and warmth, and nourishment which he should have had from her, his woman, must consume his own flesh, and so destroy himself: whether with wine, or other kindling. And she, either her surplus shall wear away her flesh, in sickness, or in lighting up and illuminating old dead Words, or she shall spend it in fighting with her man to make him take her, or she shall turn to her son, and say, "Be you my Go-between."

But the man who is the go-between from Woman to Production is the lover of that woman. And if that woman be his mother, then is he her lover in part only; he carries for her, but is never received into her for his confirmation and renewal, and so wastes himself away in the flesh. The old son-lover was Œdipus. The name of the new one is legion. And if a son-lover take a wife, then is she not his wife, she is only his bed. And his life will be torn in twain, and his wife in her despair shall hope for sons, that she may have her lover in her hour.

D. H. LAWRENCE.

Gargnano. Jan., 1913. page 104 /

The Rainbow (1915)

AUTHOR'S LETTER

Lerici, per Fiascherino,
Golfo della Spezia, Italia.
5 *Junio*, 1914.

To Edward Garnett.

DEAR GARNETT, —

First let me remember to thank you for letting the two books be sent to the Consul in Spezia.

About Pinker, I will do as you say, and tell him that the matter of the novel is not yet settled, and I will call on him in some fifteen or twenty days.

I don't agree with you about the *Wedding Ring* [*The Rainbow*]. You will find that in a while you will like the book as a

Reprinted, by permission, from *The Letters of D. H. Lawrence*, edited by Aldous Huxley (New York: The Viking Press, 1932).

whole. I don't think the psychology is wrong: it is only that I have a different attitude to my characters, and that necessitates a different attitude in you, which you are not prepared to give. As for its being my *cleverness* which would pull the thing through — that sounds odd to me, for I don't think I am so very clever, in that way. I think the book is a bit futuristic — quite unconsciously so. But when I read Marinetti — "the profound intuitions of life added one to the other, word by word, according to their illogical conception, will give us the general lines of an intuitive physiology of matter" — I see something of what I am after. I translate him clumsily, and his Italian is obfuscated — and I don't care about physiology of matter — but somehow — that which is physic — non-human, in humanity, is more interesting to me than the old-fashioned human element — which causes one to conceive a character in a certain moral **page 199 /** scheme and make him consistent. The certain moral scheme is what I object to. In Turgenev, and in Tolstoy, and in Dostoievsky, the moral scheme into which all the caracters fit — and it is nearly the same scheme — is, whatever the extraordinariness of the characters themselves, dull, old, dead. When Marinetti writes: "It is the solidity of a blade of steel that is interesting by itself, that is, the incomprehending and inhuman alliance of its molecules in resistance to, let us say, a bullet. The heat of a piece of wood or iron is in fact more passionate, for us, than the laughter or tears of a woman" — then I know what he means. He is stupid, as an artist, for contrasting the heat of the iron and the laugh of the woman. Because what is interesting in the laugh of the woman is the same as the binding of the molecules of steel or their action in heat: it is the inhuman will, call it physiology, or like Marinetti — physiology of matter, that fascinates me. I don't so much care about what the woman *feels* — in the ordinary usage of the word. That presumes an *ego* to feel with. I only care about what the woman *is* — what she IS — inhumanly, physiologically, materially — according to the use of the word: but for me, what she *is* as a phenomenon (or as representing some greater, inhuman will), instead of what she feels according to the human conception. That is where the futurists are stupid. Instead of looking for the new human phenomenon, they will only look for the phenomena of the science of physics to be found in human beings. They are crassly stupid. But if anyone would give them eyes, they would pull the right apples off the tree, for their stomachs are true in appetite. You musn't look in my novel for the old stable ego of the character. There is another ego, according to whose action the individual is unrecognizable, and passes through, as it were, allotropic states which it needs a deeper sense than any we've been used to exercise, to discover are states of the same single radically-unchanged element. (Like as diamond and coal are the same pure single element of carbon. The ordinary novel would trace the history of the diamond — but I say, "Diamond, what! This is carbon." And my diamond might be coal or soot, and my theme is carbon.) You must not say my novel is shaky — it is not perfect, because I am not expert in what I want to do. But it is the real thing, say what you like. page 200 / And I shall get my reception, if not now, then before long. Again I say, don't look for the development of the novel to follow the lines of certain characters: the characters fall into the form of some other rhythmic form, as when one draws a fiddle-bow across a fine tray delicately sanded, the sand takes lines unknown.

I hope this won't bore you. We leave here on Monday, the 8th. Frieda will stay in Baden-Baden some 10–14 days. I am not going by sea, because of the filthy weather. I am walking across Switzerland into France with Lewis, one of the skilled engineers of Vickers-Maxim works here. I shall let you know my whereabouts.

Don't get chilly and disagreeable to me.

Au revoir,

D. H. Lawrence.

I shall be awfully glad to see Bunny again — and Mrs. Garnett and you.

Please keep this letter, because I want to write on futurism and it will help me. I will come and see Duckworth. Give *Bunny* my novel — I want *him* to understand it. page 201 /

ANDRÉ GIDE

The Counterfeiters (1926)

Author's Notebooks

FIRST NOTEBOOK

17 June 1919

For two days I have been wondering whether or not to have my novel related by Lafcadio. Thus it would be a narrative of gradually revealed events in which he would act as an observer, an idler, a perverter. I do not think this would necessarily restrict the scope of the book, but it would prevent me from approaching certain subjects, entering certain circles, influencing certain characters. . . . On the other hand it would probably be foolish to collect into a single novel everything life offers me and teaches me. However closely packed I want this book to be, I cannot hope to get everything in. And yet this desire still bothers me. I am like a musician striving, in the manner of César Franck, to juxtapose and overlap an andante theme and an allegro theme.

I think I have enough material for two books, and I am starting this notebook in an effort to distinguish the elements of widely differing tonality.

The story of the two sisters. The elder, against the will of her parents (she elopes) marries a vain, worthless person who nevertheless has enough polish to win over the family after he has won over the girl. The family, deceived by the swarm of virtues their son-in-law is able to simulate, forgives her and makes due amends. Meanwhile the girl discovers little by little the basic **page 373 /** mediocrity of this person to whom she has tied herself for life. She hides from everyone the scorn and disgust she feels for him,

---

Reprinted, by permission, from *The Counterfeiters, with Journal of "The Counterfeiters"* (New York: Alfred A. Knopf, 1951). See Bibliographical Note C, page xv.

takes it upon herself as a point of honor to show off her husband to best advantage, to hide his inadequacy, and to make up for his blunders, so that she alone knows upon what a void her "happiness" rests. Everywhere this couple is cited as an ideal one; and the day when, at the end of her rope, she would like to leave this puppet and live apart, it is she whom everyone blames. (The question of the children to be examined separately).

I have noted elsewhere (gray notebook) the case of the seducer who eventually becomes the prisoner of the deed he planned to perpetrate — after he has drained all its attractions in advance in his imagination.

There would not necessarily have to be two sisters. It is never good to *oppose* one character to another, or to contrive antitheses (deplorable device of the romantics).

Never present *ideas* except in terms of temperaments and characters. I should, by the way, have this expressed by one of my characters (the novelist) — "Persuade yourself that opinions do not exist outside of individuals. The trouble with most people is that they think they have freely accepted or chosen the opinions they profess, which are actually as predetermined and ordained as the color of their hair or the odor of their breath. . . ."

Show why, to young people, the preceding generation seem so staid, so resigned, and so reasonable that it seems doubtful if they in their own youth were ever tormented by the same aspirations, the same fevers, ever cherished the same ambitions or hid the same desires.

The censure of those who "come around" for the person who remains faithful to his youth and does not *give up*. He is apparently the one in the wrong.

I am writing on a separate page the first vague outlines of the plot (one of the possible plots). page 374 /

The two characters remain nonexistent so long as they are not baptized.

There always comes a moment, just before the moment of composition, when a subject seems stripped of all attraction, all charm, all atmosphere, even bare of all significance. At last, losing all interest in it, you curse that sort of secret pact whereby you have committed yourself, and which makes it impossible for you to back out honorably. In spite of this, you would still rather quit. . . .

I say "you," but actually I do not know whether others feel this way. It is probably similar to the condition of the convert who, the last few days, on the point of approaching the altar, feels his faith suddenly falter and takes fright at the emptiness and dryness of his heart.

19 June

Probably it is not very clever to place the action of this book *before* the war, or to include *historical* considerations; I cannot be retrospective and immediate at the same time. Actually I am not trying to be *immediate;* if left to my inclination, I should rather be *future.*

"A precise portrait of the prewar state of mind" — no, even if I could succeed in that, it is not what I am trying to do. The future interests me more than the past, but even more what belongs neither to tomorrow nor to yesterday but which in all times can be said to belong to today.

Cuverville, 20 June

A day of abominable lethargy, the like of which, alas, I think I have never known except here. The influence of the weather, of the climate? I do not know; I drag myself from one task to an- page 375 / other, incapable of writing the least letter, of understanding what I read, or even of doing the simplest piano scale correctly; incapable even of sleeping when, in a desperate attempt to escape from myself, I stretch out on my bed.

As a matter of fact, the moment I start to lie down, I feel my thoughts spring to life; and, ashamed of having put my day to such poor use, I prolong my reading of Browning's *Death in the Desert* until midnight. I miss many details, but it sets my brain in ferment like the headiest of wines.

I say that man was made to grow, not stop;
That help, he needed once, and needs no more
Having grown but an inch by, is withdrawn,
For he hath new needs, and new helps to these,
(etc. V, 425)

which I copy out for the use of Lafcadio.

6 July 1919

Work cut short by the arrival at Cuverville of Copeau, back from America. I go to fetch him at Havre.

I read him the still tentative opening of the book; became rather clearly aware of the use I could make of this unusual form.

It would be wisest not to worry too much about the sterile periods. They ventilate the subject and instill into it the reality of daily life.

I think I can find a better setting than a café for the conversation on general topics I should like to use to open the book. I was tempted by the very banality of the locale. But it would be better not to make use of any setting unrelated to the action. *Everything that cannot be of use encumbers.* Thus this morning I have been considering the Luxembourg Gardens — more precisely, that page 376 / part of the park where the traffic in counterfeit gold pieces takes place behind Lafcadio's back and without his suspecting it — at the very time he is listening to and noting down that conversation on general topics, so very serious, which, however, one small definite fact is presently to render meaningless. Édouard, who sent him there to spy, is to tell him: "My boy, you don't know how to observe; this is the important thing that was going on" — thereupon producing the box full of counterfeit coins.

11 July

Furious with myself for having let so much time slip away without profit for the book. I tried in vain to persuade myself that it is ripening. I ought to be thinking about it more and not allow myself to be distracted by the petty details of everyday life. The truth is that it has not advanced a step since Cuverville. At most I have felt more urgently the need of establishing a relationship between the scattered elements. Yet I should like to avoid the artificiality of a "plot"; but events must fit into a pattern independently of Lafcadio: behind his back, so to speak. I expect too much from inspiration; it should come as the result of seeking. I am willing that the solution to a problem should appear in a sudden flash, but only after it has been studied at length.

16 July

This morning I took out once again the various newspaper clippings concerning the case of the counterfeiters. I am sorry not to have saved more of them. They are from the *Journal de Rouen* (Sept. 1906). I think I shall have to begin from there without trying any longer to construct *a priori.*

I am saving the following, which I have a notion to use as the motto for the first book: page 377 /

> When the judge asked Fréchaut if he had been a member of the Luxembourg "gang":
> "Let's call it 'the coterie,' your honor," he replied warmly. "It was a gathering where we dealt in counterfeit money, I don't deny that; but we were principally concerned with questions of politics and literature."

Essential to connect this to the case of the anarchist counterfeiters of 7 and 8 August 1907—and to the sinister account of the schoolboys' suicides at Clermont-Ferrand (5 June 1909). Weld this into a single homogeneous plot.

25 July

The pastor, upon learning that his son at twenty-six is no longer the chaste youth that he thought, exclaims: "Would to heaven he had been killed in the war! Would to God he had never been born!"

What judgment can a decent man make of a religion that puts such words into the mouth of a father?

It is out of hatred for this religion, this morality that oppressed his whole youth, out of hatred for this puritanism he himself has never been able to shed, that Z. strives to debauch and pervert the pastor's children. Some rancor is involved in this. Forced and counterfeit sentiments.

The counterfeiters' company (the "coterie") admits only *compromised* persons. Each one of the members must offer as a forfeit something by which he might be blackmailed.

Herewith a definition of friendship I got from Méral: "A friend," he says, "is somebody with whom you'd be happy to do a bad deed." page 378 /

X. (one of the pastor's sons) is led to gamble by the debaucher. To provide for the expense of M.'s childbirth (his final charitable action) he had set aside a comfortable and painfully acquired sum saved (or perhaps diverted from the family budget). He loses it; then, several days later, wins part of it back. But an odd thing takes place: during the time he had given it up for lost, he became so resigned to the loss that when he wins it back, the money seems no longer assigned to M. and he thinks only of spending it.

The periods will have to be clearly distinguished:

1ST. A noble (or charitable) motive that he advances to clothe a cheap trick. He knows very well that his family will need the money, but he is not diverting it out of selfishness (the sophism of the virtuous motive).

2ND. The sum recognized as insufficient. Chimerical hope and urgent necessity of augmenting it.

3RD. Necessity, after the loss, of feeling "above misfortune."

4TH. Renunciation of the "virtuous motive." Theory of the gratuitous and *unmotivated* action. Immediate joy.

5TH. Winner's intoxication. Absence of *reserve*.

Dudelange, 26 July

I am working in Mme. M.'s library — one of the most delightful laboratories one could imagine. Only the fear of interfering with her own work now hampers my studious satisfaction. The idea of obtaining anything whatsoever at someone else's expense paralyzes me. (Incidentally, this is no doubt one of the best of moral curbs; but it is with difficulty that I persuade myself that others can find the same joy as I do from aiding and encouraging.)

The first big question to be examined is this: can I portray all the action of my book through Lafcadio? I do not think so. Probably the point of view of Lafcadio is too narrow to make it desirable to use it all the way through without a break. But what page 379 / other way is there of presenting *the remainder*? It might be foolish to seek to avoid at all costs the simple impersonal narration.

28 July

Yesterday I spent the day convincing myself that I cannot make everything take place through Lafcadio; but I should like to have successive interpreters; for example, Lafcadio's notes would occupy the first book; the second book might consist of Édouard's notebook; the third of an attorney's file, etc.

I am trying to wind up the various threads of the plot and the complexities of my thoughts around the little living bobbins that are my characters.

30 July

I cannot aim to be simultaneously precise and timeless. If my story leaves any doubt whether it is before or after the war, it will be because I have remained too abstract.

For instance, the whole story of the counterfeit gold pieces can only occur before the war, since at the present gold pieces are outlawed. Likewise, thoughts and preoccupations are no longer the same; in seeking a more general interest, I am taking a chance of losing my footing.

It would be better to go back to my original idea: the book in two sections — before and after. This could be turned to good account: everyone finding corroboration of his ideas in the war, and emerging from the ordeal a little more rigid in his opinion. The three positions, socialist, nationalist, and Christian, each edified and strengthened by events. And all this through the fault of half-measures which allow each party to believe that if its interests had not been compromised, the thing would have worked out better and nothing disastrous would have taken place.

It is not so much by offering a solution to certain problems that I can render a real service to the reader as in actually forcing him to think for himself about these problems, for which I page 380 / am loath to admit that there can be any other solution than an individual and personal one.

The tramp that Lafcadio meets on his way back from Marseille must serve as a connecting link between him and Édouard. It would be totally useless at present to try to write the dialogue between Lafcadio and the tramp; I can't even sketch out the latter until I know a little more about the role I want him to play in the end.

1 August

Groped in the clouds for hours on end. This effort to externalize an interior creation, to objectify the subject (before having to subjectify the object) is peculiarly exhausting. For days and days you can make nothing out, and it seems as though the effort has been useless; the important thing is not to give up. To navigate for days on end without any land in sight — this image must be used in the book itself; most artists, scholars, etc. are coastwise sailors who imagine they are lost as soon as they get out of sight of land. — The dizziness of empty space.

5 August

I have been so exasperated by the difficulties of my undertaking — actually, I saw nothing else — that I have turned from the job for some time to get back to writing my Memoirs. Or at least I dissemble, I stray onto tangents, I beat about. But in spite of myself I am forever coming back to it; I think it seems the more difficult to me the more I aim to make it conform to the conventional form of the novel, and that many of these so-called difficulties will collapse as soon as I become definitely reconciled to its originality. Why, as soon as I accept it to be incomparable page 381 / with anything else (and that's the way I want it), why so much searching for a motivation, a development, the forming of a pattern around a central plot? Perhaps with the form I adopt I can find a way to have all that criticized indirectly: for example, Lafcadio could try in vain to tie the threads together; there would be unnecessary characters, ineffectual acts, pointless remarks, and the action *would not* get under way.

Dudelange, 16 August

In Stendhal no phrase evokes the one after it or takes life from the preceding one. Each one stands perpendicular to the fact or idea. Suarès speaks admirably of Stendhal; you couldn't hope for better.

9 September

A month without writing anything in this notebook. An airing out. Anything is better than a bookish odor.

Book I: *The Shrewd and Crafty*
Book II: *Old Wine and New Bottles*
Book III: *The Unfaithful Custodian*

Of all the instruments that have ever been used for sketching or writing, Stendhal's traces the most delicate line. **page 382 /**

21 November 1920

Remained several months without writing anything in this notebook; but I have hardly ever stopped thinking of the novel, although my most immediate concern is for the writing of *Si le grain ne meurt* . . . one of the most important chapters of which (the trip to Algeria with Paul) I wrote this summer. Even while writing it I was led to think that intimacy, insight, psychological investigation can in certain respects be carried even further in the "novel" than in "confessions." In the latter one is sometimes hampered by the "I"; there are some complexities one cannot try to disentangle, to expose without seeming self-centered. Everything I have seen, everything I have learned, everything that has happened to me for several months, I should like to get into this novel, where it will serve to enrich the texture. I should like events never to be related directly by the author, but instead exposed (and several times from different vantages) by those actors who will be influenced by those events. In their account of the action I should like the events to appear slightly warped; the reader will take a sort of interest from the mere fact of having to *reconstruct*. The story requires his collaboration in order to take shape properly.

Thus the whole story of the counterfeiters is to be discovered only in a gradual way through the conversations, by which all the characters will portray themselves at the same time.

Cuverville, 1 January 1921

I infinitely admire Martin du Gard's assiduity, as I do Bennett's. But I am not sure this system of notes and filing cards he recommends would have been of much help to me; the very preciseness of a recollection noted in such a way hampers it, or at page 383 / least would hamper me. I stick to Wilde's paradox: nature copies art. The artist's rule should be never to restrict himself to what nature proposes, but to propose nothing to nature but what nature can and should shortly imitate.

2 January

The treatise on the nonexistence of the Devil. The more we deny him, the more reality we give him. The Devil is affirmed in our negation.

Last night wrote several pages of dialogue on this subject—which might very well become the central subject of the whole book; in other words, the invisible point about which everything gravitates. . . .

Success in the worst, and deterioration of the most exquisite qualities.

I shall take Martin du Gard to task for the discursive gait of his narrative. His novelist's lamp, wending through the passing years, always illuminates head-on the events he is considering as each one in succession moves into the foreground. Their lives never mingle and there is no more perspective than there is shadow. This is just what bothers me in Tolstoy. They both paint panoramas; art lies in creating a picture. *First* study the source of the light; all the shadows depend on that. Every form rests on and finds support in its shadow.

Admit that a character who is exiting can only be seen from the rear.

To write this book properly I must persuade myself that it is the only novel and final book I shall write. I want to pour everything into it without reservation. page 384 /

If Stendhal's "crystallization" is sudden, the pathetic element lies in the gradual contrary process of *decrystallization*; worth examining. When time and age strip from love one by one all its *points of reference* and force it to take refuge in some mystical adoration or other, some altar upon which the lover hangs as an ex-voto all the souvenirs of the past: her smile, her bearing, her voice, the details of her beauty.

He comes to the point of asking himself: what does he still love in her? The surprising thing is that he still feels that he loves her *desperately* — I mean to say: with a hopeless love, for she no longer believes in his love because of his previous "infidelities" (I am purposely using the most deceptive term) of a purely carnal sort. But precisely because he loved her above and beyond sensuality (of a gross sort, at least), his love remains safe from any danger of ruin.

He is jealous of God, who is stealing his wife from him. Vanquished in advance, he feels incapable of struggle; but he conceives a hatred for this rival and everything connected with Him. What a paltry thing is this petty human happiness he is offering her, compared with eternal bliss!

13 January

I must note here nothing but remarks of a general sort on the planning, composition, and guiding motive of the novel. This journal must become to some extent "Édouard's notebook." In addition I am noting on cards things that might be of help: various materials, dialogues, scraps of conversation, and especially anything that may help me in sketching characters.

Of these I should like one character (the Devil) to circulate incognito throughout the entire book, his reality growing stronger the less the other characters believe in him. This is the distin-
page 385 / guishing feature of the devil, whose introductory motif is: "Why should you be afraid of me? You know very well I don't exist."

I have already written a section of dialogue the sole purpose of which is to introduce and explain this extremely important remark, one of the catchwords of the book. But the dialogue itself (such as I have scribbled it down) is very poor and will have to be completely recast in the book, set into the action.

The great error of the dialogues in X.'s book is that his characters are forever speaking to the reader; the author has given them his job of explaining everything. Take constant care that a character speak only for the benefit of the one to whom he is addressing himself.

There is one sort of character who can speak only for an imaginary "gallery" (impossibility of being sincere, even in a monologue) — but this case is quite special and can stand out only if the others, on the contrary, remain utterly natural.

Paris, 22 April 1921

While I waited for my luggage, on the arrival of the train that brought me back from Brignoles, the opening scene of *The Counterfeiters* became clear to me in a sudden flash: Édouard and Lafcadio meeting on a station platform, the ice broken with the sentence: "I'll bet you are traveling without a ticket." (I used this sentence to approach the odd vagrant in the Tarascon station I speak about in my journal.) All this now seems quite mediocre to me, at least greatly inferior to what I visualize at present.

(There follows the draft of the episode that now appears in the book.) page 386 /

To tell the truth, Édouard feels that Lafcadio, although he has returned all the letters, has an advantage over him; he feels that the most gallant way to disarm him is to win him over — and Lafcadio, offhandedly and tactfully, gives him to understand this. But soon this forced intimacy gives way to a genuine feeling. After all, Lafcadio is most attractive (he is not yet fully aware of this).

Yesterday I left Dent's before noon and was not expected until 1.30 at Charles Du Bos's. As I was dawdling in front of a second-hand bookshop, I caught an urchin in the act of pocketing a book. He took advantage of a moment when the proprietor, or at least the clerk in charge of the sidewalk exhibit, had his back turned; but only after he had crammed the book into his pocket did he become aware of my glance and realize that I was keeping an eye on him. Immediately I saw him blush slightly, then strive by some sort of hesitant gesture to explain his act. He drew back a few steps, seemed to be considering, returned, then ostensibly, and *for my benefit*, drew a little threadbare wallet from the inside pocket of his jacket and made a pretense of looking for the money he knew very well wasn't there. He made, still for my benefit, a little grimace that meant: "Not enough!" shook his head, went back to the clerk in charge, and, as naturally as he could (in other words, with a sort of slow-motion, like an actor who has been told: "You're going through it much too fast" and who forces himself to "put in pauses"), he finally pulled the book out of his pocket and put it back in its original place. Since he felt that I had never stopped watching him, he could not make up his mind to leave and continued to pretend an interest in the bookstall. I think he would have stayed there a great deal longer had I not drawn back a few steps, as though I were the cat in **page 387 /** the game of "cat in the corner," giving the mouse a chance to change corners. But he had no sooner broken away than I accosted him.

"What was that book?" I asked, with as much smile as I could muster.

"A guide to Algeria. But it costs too much."

"How much?"

"Two francs fifty. I'm not that rich."

"If I hadn't been watching you, you'd have slipped out with the book in your pocket, eh?"

The boy protested energetically. He had never stolen anything, he had no wish to start, etc. I took a two-franc note from my pocket:

"Here you are. Go ahead and buy the book."

A couple of minutes later he emerged from the shop thumbing through the book, which he had just paid for: an old 1871 Joanne bound in blue.

"It's dreadfully old. That's no good for anything."

"Oh, yes; it's got maps. That's the thing I get the most fun out of — geography."

I suspect that the book flattered an instinct for wanderlust; I talk a little more with him. He is about fifteen or sixteen, very modestly clad in a scanty brown jacket, stained and threadbare. He carries a schoolboy's satchel under his arm. I discover that he is at Henri IV in his next to last year. Not very attractive to look at; but I reproach myself for having left him too quickly.

If I am able to use the anecdote, it seems to me it would be much more interesting told by the boy himself, for this would no doubt permit more detours and dodges. **page 388 /**

Brussels, 16 June

Finished the preface for *Armance* in Paris.

At present there is nothing to keep me from the novel with the possible exception of the *Curieux malavisé*, the rough draft of which I took out before I left, and hope to finish up this summer; and the last chapter of *Si le grain ne meurt*. . . .

Z. told me the story of his sister. She married his wife's brother; her husband's health is extremely delicate and she, considerably older, cares for him. She nurses him so well that he finally recovers and runs off with another woman, leaving his exhausted wife behind. The most painful part for her is that she soon learns that her husband has a child by the other woman (he had been too delicate during the time he was faithful, and she had abandoned any hope of ever being a mother).

And I imagine further: the two women are sisters; he has married the elder (considerably older than her sister), but gets the younger with child. And the elder sister cannot rest until she has won over the child. . . .

This afternoon all this seemed lucid; but this evening I am tired, the thing seems quite flat — and I am putting all this down as a matter of duty.

Cuverville, 9 July 1921

The first thing to do is to establish the field of action and smooth off a space upon which to erect the book.

Difficult to explain this properly in metaphors; might as well say more simply: "lay the bases."

1. First the Artistic bases: the problem of the book will be set forth through Édouard's meditation. page 389 /

2. The Intellectual bases: the subject of the baccalaureate composition ("to skim the surface — *effleurer* — to take only the flower").

3. The Moral bases: filial insubordination; the opposition of the parents (who apply in this regard the sophistry of England with respect to Egypt or Ireland: if they were given the liberty they demand, they would be the first to repent of it, etc.).

It must be considered whether that is not where the book should begin.

22 July

Note: William James's extremely remarkable observations on habit (in his psychology text, which I am reading at the moment):

> But every one of us in his measure, whenever, after glowing for an abstractly formulated Good, he practically ignores some actual case, *among the squalid "other particulars" of which that same Good lurks disguised*, treads straight on Rousseau's path. *All Goods are disguised by the vulgarity of their concomitants, in this work-a-day world.*

Cuverville, 25 November 1921

Back here since last night, after a stay in Rome, which, although it greatly distracted me from my work, nevertheless left me with a feeling that I now see much more clearly what I want. During my last stay at Cuverville, in October, I had already worked out the first chapters; unfortunately I had had to stop at the moment when the inert mass was beginning to stir into motion. This comparison is not very good. I prefer the image of the churn. Yes; I churned the subject in my head for several evenings on end without getting the least bit of butter, but without losing my conviction that the curds were indeed going to form in the end. A strange liquid substance which, long after you page 390 / begin, refuses to acquire consistency, but in which solid particles, stirred and shaken every which way, at last clot together and separate from the whey. At present I have the raw materials, which I must work together and knead. If he didn't know beforehand from experience that through beating and shaking this creamy chaos he was going to see the miracle repeated—who wouldn't throw up the job?

Cuverville, 7 December

During the thirteen days that I have been here I have written the first thirty pages of my book with hardly any difficulty and *currente calamo*—although it's true that for a long time I have had it all worked out in my head. At present I am at a standstill. Looking back over yesterday's work, it seems to me that I am on the wrong track; the dialogue with Édouard, especially (however successful it may be), leads the reader as well as myself into a region from which I am not going to be able to get back down to real life. Or else I should have to put the principal irony of the tale into the words: "toward real life" — implying plainly that real life exists equally in the region of thought, along with anxiety, passion, and suffering. . . .

Of the need to go farther and farther back to explain any given incident. The slightest act requires an infinite motivation.

I am continually wondering: might such an effect have been the result of other causes? Each time I am forced to acknowledge that it could not; that anything less than all that — and precisely *that* — would not do, and that I cannot change the least figure without immediately falsifying the end product.

The problem for me is not *how to succeed* — but rather how to *survive.*

For some time now I have aimed to win my case only on appeal. I write only to be *re*read. page 391 /

SECOND NOTEBOOK

Colpach, August 1921

The extreme difficulty I am encountering in making my book progress is perhaps but the natural result of an initial vice. From time to time I am convinced that the very idea of the book is ridiculous, and I come to the point where I no longer even understand what I want. Properly speaking, the book has no one single center for my various efforts to converge upon; those efforts center about two foci, as in an ellipse. On one side, the event, the fact, the external datum; on the other side, the very effort of the novelist to make a book out of it all. The latter is the main subject, the new focus that throws the plot off center and leads it toward the imaginative. In short, I see this notebook in which I am writing the very history of the novel poured into the book in its entirety and forming its principal interest — for the greater irritation of the reader.

The most questionable strayings of the flesh have left my soul more tranquil than the slightest intellectual error. When I feel uneasy in conscience, it is upon leaving the fashionable salon, not the brothel.

The more G. sinks into devotion, the more he loses his sense of truth. The state of deception in which a pious soul can live — a certain mystic splendor turns his gaze away from reality. He page 392 / no longer seeks to see things as they are; he no longer can. When Édouard tells X. that G. seems to him to have lost all love of truth, X. presents the Catholic thesis:

It is not Truth we must love, but God. Truth is only one of God's attributes, as is Beauty, which is worshipped exclusively by certain artists. The exclusive worship of one of God's attributes is a form of paganism, etc.

The forming into groups.

The Argonauts. They devote themselves to the "nation"; but there are manifold dissensions in the very heart of the group: *how* can France be best served?

On the other hand, the grouping of enemies of society. Partnership for crime. In opposition to these, the conservatives look like cads. The important thing is to know what is worth protecting, what is worth the trouble of . . .

As for personal opinions — in short, Valentin simply had none. Or, more precisely, he had them all and tried them out one by one, if indeed not simultaneously. He would follow a discussion as though it were a chess game, ready to advise one or the other of the adversaries, thinking only of the proper way of playing the game and of not giving unjust (that is to say, illogical) advantage to anyone.

What we call "wrong-headedness' (the other shrugged his shoulders at this ready-made expression and declared it had no meaning) — well, I am going to tell you: it is the person who finds it necessary to convince himself he has a *reason* for committing every act he wants to commit, the person who enslaves his reason to his instincts, to his interests (and this is worse), or to his temperament. So long as Lucien tries only to convince others, the evil is merely embryonic; this is the first step toward hypocrisy. But have you noticed that, with Lucien, the hypocrisy becomes deeper day by day. He is the first victim of all the false motives he brings forth; eventually he convinces himself that it is these false motives that are guiding him, whereas in reality it is he who bends and guides them. The true hypocrite is the one **page 393 /** who ceases to perceive his deception, the one who lies with sincerity.

M. says of Lucien that he is "completely penetrated by his façade."

Jude had this intellectual shortcoming, shared by so many young men — which often makes them insufferable to their elders — of exaggerating his praise or his blame. His judgment admitted no purgatory. Everything he didn't find "admirable" was "frightful."

Édouard might very well have encountered on the train that extraordinary creature who forced us to give up our reserved seats. I felt it was beyond my power to spend the night in the same compartment with her. . . . Imagine a person of indeterminate age and sex, with an absent expression and a flabby body propped up with an assortment of pillows; to *this* clung two middle-aged women. The compartment closed and overheated, the atmosphere stifling; an odor of medicine and sickness. . . . I immediately shut the door again. But the car in which we then ensconced ourselves, Marc and I, went only as far as Marseille. When we got there we had to change; and in the packed train the only space we could find was in the compartment where our seats were still reserved. The window was open; one could breathe . . . and perhaps, after all, I had imagined the bad odor.

The young girl now seemed to me almost pretty. Her hair, cut page-boy fashion, clung to her temples with perspiration. From time to time she smiled at the two women who accompanied her, who might have been her mother and her aunt. Whereupon the aunt would ask:

"How do you feel?"

But the mother would immediately exclaim: "Now, don't keep asking her how she feels. The less she thinks about it, the better."

At times the girl tried to talk, but immediately a shadow seemed to creep over her face, and an expression of insufferable **page 394 /** weariness strained her features. A little before we got to Nice, the two women began their preparations for leaving, and when the train pulled into the station they struggled to raise their companion's inert body; but she began to weep — or not exactly to weep, but to moan — a sort of whining lamentation, so strange that the startled passengers began running up from all sides.

"Here we go! The same old song again," exclaimed the mother. "Come, come! You know very well it won't do any good to cry. . . ."

I offered to assist the women in lifting the patient, in dragging her to the door; but at the end of the corridor, right in front of the open door of the lavatory, she literally crumpled. It was all I could do to hold her by bracing myself against the door-jamb. Then with a huge effort I hoisted her, held her on the steps, getting off with her, while the aunt, who had got off ahead of us, caught her in her arms.

"She's been that way now for eighteen months," the aunt told me when I had joined her. "Such a shame! A girl of seventeen! . . . And it isn't a case of real paralysis at all — just a nervous paralysis."

"I suppose there were mental causes?" I asked rather indiscreetly.

"Yes; it came from a fright she had, one night when she was sleeping in the room with my brother's children. . . ."

I realized that the good woman would have liked nothing better than to talk, and regretted that I had not questioned her sooner. But a porter came up with a wheelchair, and the patient was put into it; the aunt, thanking me, drew away.

Édouard might encounter her later and reconstruct the past.

Make Édouard say, perhaps:

"The bore, you see, is having to condition one's characters. They live powerfully within me and I will even admit that they live at my expense. I know how they think, how they speak; I distinguish the slightest intonations of their voices. I know that they are to commit certain acts, and that certain others are forbidden them. . . . But as soon as I must clothe them, establish

page 395 / their position in the social scale, their careers, the amount of their income — above all, invent relationships, parents, a family, friends — I throw up the job. I confess to you that I see each one of my characters as an orphan, an only son, unmarried, and childless. Perhaps that is why I see such a fine hero in you, Lafcadio. But then — imagine yourself having what we call "responsibilities" — with aged parents to support, for example; a paralytic mother, a blind father. . . . Such things happen, you know. Or better yet, a young sister in delicate health, who needs mountain air."

"Might as well make her a bedridden cripple."

"Imagine what it would be to have a sister! There you are with a little sister on your hands, who had once said to you: 'Cadio, my little Cadio, since our parents died, you are all I have left in the world. . . .' "

"I would hasten to find her a seducer."

"You say that because you don't love her. But if she were real, you would love her."

The symbolist school. The worst thing against it is its lack of curiosity toward life. With the single possible exception of Vielé-Griffin (whose verses consequently partake of a special savor), they were all pessimists, forsaking and resigned,

Tired of the sorry hospital

that our country (I should say the earth) — "monotonous and undeserved," as Laforgue said — was for them. For them poetry became a refuge, their only sanctuary from the squalor of reality; they plunged into it with the fervor of desperation.

Disenchanting life of everything they considered to be mere deception, wondering whether it was worth the trouble of "being lived," no wonder they brought no new moral code (being satis- **page 396 /** fied with Vigny's, which at most they dressed up in irony), but merely an æsthetic.

A character may well describe himself wonderfully while describing someone else or speaking of someone else — according to the rule that each of us really understands in others only those feelings he is capable of producing himself.

Each time Édouard is called upon to outline his novel, he talks of it in a different way. In short, he is bluffing; in his heart he is afraid of never being able to finish it.

"Why try to conceal it? The form that tempts me is the epic. The epic tone alone suits me and has the power to satisfy me; it alone can free the novel from its realistic rut. For a great many years it was possible to think that Fielding and Richardson occupied opposite poles. Actually one is as realistic as the other. Until now the novel in every country has always clung to reality. Our great literary period found it possible to carry out its effort toward idealization only in the drama. *La Princesse de Clèves* is without a successor; when the French novel really launches out, it does so in the direction of the *Roman bourgeois*."

28 November 1921

"These young men had a very hazy idea of the limits of their power" — this from *The Idiot*, which I am rereading at present. An excellent epigraph for one of the chapters. **page 397 /**

Pontigny, 20 August 1922

Bernard has taken for his motto:

> *If not you, who will do it?*
> *If not now, then when?*

He tries to work this out in Latin. And when he is thinking about getting Édouard's suitcase out of the checkroom: "If you don't do it now, you run the risk of letting Édouard do it."

The charming thing about these maxims is that they are equally the key to heaven as to hell.

Cuverville, 11 October 1922

Oddly enough, my novel is taking shape in reverse. I mean to say that I am constantly discovering that this or that which has happened previously ought to be included. Thus the chapters are not added one after the other at all; but they are continually pushing back the chapter I originally conceived as the first.

28 October

Do not bring the most important characters too much into the foreground — at least not too soon. Better to hold them back, make the reader wait for them. Do not describe them, but make it necessary for the reader to imagine them, as is fitting. On the other hand, describe the various supernumeraries with precision; lead them boldly to the fore, to let them get that much ahead of the others.

In the first Luxembourg scene I have characters of no importance talking; Olivier's monologue is unique. He must not be heard; scarcely be glimpsed; but already begin to be liked. You page 398 / must associate yourself with him, wish to see and hear him. In this case feeling must precede knowledge.

All this I do by instinct. It is only later that I analyze.

1 November

Purge the novel of all elements that do not belong specifically to the novel. Nothing good ever comes from a hodgepodge. I have always had a horror of what they call "the synthesis of the arts," which, according to Wagner, was to take place in the theater. This gave me a horror of the theater — and of Wagner. (It was in that period that symphonies were played and verses recited behind a Munkacsy landscape; that, at the Théâtre des Arts, perfumes were sprayed into the theater during the performance of *The Song of Songs.*) The only theater I can bear is the one that offers itself simply for what it is, and does not claim to be more than a theater.

In the seventeenth century, tragedy and comedy attained a magnificent purity (and *purity*, in art as elsewhere, is what matters) — and in addition almost all the genres, big and little: fables, characters, maxims, sermons, memoirs, letters. Lyric poetry, purely lyrical — and not the novel? (No, do not make too much of *La Princesse de Clèves;* it is chiefly a marvel of tact and taste. . . .)

As for this *pure* novel, no one has produced it since either — not even that admirable Stendhal, who of all novelists perhaps approached it the closest. But is it not remarkable that Balzac, possibly our greatest novelist, is beyond doubt the one who mingled with the novel, annexed to it and amalgamated with it, more heterogeneous and inherently indigestible elements than anyone else? Hence the very bulk of one of his books is simultaneously **page 399 /** one of the most powerful, but also one of the most turgid, most imperfect, and most dross-laden things in all our literature. It is worthy of note that the English, who have never known how to *purify* their drama in the sense that Racine's tragedy is purified, yet achieved at the very outset a much greater purity in the novels of Defoe, Fielding, and even Richardson.

I think all this will have to go into Édouard's mouth — which would allow me to add that I do not grant him all these points, however judicious his remarks may be; that, as far as I am concerned, I doubt whether there could be imagined a *purer* novel than, for instance, Mérimée's *La double Méprise.* But in order for Édouard to be stimulated to produce the pure novel he envisaged, it was necessary for him to be convinced that such a thing had never been done.

What is more, he will never succeed in writing this pure novel.

I must be careful to respect in Édouard everything that makes him unable to write his book. He understands a great many things, but he is forever pursuing himself — through everyone and everything. Real devotion is almost impossible for him. He is a dabbler, a failure.

A character all the more difficult to establish since I am lending him much of myself. I have to step back and put him at some distance from me to see him properly.

Classic art:

"*You both love each other more than you think.*"

(TARTUFFE)

Sarah says: "so as not" — a horrible mistake, so common today, that no one ever seems to denounce — "I closed the door so as not to let him out," etc. **page 400 /**

Olivier took great care not to talk about things he did not know well. But since this precaution was not shared by the others of Robert's circle, who were not in the least embarrassed at offering peremptory judgments on books they had never read, Olivier chose to think he was much more ignorant than they, when actually he was only more conscientious.

"I admire the background your friends have," he told Robert. "I feel so ignorant in comparison that I hardly dare open my mouth. What is this book you have all just been saying such fine things about?"

"It's a book almost none of us has read," said Robert, laughing. "But it's been tacitly agreed to find all those qualities in it, and to look at everyone who doesn't recognize its merits as a fool."

A month before, an answer like that would have made Olivier indignant. He smiled.

Annecy, 23 February

Bernard: his character still uncertain. Completely insubordinate in the beginning. Becomes motivated, limited, and defined throughout the book, thanks to his love affairs. Each love, each adoration, brings with it a devotion, a sacrifice. At first he is grieved by this, but he readily realizes that it is only by limiting his field of action that he can define it precisely.

Olivier: his character is distorted little by little. He commits actions altogether contrary to his nature and tastes — out of spite and ferocity. There follows an abominable disgust for himself. The progressive blunting of his personality — likewise that of his brother Vincent. (Stress the defeat of his virtue at the moment he begins to win at gambling.) I have not been able to indicate this clearly enough.

Vincent and Olivier have quite fine and noble instincts and plunge into life with a lofty concept of what they are to do — but they are weak characters and allow themselves to be deflected. Bernard, on the contrary, reacts to each influence by fighting page 401 / back at it. The cards were dealt out wrong: Édouard should have adopted Olivier; it is Olivier he really loved.

Vincent gradually lets himself be permeated by the diabolic spirit. He imagines he is becoming the Devil; it is when things go best for him that he feels the most damned. He tries to *warn off* his brother Olivier, and every attempt to save him acts to Olivier's prejudice and to his own profit. He actually feels he has *taken sides* with Satan. He feels that the more he succeeds in disbelieving in the real existence of the Evil One, the more he becomes the pawn of Satan. This is always an easy metaphorical way for him to explain things; but one theme always returns to his mind: "Why should you be afraid of me? You know very well I don't exist." In the end he believes in the existence of Satan *as in his own;* in other words, he eventually believes he is Satan.

It is this very assurance (the assurance that the Devil is backing his game) that makes him succeed in everything he undertakes. He is frightened by this; he gets to the point of almost hoping for a measure of failure; but he knows he will succeed, no matter what he undertakes. He knows that in gaining the world he is losing his own soul.

He realizes by what arguments the Devil *tricked* him when he first found himself with Laura in the sanatorium neither of them expected to be able to leave — he knows he took sides with him from the instant he used a sophism as the basis of argument: "Since we aren't going to live on, and since, therefore, nothing we might do henceforth could be of any consequence . . ."

I am unable to admire fully the courage of the man who scorns life.

It is appropriate, in opposition to the manner of Meredith or James, to let the reader get the advantage over me — to go about it in such a way as to allow him to think he is more intelligent, more moral, more perspicacious than the author, and that he is discovering many things in the characters, and many truths in **page 402 /** the course of the narrative, in spite of the author and, so to speak, behind the author's back.

Annecy, 5 March 1923

Dreamed last night:

A servant in livery came with a tray to carry away the remains of the meal we had been served. I was sitting on a plain stool beside a low coffee table, almost in the center of a large, dimly lighted room. The person I was talking to, his face half hidden by the wings of a large armchair, was Marcel Proust. The attention I was paying to him was distracted by the departure of the servant, who, as I noticed, was dragging behind him a piece of string, one end of which was in my hand, while the other end led off between the books on one of the bookshelves. The bookcase covered one of the walls of the room. Proust had his back to it, and I was facing it. I pulled the string and saw two huge, old, and sumptuously bound volumes move. I pulled a little more and the books came half out of the shelf, ready to fall; I pulled still a little more and they fell. The noise of their falling made my heart pound and cut short the story that Proust was telling. I leaped to the bookcase and picked up one of the books to make sure the full morocco binding had not been bent at the corners, so I might immediately reassure my friend that the book was undamaged. But the boards were half torn from the back; the binding, in short, was in a lamentable state. I realized intuitively that Proust thought a lot of the books, this one especially. But in a tone of exquisite kindness befitting the well-bred gentleman: "It's nothing. It's a Saint-Simon in the edition of . . . " He told me the date, and I immediately recognized it to be one of the rarest and most sought-after editions. I tried to stammer excuses, but Proust cut them short and began showing me, with many a comment, some of the numerous illustrations of the book he had kept on his knees.

A moment later (I don't know where Proust had gone) I found myself alone in the room. A sort of majordomo clad in a long green and black frock-coat came to close the shutters, like a museum attendant when it is about to strike five. I got up to leave page 403 / and had to file through a series of lavish drawing-rooms at the side of the majordomo. I slipped on the polished floor, almost fell, and finally, losing my balance, fell sobbing to the floor at the feet of the majordomo. I then began to explain, with a great display of bombast and rhetoric, which I considered proper to cover the absurdity of my confession:

"I lied just now when I pretended I pulled the books down by mistake; I knew they would fall if I pulled the string, and I pulled it just the same. I could not resist."

I had got back to my feet, and the majordomo, supporting me in his arms, slapped me on the shoulder several times in the Russian manner.

In the compartment of the Annecy train a worker, after having tried in vain to light his pipe:

"At the price matches are, it really counts when they don't light."

I am so afraid (and I should dislike it so much) of letting my emotions bend my thinking that it is often precisely when someone is most inclined against me that I am tempted to speak most highly of him.

Cuverville, 3 November

At the time of my reading to R. Martin du Gard (August, Pontigny), I was obliged to recognize that the best parts of my book are parts of pure invention. If I spoiled the portrait of old La Pérouse, it was because I clung too closely to reality; I neither knew how nor was able to lose sight of my model. The narrative of that first visit will have to be done over. La Pérouse will not come to life nor shall I really visualize him until he completely displaces his original. Nothing so far has given me so **page 404 /** much trouble. The difficult thing is inventing when you are encumbered by memory.

15 November

Have completely gone over this chapter; I think it is rather good now.

Certainly it is easier for me to put words into a character's mouth than to express myself in my own name — and particularly when the character I am creating differs most from me. I have written nothing better or with more facility than Lafcadio's monologues, or Alissa's journal. In this sort of thing I forget who I am, if indeed I have ever known. I become the other person. (They try to find out my opinion; I have no interest in my own opinion. I am no longer someone, but several — whence the reproaches for my restlessness, my instability, my fickleness, my inconstancy.) Push abnegation to the point of complete self-oblivion.

(I told Claudel, one night when he, as a friend, was worried about the salvation of my soul: "I have lost all interest in my soul and its salvation." "But God," he replied, "He hasn't lost interest in you.")

In life as well, the thoughts and emotions of others dwell in me; my heart beats only through sympathy. This is what makes any discussion so difficult for me. I immediately abandon *my* point of view. I get away from myself — and so be it. page 405 /

This is the key to my character and work. The critic who fails to grasp this will botch the job — and this too: I am not drawn toward what resembles me, but toward what differs from me.

Cuverville, 27 December

Jacques Rivière has just left me. He has been staying here for three days. I read him the first seventeen chapters of *Les Faux-Monnayeurs* (chapters one and two are to be completely redone).

It might be well to introduce into the very first chapter a fantastic and supernatural element — an element that will later authorize certain deviations in the plot, certain unrealities. I think it would be best to do a "poetic" description of the Luxembourg — which must be as mythical a place as the Forest of Arden in the fantasies of Shakespeare.

Cuverville, 3 January 1924

The difficulty arises from the fact that I must start anew with each chapter. *Never take advantage of momentum* — such is the rule of my game.

6 January

The book now seems frequently animated with its own life; it reminds one of a plant developing, and my brain is simply the earth-filled pot that contains and feeds it. It even seems to me unwise to try to "force" the plant, that it is better to let its buds page 406 / swell, its stalks stretch out, its fruits ripen slowly. If you try to advance the hour of natural maturity you impair the fullness of their flavor.

In the train to Cuverville, 8 February 1924

Since they are preventing me from reading and meditating, I

shall note as they come the remarks of the fat lady who, with her husband, is occupying two of the other seats in my compartment:

"Just the same, they're convenient, these cars with exits in each compartment — in case of an accident" (our car is one with a corridor). "Look! You'd think it was a fellow on top of the roof — that weathervane. I didn't know Amer-Picon had a factory at Batignolles."

THE HUSBAND: "We're in the suburbs. The suburbs, which already . . ."

THE WIFE: "There are a few clouds, but it won't rain. You might as well take off your coat. La! la, la, la."

THE HUSBAND: "Eh?"

THE WIFE: "La, la, la, la. Isn't that Rouen over there?"

THE HUSBAND: "Oh, la, la! Two hours from here."

THE WIFE: "Look at the shape of those chimneys."

THE HUSBAND: "Argenteuil . . . asparagus."

The lady caught my eye. She bent over toward her husband, and from that moment on they spoke only in a whisper. So much the better. Nevertheless I heard:

THE HUSBAND: "It isn't sincere."

THE WIFE: "Of course not. To be sincere it would have to be . . ."

Admirable — the person who never finishes his sentences. Mme Vedel, the pastor's wife.

14 February

The translation of *Tom Jones*, the proofs of which Dent has just sent me, is most mediocre. I decline to write the introduc-
page 407 / tion. After a long parley involving Rhys (Dent's representative), Valery Larbaud, and myself, the Dent firm abandons the undertaking. I find myself again confronted with my *Faux-Monnayeurs*, but this brief plunge into Fielding has enlightened me as to the insufficiencies of my book. I am wondering whether I shouldn't expand the text, intrude myself (in spite of what Martin du Gard says), make comments. I have lost touch.

Brignoles, 27 March

The style of *Les Faux-Monnayeurs* should offer no surface interest — no handhold. Everything must be said in the flattest manner possible, which will cause certain sleight-of-hand artists to ask: what do you find to admire in that?

Vence, 29 March

From the very first line of my first book I have sought a direct expression of the state of my character — some sentence that would be a direct revelation of his inner state — rather than to portray that state. The expression might have been clumsy and weak, but the principle was right.

30 March

All those heroes I have hewn out of my own flesh lack this one thing: the modicum of common sense that keeps me from carrying my follies as far as they do. page 408 /

31 March

Lady Griffith's character is and must remain somewhat outside the book. She has no moral existence, or even, as a matter of fact, any personality; this is what is soon going to irritate Vincent. Those two lovers are made to hate each other.

Roquebrune, 10 April 1924

The difficulty lies in not constructing the rest of my novel as a prolongation of the lines already traced. A perpetual upheaval; each new chapter must pose a new problem, be an overture, a new direction, a new impulse, a forward plunge — of the reader's mind. But the reader must leave me as the stone leaves the sling-shot. I am even willing that, like a boomerang, he should come back and strike me.

Paris, 17 May

Wrote the three chapters to precede the opening of the school year at the *pension* (Édouard's Journal: conversations with Molinier, with the Vedel-Azaïs family, with La Pérouse).

I want to bring each of my characters successively before the footlights to allow him the place of honor for a few moments. A breathing-space necessary between the chapters (but I'd have to make the reader take one too).

27 May

Bernard's elder brother convinces himself he must be a "man of action." In other words, he becomes a partisan. He has his riposte ready before his adversary has spoken; he hardly lets his **page 409 /** interlocutor finish his sentence. Listening to others might weaken him. He works steadily and aims to teach himself, but in his reading he seeks only ammunition for his cause. In the beginning he still suffered from a slight discrepancy he felt between his thoughts and his words; I mean that his words, his statements before like-minded friends, were often ahead of his thoughts. But he took care to get his thoughts into step with his words. Now he really *believes* what he affirms, and doesn't even feel it necessary to add "sincerely" to each of his declarations as he used to do.

Bernard has a talk with him after his bachelor's exam. He was on the point of going back to his father. The conversation he has with his conservative brother throws him back into revolt.

The poor novelist constructs his characters; he controls them and makes them speak. The true novelist listens to them and watches them function; he eavesdrops on them even before he knows them. It is only according to what he hears them say that he begins to understand *who* they are.

I have put "watches them function" second — because, for me, speech tells me more than action. I think I should lose less if I went blind than if I became deaf. Nevertheless I do *see* my characters — not so much in their details as in their general effect, and even more in their actions, their gait, the rhythm of their movements. I do not worry if the lenses of my glasses fail to show them completely "in focus"; whereas I perceive the least inflections of their voices with the greatest sharpness.

I wrote the first dialogue between Olivier and Bernard and the scenes between Passavant and Vincent without having the slightest idea what I was going to do with those characters, or even who they were. They thrust themselves upon me, despite me. Nothing miraculous in this. I understand rather well the formation of an imaginary character, and of what cast-off part of oneself he is made.

There is no act, however foolish or harmful, that is not the result of interacting causes, connections, and concomitances. No doubt there are very few crimes of which the responsibility can- **page 410 /** not be shared, to the success of which several did not contribute — albeit without their knowledge or will. The sources of our slightest acts are as diverse and remote as those of the Nile.

The renouncement of virtue through the surrender of pride.

Coxyde, 6 July

Profitendieu must be completely redrawn. When he first launched into my book, I didn't properly understand him. He is much more interesting than I thought.

Cuverville, 27 July

Boris. The poor child realizes that there is not one of his qualities, not one of his virtues, that his companions cannot turn into a shortcoming: his chastity into impotence, his sobriety into absence of appetite, his general abstinence into cowardice, his sensitiveness into weakness. Just as there are no bonds like shortcomings or vices held in common, likewise nobility of soul prevents easy acceptance (being accepted as well as accepting).

Jarry. He had a keen sense of language; or rather, of the weight of words. He constructed massive, stable sentences, their full length touching the ground.

Cuverville, 10 August

Another article of their code was what I might call "the doctrine of least effort." With the exception of a small minority, who were considered show-offs and malcontents, all of these children made it a point of honor, or of self-esteem, to obtain everything

page 411 / by paying or straining as little as possible. One of them might be proud of having obtained a desired object at a bargain, another might have discovered the solution of a problem without having devoted any effort to calculating, perhaps a means of locomotion that will allow him to leave for class five minutes later — the principle remained the same. "No useless effort" was their foolish motto. None of them had been able to comprehend that there can be reward in effort itself, that there can be any other recompense than the goal achieved.

There is a possibility that this attitude of mind (which I personally consider one of the most tiresome) becomes less dangerous as soon as it is catalogued. It happens that we name things only when we are breaking with them; this formula may quite well presage a new departure.

The clothing of these children reflected the same ethics. Everything about them breathed strictness; everything was parsimoniously measured. Their jackets (I speak of those who were most elegant) circled them like the bark of a tree burst in front by the growth of the trunk. Their collars left their neckties only the tiniest space for the tiniest knot. This even applied to their shoes, of which several of these young fellows artfully tucked in the laces so as to let only the indispensable be seen.

Cuverville, 1 November 1924

I was to have left on 6 November for the Congo; all the arrangements were made, cabin space booked, etc. I put off the departure until July. Hope of finishing my book (this, however, is not the principal reason for my staying).

I have just written Chapter x of Part Two (Olivier's unsuccessful suicide). Ahead I can see only a terrible confusion — underbrush so thick I don't know which branch to begin hacking. According to my method, I take patience and study the thicket carefully before attacking it.

On all sides life offers us many beginnings of drama, but only rarely do these continue and take shape as the novelist is accus- **page 412 /** tomed to spin them out. And this is exactly the idea I want to give in this book, which I shall have Édouard express.

Cuverville, 20 November

That many acts of a particular generation find their *explanation* in the generation that follows — this is what I started out to show, but my characters run away with me and I was unable to give myself complete satisfaction on this point. If I write another novel I should like to give more importance to this: the way those of a new generation, after having criticized and blamed the actions and attitudes (conjugal, for ex.) of their predecessors, find themselves gradually led to do almost the same things over again. André sees taking shape again in his own marriage everything that seemed to him monstrous in the family of Guillaume during his childhood.

Hospital, 3 January 1925

Bernard endures the indoctrination of a traditionalist who, ignorant of Bernard's illegitimacy, wants to convince him that wisdom consists in everyone's prolonging the line his father has begun to trace, etc. Bernard hardly dares come forth with his objection:

"But, after all, suppose I don't know that father?"

And almost immediately he gets to the point of congratulating himself for not knowing him, and for consequently being forced to seek a moral rule in himself. page 413 /

But will he know enough to rise to the point of accepting and assuming all the contradictions of his too rich nature? To the point of seeking not to resolve them but to feed them — to the point of realizing that for a taut string the amplitude of vibration and the extent of the stretch represent the power of the sound it can produce, that it can come to rest only at dead center?

A like comparison with the two magnetic poles, between which flashes the spark of life.

Bernard thinks: "Strive toward a goal? — No! Rather, go forward."

Cuverville, end of January

How an ideal team is formed:

The first condition for joining it is that you must give up your name and become simply an anonymous force; to seek victory for the team, but not to distinguish yourself.

Without this there will be only prima donnas — freaks. To win, a high average always helps more than a few exceptional members — who seem all the more extraordinary and are noticed all the more when the team in general is more mediocre.

Classical art:

I complain of my fate less than you think.
(BAJAZET)

8 March 1925

Saw Martin du Gard at Hyères. He would like to see my novel stretch out indefinitely. He encourages me to take more "advantage" of the characters I have created. I don't think I shall follow his advice. page 414 /

What will attract me to a new book is not so much new characters as a new way of presenting them. This novel will end sharply, not through exhaustion of the subject, which must give the impression of inexhaustibility, but on the contrary through its expansion and by a sort of blurring of its outline. It must not be neatly rounded off, but rather disperse, disintegrate. . . .

La Bastide, 29 March 1925

Worked rather well for almost a month. Wrote several chapters, which at first seemed particularly hard to me. But one of the peculiarities of this book (which certainly comes from the fact that I constantly refuse to "take advantage of the momentum") is the excessive difficulty I find in beginning each new chapter — a difficulty almost equal to the one that held me marking time on the threshold of the book for so long. Yes, it has actually occurred to me for days on end to wonder whether I should be able to get the wheels turning again. As far as I can remember, there was nothing like this with *Les Caves du Vatican*, or with any other book. Or has the trouble I had in writing them been effaced from my memory, like the labor pains after the birth of the child?

I have been wondering since last night (I finished the day before Chapter xvii of the Second Part: Armand's visit to Olivier) if it would not be well to condense into one the several chapters I had planned. It seems to me that the ghastly scene of the suicide would gain from not being too much announced. With too much preparation you slip into bleakness. This morning I can see only advantage in a condensation that would present the suicide and its motivation in a single chapter.

It can be said of almost all "rules of life" that it would be wiser to take the opposite course than to follow them.

First take the inventory. We can balance the books later. It's not well to mix them up. As soon as my book is finished, I shall **page 415 /** draw a line and leave the rest to the reader — addition, subtraction, it matters but little; I do not think this ought to be up to me. So much the worse for the lazy reader; it's the others I want. To disturb is my function. The public always prefers to be reassured. There are those whose job this is. There are only too many.

Cuverville, May 1925

I am afraid of the disproportion between the first and second parts — and that the latter, in the end, will seem noticeably shorter. Still, I am fond of sudden endings; I like to give my books the appearance of the sonnet which begins with an octave and ends with a sestet. It always seems useless to me to explain at length what the attentive reader has understood; it is an insult to him. The imagination shoots higher the narrower the end of the tube is, etc. Nevertheless, this morning I have come to the point of considering the possible advantage of dividing the book into three parts: the first (Paris) ending with Chapter xvi, the second comprising the eight chapters of Saas-Fée — which would make the third the most considerable.

Yesterday, 8 June, finished *Les Faux-Monnayeurs.*

Martin du Gard sends me this quotation from Thibaudet:

> It is rare for an author who depicts himself in a novel to make of

> himself a convincing figure, by which I mean a living person. . . . The authentic novelist creates his characters according to the infinite directions of his possible life; the false novelist creates them from the single line of his real life. The genius of the novel makes the possible come to life: it does not revive the real. **page 416 /**

And this seems so true to me that I am thinking of setting these sentences at the head of *Les Faux-Monnayeurs* as a preface alongside the following, which Vauvenargues wrote, undoubtedly thinking of Henri Massis:

> Those who do not get outside themselves are all of a piece.

But in the final analysis it is better to let the reader think what he will — though it be against me. **page 417 /**

ELIZABETH BOWEN

Notes on Writing a Novel (1946)

PLOT — *Essential. The Pre-Essential.*

Plot might seem to be a matter of choice. It is not. The particular plot is something the novelist is driven to. It is what is left after the whittling-away of alternatives. The novelist is confronted, at a moment (or at what appears to the moment: actually its extension may be indefinite) by the impossibility of saying what is to be said in any other way.

He is forced towards his plot. By what? By the 'what is to be said.' What is 'what is to be said?' A mass of subjective matter that has accumulated — impressions received, feelings about experience, distorted results of ordinary observation, and something else — *x*. This matter is *extra* matter. It is superfluous to the non-writing life of the writer. It is luggage left in the hall between two journeys, as opposed to the perpetual furniture of rooms. It is destined to be elsewhere. It cannot move till its destination is known. Plot is the knowing of destination.

Plot is diction. Action of language, language of action.

Plot is story. It is also 'a story' in the nursery sense = lie. The novel lies, in saying that something happened that did not. It must, therefore, contain uncontradictable truth, to warrant the original lie.

Story involves action. Action towards an end not to be foreseen (by the reader) but also towards an end which, having *been* reached, must be seen to have been from the start inevitable.

Action by whom? The Characters (see CHARACTERS). Action in view of what, and because of what? The 'what is to be said.'

What about the idea that the function of action is to *express* the characters? This is wrong. The characters are there to provide the action. Each character is created, and must only be so

---

Reprinted, by permission, from *Collected Impressions*, by Elizabeth Bowen (New York: Alfred A. Knopf, Inc., 1950).

created, as to give his or her action (or rather, contributory part in the novel's action) verisimilitude.

What about the idea that plot should be ingenious, complicated — a display of ingenuity remarkable enough to command attention? If more than such a display, what? Tension, or mystification towards tension, are good for emphasis. For their own sakes, bad. page 249 /

Plot must further the novel towards its object. What object? The non-poetic statement of a poetic truth.

Have not all poetic truths been already stated? The essence of a poetic truth is that no statement of it can be final.

Plot, story, is in itself un-poetic. At best it can only be not anti-poetic. It cannot claim a single poetic license. It must be reasoned — onward from the moment when its non-otherness, its only-possibleness has become apparent. Novelist must always have one foot, sheer circumstantiality, to stand on, whatever the other foot may be doing. (*N.B.* — Much to be learnt from story-telling to children. Much to be learnt from the detective story — especially non-irrelevance. (See RELEVANCE))

Flaubert's '*Il faut intéresser.*' Stress on manner of telling: keep in mind, 'I will a tale *unfold.*' Interest of watching silk handkerchief drawn from a conjuror's watch.

Plot must not cease to move forward. (See ADVANCE.) The *actual* speed of the movement must be even. *Apparent* variations in speed are good, necessary, but there must be no actual variations in speed. To obtain those apparent variations is part of the illusion-task of the novel. Variations in texture can be made to give the effect of variations in speed. Why are *apparent* variations in speed necessary? (a) For emphasis. (b) For non-resistance, or 'give,' to the nervous time-variations of the reader. Why is *actual* evenness, non-variation, of speed necessary? For the sake of internal evenness for its own sake. Perfection of evenness = perfection of control. The evenness of the speed should be the evenness inseparable from tautness. The tautness of the taut string is equal (or even) all along and at any part of the string's length.

CHARACTERS

Are the characters, then, to be constructed to formula — the formula pre-decided by the plot? Are they to be drawn, cut out, jointed, wired, in order to be manipulated for the plot?

No. There is no question as to whether this would be right or wrong. It would be impossible. One cannot 'make' characters, only marionettes. The manipulated movement of the marionette is not the 'action' necessary for plot. Characterless action is not action at all, in the plot sense. It is the indivisibility of the act from the actor, and the inevitability of *that* act on the part of *that* actor, page 250 / that gives action verisimilitude. Without that, action is without force or reason. Forceless, reasonless action disrupts plot. The term 'creation of character' (or characters) is misleading. Characters pre-exist. They are *found.* They reveal themselves slowly to the novelist's perception — as might fellow-travellers seated opposite one in a very dimly-lit railway carriage.

The novelist's perceptions of his characters take place *in the course of the actual writing of the novel.* To an extent, the novelist is in the same postion as his reader. But his perceptions should be always just in advance.

The ideal way of presenting character is to invite perception.

In what do the characters pre-exist? I should say, in the mass of matter (see Plot) that had accumulated before the inception of the novel.

(*N.B.* — The unanswerability of the question, from an outsider: 'Are the characters in your novel invented, or are they from real life?' Obviously, neither is true. The outsider's notion of 'real life' and the novelist's are hopelessly apart.)

How, then, is the pre-existing character — with its own inner spring of action, its contrarieties — to be made to play a preassigned rôle? In relation to character, or characters, once these have been contemplated, *plot* must at once seem over-rigid, arbitrary.

What about the statement (in relation to Plot) that 'each character is created in order, and only in order, that he or she may supply the required action?' To begin with, strike out 'created.' Better, the character is *recognized* (by the novelist) by the signs he or she gives of unique capacity to act in a certain way, which 'certain way' fulfils a need of the plot.

The character is there (in the novel) for the sake of the action he or she is to contribute to the plot. Yes. But also, he or she exists *outside* the action being contributed to the plot.

Without that existence of the character outside the (necessarily limited) action, the action itself would be invalid.

Action is the simplification (for story purposes) of complexity. For each one act, there are an *x* number of rejected alternatives. It is the palpable presence of the alternatives that gives action interest. Therefore, in each of the characters, while he or she is acting, the play and pull of alternatives must be felt. It is in being seen to be capable of alternatives that the character becomes, for the reader, valid. **page 251 /**

Roughly, the action of a character should be unpredictable before it has been shown, inevitable when it has been shown. In the first half of a novel, the unpredictability should be the more striking. In the second half, the inevitability should be the more striking.

(Most exceptions to this are, however, masterpiece-novels. In *War and Peace*, *L'Education Sentimentale* and *La Recherche du Temps Perdu*, unpredictability dominates up to the end.)

The character's prominence in the novel (pre-decided by the plot) decides the character's range — of alternatives. The novelist must allot (to the point of rationing) psychological space. The 'hero,' 'heroine' and 'villain' (if any) are, by agreement, allowed most range. They are entitled, for the portrayal of their alternatives, to time and space. Placing the characters in receding order of their importance to the plot, the number of their alternatives may be seen to diminish. What E. M. Forster has called the 'flat' character has no alternatives at all.

The ideal novel is without 'flat' characters.

Characters must *materialize* — *i.e.*, must have a palpable physical reality. They must be not only see-able (visualizable); they must be to be felt. Power to give physical reality is probably a matter of the extent and nature of the novelist's physical sensibility, or susceptibility. In the main, English novelists are weak in this, as compared to French and Russians. Why?

Hopelessness of categoric 'description.' Why? Because this is static. Physical personality belongs to action: cannot be separated from it. Pictures must be in movement. Eyes, hands, stature, etc., must appear, and only appear, *in play*. Reaction to physical personality is part of action — love, or sexual passages, only more marked application of this general rule.

(Conrad an example of strong, non-sexual use of physical personality.)

The materialization (in the above sense) of the character for the novelist must be instantaneous. It happens. No effort of will — and obviously no effort of intellect — can induce it. The novelist can *use* a character that has not yet materialized. But the unmaterialized character represents an enemy pocket in an area that has been otherwise cleared. This cannot go on for long. It produces a halt in plot.

When the materialization *has* happened, the chapters written **page 252 /** before it happened will almost certainly have to be recast. From the plot point of view, they will be found invalid.

Also, it is essential that for the reader the materialization of the character should begin early. I say begin, because for the *reader* it may, without harm, be gradual.

Is it from this failure, or tendency to fail, in materialization that the English novelist depends so much on engaging emotional sympathy for his characters?

Ruling sympathy out, a novel must contain at least one *magnetic* character. At least one character capable of keying the reader up, as though he (the reader) were in the presence of someone he is in love with. This is not a rule of salesmanship but a pre-essential of *interest.* The character must do to the reader what he has done to the novelist — magnetize towards himself perceptions, sense-impressions, desires.

The unfortunate case is, where the character has, obviously, acted magnetically upon the author, but fails to do so upon the reader.

There must be combustion. Plot depends for its movement on internal combustion.

Physically, characters are almost always copies, or composite copies. Traits, gestures, etc., are searched for in, and assembled from, the novelist's memory. Or, a picture, a photograph or the cinema screen may be drawn on. Nothing physical can be *invented.* (Invented physique stigmatizes the inferior novel.) Proust (in last volume) speaks of this assemblage of traits. Though much may be lifted from a specific person in 'real life,' no person in 'real life' could supply everything (physical) necessary for the character in the novel. No such person could have just that exact degree of physical intensity required for the character.

Greatness of characters is the measure of the unconscious greatness of the novelist's vision. They are 'true' in so far as he is occupied with poetic truth. Their degrees in realness show the degrees of his concentration.

SCENE — *Is a derivative of Plot. Gives actuality to Plot.*

Nothing can happen nowhere. The locale of the happening always colours the happening, and often, to a degree, shapes it.

Plot having pre-decided what is to happen, scene, scenes, **page 253 /** must be so found, so chosen, as to give the happening the desired force.

Scene, being physical, is, like the physical traits of the characters, generally a copy, or a composite copy. It, too, is assembled — out of memories which, in the first place, may have had no rational connection with one another. Again, pictures, photographs, the screen are sources of supply. Also dreams.

Almost anything drawn from 'real life' — house, town, room, park, landscape — will almost certainly be found to require *some* distortion for the purposes of the plot. Remote memories, already distorted by the imagination, are most useful for the purposes of scene. Unfamiliar or once-seen places yield more than do familiar, often-seen places.

Wholly invented scene is as unsatisfactory (thin) as wholly invented physique for a character.

Scene, much more than character, is inside the novelist's conscious power. More than any other constituent of the novel, it makes him conscious *of* his power.

This can be dangerous. The weak novelist is always, compensatorily, scene-minded. (Jane Austen's economy of scene-painting, and her abstentions from it in what might be expected contexts, could in itself be proof of her mastery of the novel.)

Scene is only justified in the novel where it can be shown, or at least felt, to act upon action or character. In fact, where it has dramatic use.

Where not intended for dramatic use, scene is a sheer slower-down. Its staticness is a dead weight. It cannot make part of the plot's movement by being shown *in play*. (Thunderstorms, the sea, landscape flying past car or railway-carriage windows are not scene but *happenings*.)

The deadeningness of straight and prolonged 'description' is as apparent with regard to scene as it is with regard to character. Scene must be evoked. For its details relevance (see RELEVANCE) is essential. Scene must, like the characters, not fail to materialize. In this it follows the same law — instantaneous for the novelist, gradual for the reader.

In 'setting a scene' the novelist directs, or attempts to direct, the reader's visual imagination. He must allow for the fact that **page 254 /** the reader's memories will not correspond with his own. Or, at least, not at all far along the way.

DIALOGUE — *Must* (1) Further Plot. (2) Express Character.

Should not on any account be a vehicle for ideas for their own sake. Ideas only permissible where they provide a key to the character who expresses them.

Dialogue requires more art than does any other constituent of the novel. Art in the *celare artem* sense. Art in the trickery, self-justifying distortion sense. Why? Because dialogue must appear realistic without being so. Actual realism — the lifting, as it were, of passages from a stenographer's take-down of a 'real life' conversation — would be disruptive. Of what? Of the illusion of the novel. In 'real life' everything is diluted; in the novel everything is condensed.

What are the realistic qualities to be imitated (or faked) in novel dialogue? — Spontaneity. Artless or hit-or-miss arrival at words used. Ambiguity (speaker not sure, himself, what he means). Effect of choking (as in engine): more to be said than can come through. Irrelevance. Allusiveness. Erraticness: unpredictable course. Repercussion.

What must novel dialogue, behind mask of these faked realistic qualities, really be and do? It must be pointed, intentional, relevant. It must crystallize situation. It must express character. It must advance plot.

During dialogue, the characters confront one another. The confrontation is in itself an occasion. Each one of these occasions, throughout the novel, is unique. Since the last confrontation, something has changed, advanced. What is being said is the effect of something that has happened; at the same time, what is being said *is in itself something happening,* which will, in turn, leave its effect.

Dialogue is the ideal means of showing what is between the

characters. It crystallizes relationships. It *should*, ideally, so be effective as to make analysis or explanation of the relationships between the characters unnecessary.

Short of a small range of physical acts — a fight, murder, love-making — dialogue is the most vigorous and visible inter-action of which characters in a novel are capable. Speech is what the characters *do to each other*.

Dialogue provides means for the psychological materialization of the characters. It should short-circuit description of mental traits. Every sentence in dialogue should be descriptive **page 255 /** of the character who is speaking. Idiom, tempo, and shape of each spoken sentence should be calculated by novelist, towards this descriptive end.

Dialogue is the first case of the novelist's need for notation from real life. Remarks or turns of phrase indicatory of class, age, degree of intellectual pretension, *idées reçues*, nature and strength of governing fantasy, sexual temperament, persecution-sense or acumen (fortuitous arrival at general or poetic truth) should be collected. (*N.B.* — Proust, example of this semi-conscious notation and putting to use of it.)

All the above, from *class* to *acumen*, may already have been established, with regard to each character, by a direct statement by the novelist to the reader. It is still, however, the business of dialogue to show these factors, or qualities, in play.

There must be present in dialogue — *i.e.*, in each sentence spoken by each character — *either* (a) calculation, or (b) involuntary self-revelation.

Each piece of dialogue *must* be 'something happening.' Dialogue *may* justify its presence by being 'illustrative' — but this secondary use of it must be watched closely, challenged. Illustrativeness can be stretched too far. Like straight description, it then becomes static, a dead weight — halting the movement of the plot. The 'amusing' for its *own* sake, should above all be censored. So should infatuation with any idiom.

The functional use of dialogue for the plot must be the first thing in the novelist's mind. Where functional usefulness cannot be established, dialogue must be left out.

What is this functional use? That of a bridge.

Dialogue is the thin bridge which must, from time to time, carry the entire weight of the novel. Two things to be kept in mind — (a) the bridge is there to permit *advance*, (b) the bridge must be strong enough for the weight.

Failure in any one piece of dialogue is a loss, at once to the continuity and the comprehensibility of the novel.

Characters should, on the whole, be under rather than over-articulate. What they *intend* to say should be more evident, more striking (because of its greater inner importance to the plot) than what they arrive at *saying*. page 256 /

ANGLE

The question of *angle* comes up twice over in the novel.

Angle has two senses — (a) visual; (b) moral.

(a) *Visual Angle.* — This has been much discussed — particularly, I think, by Henry James. Where is the camera-eye to be located? (1) In the breast or brow of *one* of the characters? This is, of course, simplifying and integrating. But it imposes on the novel the limitations of the 'I' — whether the first person is explicitly used or not. Also, with regard to any matter that the specific character does not (cannot) know, it involves the novelist in long cumbrous passages of cogitation, speculation and guesses. *E.g.* — of any character other than the specific (or virtual) 'I' it must always be 'he appeared to feel,' 'he could be seen to see,' rather than 'he felt,' 'he saw.' (2) In the breast or brow of a succession of characters? This is better. It *must*, if used, involve very careful, considered division of the characters, by the novelist, in the *seeing* and the *seen*. Certain characters gain in importance and magnetism by being only *seen*: this makes them more romantic, fatal-seeming, sinister. In fact, no character in which these qualities are, for the plot, essential should be allowed to enter the *seeing* class. (3) In the breast or brow of omniscient story-teller (the novelist)? This, though appearing naïve, would appear best. The novelist should retain right of entry, at will, into any of the characters: their memories, sensations and thought-processes should remain his, to requisition for appropriate use. What conditions 'appropriateness'? The demands of the plot. Even so, the novelist must not lose sight of point made above — the gain in necessary effect, for some characters, of their remaining *seen* — their remaining closed, apparently, even to the omniscience of the novelist.

The cinema, with its actual camera-work, is interesting study for the novelist. In a good film, the camera's movement, angle and distance have all worked towards one thing — the fullest possible realization of the director's idea, the completest possible surrounding of the subject. Any trick is justified if it adds a statement. With both film and novel, plot is the pre-imperative. The novelist's relation to the novel is that of the director's relation to the film. The cinema, cinema-going, has no doubt built up in novelists a great authoritarianism. This seems to me good. **page 257 /** (b) *Moral Angle.* — This too often means, pre-assumptions — social, political, sexual, national, aesthetic, and so on. These may all exist, sunk at different depths, in the same novelist. Their existence cannot fail to be palpable; and their nature determines, more than anything else, the sympatheticness or antipatheticness of a given novel to a given circle of readers.

Pre-assumptions are bad. They limit the novel to a given circle of readers. They cause the novel to act immorally *on* that given circle. (The lady asking the librarian for a 'nice' novel to take home is, virtually, asking for a novel whose pre-assumptions will be identical with her own.) Outside the given circle, a novel's pre-assumptions must invalidate it for all other readers. The increasingly bad smell of most pre-assumptions probably accounts for the growing prestige of the detective story: the detective story works on the single, and universally acceptable, pre-assumption that an act of violence is anti-social, and that the doer, in the name of injured society, must be traced.

Great novelists write without pre-assumption. They write from outside their own nationality, class or sex.

To write thus should be the ambition of any novelist who wishes to state poetic truth.

Does this mean he must have no angle, no moral view-point? No, surely. Without these, he would be (a) incapable of maintaining the *conviction* necessary for the novel; (b) incapable of *lighting* the characters, who to be seen at all must necessarily be seen in a moral light.

From what source, then, must the conviction come? and from *what* morality is to come the light to be cast on the characters?

The conviction must come from certainty of the validity of the truth the novel is to present. The 'moral light' has not, actually, a moral source; it is moral (morally powerful) according to the strength of its power of revelation. Revelation of what? The virtuousness or non-virtuousness of the action of the character. What is virtue in action? Truth in action. Truth by what ruling, in relation to what? Truth by the ruling of, and in relation to, the inherent poetic truth that the novel states.

The presence, and action, of the poetic truth is the motive (or motor) morality of the novel.

The direction of the action of the poetic truth provides — in **page 258 /** fact, *is* — the moral angle of the novel. If he remains with that truth in view, the novelist has no option as to his angle.

The action, or continuous line of action, of a character is 'bad' in so far as it runs counter to, resists, or attempts to deny, the action of the poetic truth. It is predisposition towards such action that constitutes 'badness' in a character.

'Good' action, or 'goodness' in the character, from predisposition towards such action, is movement along with, expressive of and contributory to, the action of the poetic truth.

If the novelist's moral angle is (a) decided by recognition of the poetic truth, and (b) maintained by the necessity of stating the truth by showing the truth's action, it will be, as it should be, impersonal. It will be, and (from the 'interest' point of view) will be able to stand being, pure of pre-assumptions — national, social, sexual, etc.

N.B. — 'Humour' is the weak point in the front against pre-assumptions. Almost all English humour shows social (sometimes, now, backed by political) pre-assumptions. (Extreme cases — that the lower, or employed, classes are quaint or funny — that aristocrats, served by butlers, are absurd. National pre-assumptions show in treatment of foreigners.)

Advance

It has been said that the plot must advance; that the underlying (or inner) speed of the advance must be even. How is this arrived at?

(1) Obviously, first, by the succession, the succeedingness, of events or happenings. It is to be remembered that *everything* put on record at all — an image, a word spoken, an interior movement of thought or feeling on the part of a character — is an event or happening. These proceed out of one another, give birth to one another, in a continuity that must be (a) obvious, (b) unbroken.

(2) Every happening cannot be described, stated. The reader must be made to feel that what has not been described or stated has, none the less, happened. How? By the showing of subsequent events or happenings whose source *could* only have been in what has not actually been stated. Tuesday is Tuesday by virtue of being the day following Monday. The stated Tuesday must be shown as a derivative of the unstated Monday.

(3) For the sake of emphasis, time must be falsified. But **page 259 /** the novelist's consciousness of the subjective, arbitrary and emotional nature of the falsification should be evident to the reader. Against this falsification — in fact, increasing the force of its effect by contrast — a clock should be heard always impassively ticking away at the same speed. The passage of time, and its demarcation, should be a factor in plot. The either concentration or even or uneven spacing-out of events along time is important.

The statement 'Ten years had passed,' or the statement 'It was now the next day' — each of these is an event.

(4) Characters most of all promote, by showing, the advance of the plot. How? By the advances, from act to act, in their action. By their showing (by emotional or physical changes) the effects both of action and of the passage of time. The diminution of the character's alternatives shows (because it is the work of) advance — by the end of a novel the character's alternatives, many at the beginning, have been reduced to almost none. In the novel, everything that happens happens either *to* or *because* of one of the characters. By the end of the novel, the character has, like the silkworm at work on the cocoon, spun itself out. Completed action is marked by the exhaustion (from one point of view) of the character. Throughout the novel, each character is expending potentiality. This expense of potentiality must be felt.

(5) Scene promotes, or contributes to, advance by its freshness. Generically, it is fresh, striking, from being unlike the scene before. It is the new 'here and now.' Once a scene ceases to offer freshness, it is a point-blank enemy to advance. Frequent change of scene *not* being an imperative of the novel — in fact, many novels by choice, and by wise choice, limiting themselves severely in this matter — how is there to continue to be freshness? By means of ever-differing presentation. Differing because of what?

Season of year, time of day, effects of a happening (*e.g.*, with house, rise or fall in family fortunes, an arrival, a departure, a death), beholding character's mood. At the first presentation, the *scene* has freshness; afterwards, the freshness must be in the *presentation.* The same scene can, by means of a series of presentations, each having freshness, be made to ripen, mature, to actually advance. The *static* properties in scene can be good for advance when so stressed as to show advance by contrast — advance on the part of the characters. Striking 'unchangingness' gives useful emphasis to change. Change should not be a factor, at once, in page 260 / *both* scene and character; either unchanged character should see, or be seen against, changed scene, or changed character should see, or be seen, against unchanged scene. *Two* changes obviously cancel each other out, and would cancel each other's contribution to the advance of plot.

RELEVANCE

Relevance — the question of it — is the headache of novel-writing.

As has been said, the model for relevance is the well-constructed detective story: nothing is 'in' that does not tell. But the detective story is, or would appear to be, simplified by having *fact* as its kernel. The detective story makes towards concrete truth; the novel makes towards abstract truth.

With the detective story, the question 'relevant to *what?*' can be answered by the intelligence. With the novel, the same question must constantly, and in every context, be referred to the intuition. The intelligence, in a subsequent check over, may detect, but cannot itself put right, blunders, lapses or false starts on the part of the intuition.

In the notes on Plot, Character, Scene and Dialogue, everything has come to turn, by the end, on relevance. It is seen that all other relevances are subsidiary to the relevance of the plot — *i.e.*, the relevance to itself that the plot demands. It is as contributory, in fact relevant, to plot that character, scene and dialogue are examined. To be perfectly contributory, these three must be perfectly relevant. If character, scene or dialogue has been weakened by anything irrelevant *to itself*, it can only be imperfectly relevant — which must mean, to a degree disruptive — to the plot.

The main hope for character (for each character) is that it

should be magnetic — *i.e.*, that it should *attract* its parts. This living propensity of the character to assemble itself, to integrate itself, to make itself in order to *be* itself will not, obviously, be resisted by the novelist. The magnetic, or magnetizing, character can be trusted as to what is relevant *to itself*. The trouble comes when what is relevant to the character is found to be not relevant to the plot. At this point, the novelist must adjudicate. It is possible that the character may be right; it is possible that there page 261 / may be some flaw in the novelist's sense of what is relevant to the plot.

Again, the character may, in fact must, decide one half of the question of relevance in dialogue. The character attracts to itself the right, in fact the only possible, idiom, tempo and phraseology for *that* particular character in speech. In so far as dialogue is *illustrative*, the character's, or characters', pull on it must not be resisted.

But in so far as dialogue must be 'something happening' — part of action, a means of advancing plot — the other half of the question of dialogue-relevance comes up. Here, the pull from the characters may conflict with the pull fom the plot. Here again the novelist must adjudicate. The recasting and recasting of dialogue that is so often necessary is, probably, the search for ideal compromise.

Relevance in scene is more straightforward. Chiefly, the novelist must control his infatuation with his own visual power. *No* non-contributory image, must be the rule. Contributory to what? To the mood of the 'now,' the mood that either projects or reflects action. It is a good main rule that objects — chairs, trees, glasses, mountains, cushions — introduced into the novel should be stage-properties, necessary for 'business.' It will be also recalled that the well-set stage shows many objects *not* actually necessary for 'business,' but that these have a right to place by being descriptive — explanatory. In a play, the absence of the narrating voice makes it necessary to establish the class, period and general psychology of the characters by means of objects that can be seen. In the novel, such putting of objects to a descriptive (explanatory) use is excellent — alternative to the narrator's voice.

In scene, then, relevance demands either usefulness for action or else explanatory power in what is shown. There is no doubt that with some writers (Balzac, sometimes Arnold Bennett) categoricalness, in the presentation of scene, is effective. The aim is, usually, to suggest, by multiplication and exactitude of detail, either a scene's material oppressiveness or its intrinsic authority. But in general, for the purposes of most novelists, the number of objects genuinely necessary for explanation will be found to be very small.

Irrelevance, in any part, is a cloud and a drag on, a weakener of, the novel. It dilutes meaning. Relevance crystallizes meaning. **page 262 /**

The novelist's — any writer's — object is, to whittle down his meaning to the exactest and finest possible point. What, of course, is fatal is when he does not know what he does mean: he has no point to sharpen.

Much irrelevance is introduced into novels by the writer's vague hope that at least some of this *may* turn out to be relevant, after all. A good deal of what might be called provisional writing goes to the first drafts of first chapters of most novels. At a point in the novel's progress, relevance becomes clearer. The provisional chapters are then recast.

The most striking fault in work by young or beginning novelists submitted for criticism, is irrrelevance — due either to infatuation or indecision. To direct such an author's attention to the imperative of relevance is certainly the most useful — and possibly the only — help that can be given. **page 263 /**